The Devil's Plantation
East Anglian Lore,
Witchcraft & Folk-Magic

The Devil's Plantation

East Anglian Lore, Witchcraft & Folk-Magic

by
Nigel G. Pearson

TROY BOOKS

© 2015 Nigel G. Pearson

First printing in paperback
January 2016

All rights reserved.
No part of this publication may be reproduced, stored within a retrieval system or transmitted in any form or by any means, electronic, mechanical, photocopying, scanning, recording or otherwise, without the prior written permission of the author and the publisher.

Any practices or substances described within this publication are presented as items of interest. The author and the publisher accept no responsibility for any results arising from their enactment or use. Readers are self responsible for their actions.

Published by Troy Books
www.troybooks.co.uk

Troy Books Publishing
BM Box 8003
London WC1N 3XX

Printed and bound in Great Britain

Dedication

This book is dedicated with deepest love
and remembrance to;
Fionn Puca MacGereilt Pearson,
1998 – 2013.
Best Boy, Special, Precious, my very own Black Shuck

Acknowledgements

I am deeply indebted to the following people for their help and advice throughout the research and writing of this book.
Gemma Gary and Jane Cox, for inviting me to write this book in the first place, and Christine Gary for casting a helpful eye over the manuscript.
Stuart Inman, Richard Parkinson and Michael Clarke for information and background on the Toad Bone Ritual and Traditional Craft in East Anglia.
Graham King and Hannah Fox of the Museum of Witchcraft, Boscastle, Cornwall, for permission to peruse their archives.
Michael Howard for kindly allowing me to use the material on Monica English from his book 'Children of Cain'.
Pete Jennings, Val Thomas, Chris Wood and Rod Chapman for volunteering information on contemporary witchcraft practices and personalities.
All those people in East Anglia who are either unknown or who wish to remain unnamed, who contributed their knowledge to this book.
And Anthony who, as usual, stood beside and behind me all the way.
To all, my thanks and gratitude.

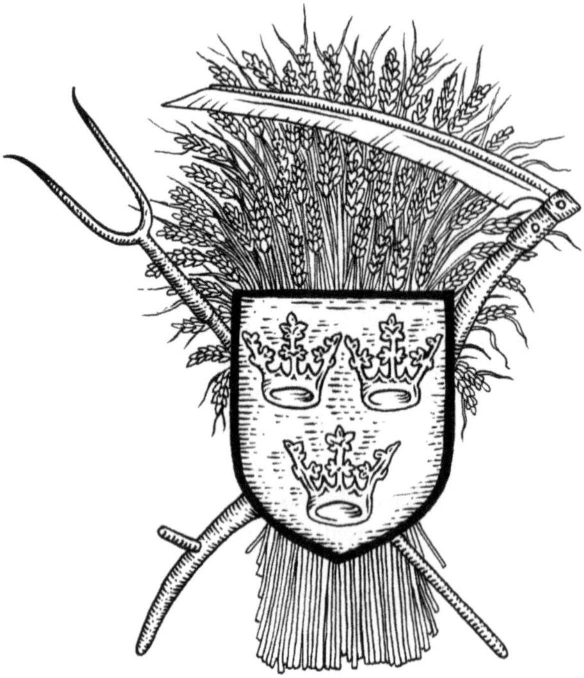

Contents

Dedication and Acknowledgements	5
Introduction	11
Chapter 1 – The Living Landscape	19
Echoes of the Ancestors	19
Graven Images	23
Spirits in the Landscape	25
The Good Folk and their Kin	28
Land Drakes	35
Chapter 2 – Meremaids, Giants and Spectral Hounds	39
Maids of the Meres	39
Herculean Labourers	43
Dark and Demon Dogs	52
Chapter 3 – Characters of Craft	63
Witch Country	63
Dual Faith	64
Witchfinder General	68
Mother Lakeland	71
Old Winter	73
Jabez Few	76
Tilly Baldrey	77
Using the "Eye"	79
A Little Learning	81
Daddy Witch	83
Try to remember…	85
By Royal Appointment	86
Spying on the Witches	88
Monica English	91
Today's Characters	94
Chapter 4 – Speak of the Devil … (and He will appear)	99
The Devil in Cambridgeshire	99
Suffolk's Stones	101
Norfolk's Hills and Hollows	105
Liminality	109
Cunning and Mighty is His Nature	110
Men In Black	113

Chapter 5 – Witch Ways *119*
    Circles of Might *120*
    Toads and Bones *122*
    Toads in Magic *129*
    With the help of the Dead *131*
    Working with Familiars *135*
    Prevention, Healing and Cure of all Ills *142*
    The Craft of Contact *148*
    The Arte of Ligature *157*

Chapter 6 – Green Ways *161*
    Specialist Collectors and Gatherers *161*
    The Dark Orders *164*
    Plant Lore *168*
    Arboreal Lore *179*
    Healing Lore *186*
    Some Recipes *188*

Chapter 7 – Folk Ways *191*
    Defence by Boiling and Bottle *191*
    Salt, Shoes and Spheres *198*
    Blood, Bones, Burning and Baking *200*
    Special Stones *204*
    The Wake of Freya *208*
    Charms of Love *211*
    St. Mark's Eve *213*
    Curious Cures *218*
    The Tides of Life *221*

Chapter 8 – Three Crowns and Several Halos *227*
    Legendary regalia *228*
    East Anglian Holy Land *229*
    St. Felix *231*
    St. Fursey *234*
    St. Botolph *238*
    St. Etheldreda *242*
    St. Withburga *244*
    St. Edmund *247*
    St. Walstan *252*
    Walsingham *255*
    Petitioning the Saints *258*

Appendix – Removing a Witch's Curse *260*

Bibliography. *264*

Index. *267*

Photoplates
between pages 136 – 137

1. *Ancient Yew grove, on the cliffs at the ancient town of Dunwich.*
2. *Arrangement of human bones, on the cliffs at Dunwich.*
3. *Grave mound at the Anglo-Saxon burial site of Sutton Hoo.*
4. *Wooden carving of a Meremaid.*
5. *North door of Blythburgh Church, scorched by Black Shuck.*
6. *Tapestry depicting the Black Dog, St. Mary's Church, Bungay.*
7. *Weather vane of Black Shuck, Bungay, Suffolk.*
8. *The Devil's Stone/Druid's Stone, Church of St. Mary, Bungay.*
9. *The Devil's Stone, Church of St. Andrew, Westleton.*
10. *Protective Hagstones, hung up outside a cottage in Suffolk.*
11. *'Thunderbolts' & 'Frairy Loaves', used in East Anglian magic.*
12. *Horse Brasses, used as protective charms & a divination tool.*
13. *Witch Bottles, used as protective & curse-breaking devices.*
14. *Preserved toad, for casting spells & acquiring magical benefits.*
15. *Working tools on a typical East Anglian Witch's altar.*
16. *The Three Crowns of East Anglia, on church font, Suffolk.*
17. *St. Botolph's Church, Iken, Suffolk.*
18. *'Frairy Ring', outside the main door of St. Botolph's Church.*
19. *9th/10th century cross shaft, discovered at St. Botolph's Church.*
20. *Painted panel, depicting St. Withburga.*
21. *Martyr King, Edmund, St. Edmunds Church, Southwold.*
22. *The Wuffingas royal Wolf, in pargetting, from Suffolk.*
23. *Magical charm carved into the stonework of Orford Castle.*
24. *Ritual mask used by modern East Anglian witches.*
25. *'Ferisher Tree', Ferisher entrance, or 'Green Country' opening.*

All photography by the author,
except image no. 20

Introduction

The 'Devil's Plantation' has two particular meanings, both with especial interest to this book. Firstly, it is the name of a manual of magic, reputedly owned by an old woman known as 'Daddy Witch', who lived in the village of Horseheath, in Cambridgeshire, in the 19th century. This is one version of what are known as 'Black Books'; books of knowledge, ritual, lore and magic, that are hand-written, copied out by individuals for their own use, either from available, printed sources, and/or from other practitioners' books. Daddy Witch's book was said to be a collection of East Anglian lore and magic of this type, but it has disappeared without trace and no one knows its whereabouts ('Daddy', by the way, is an old Cambridgeshire term for the entity known in popular folklore as the Devil).

The second meaning of 'Devil's Plantation' is a plot of land that is set aside by farmers or a community, on which no crops are grown or livestock are grazed. It is often triangular in shape, at the corner of a field, or where two or more fields meet, and is sometimes fenced off from the surrounding land. It is a place where the Spirits, Land Wight's, or other beings live, and where the normal rules of humanity do not apply. Humans are sometimes not terribly welcome and enter the area at their own risk. Some of these plots contain ancient stone crosses, and were also thought to be places of pagan worship in times gone by.

The Devil's Plantation

In Scotland they are known as the 'Guidman's Croft' and in Cornwall as 'Chy Bucca', both referring to the House of the Horned One.

It is not the intention of this book to pretend to the level of a magical grimoire, nor to infer that East Anglia is home to the Devil Himself; but as an isolated area where magical practice has not been, and is still not, uncommon, then The Devil's Plantation lends itself well to describing the area and some of its Ways. I do, however, intend this book to be an evocation of the Spirit of the Land of East Anglia and, to that end, it is indeed, a magical book.

East Anglia is an ancient, self-contained region of the British Isles and one that has been home to various peoples, beliefs and practices during its long life. Its boundaries have been somewhat fluid, changing with the prevailing political and military strength of the time, but it has largely consisted of the core counties of Suffolk and Norfolk and the eastern part of Cambridgeshire, known as the Fenlands. Its southern boundary has always been the river Stour, the dividing line between Suffolk and Essex. At its inception, around 450 CE, the Kingdom of East Anglia became the home of the invading peoples known as the Anglii, hailing as they did from the region of Angeln in what is now Northern Germany. In the wake of the Roman departure from Britain, these people colonised the vacuum that was left in what was previously the land of the Iron Age Iceni tribe. Their royal house took its name of 'Wuffingas', meaning 'descendants of the Wolf', from their semi-mythical founding king, Wuffa. These people spoke an ancient dialect of Old English, distinct from their surroundings, and East Anglia can, with some justification, claim to be the first place in England where the English language was actually spoken.

In the following centuries, East Anglia and its kings, notably Raedwald, rose to prominence amongst the Anglo Saxon Kingdoms of the rest of Britain. Raedwald himself, after defeating the Kingdom of Northumbria and placing

Introduction

his puppet king, Edwin, on the throne, briefly became the 'Bretwalda', or overlord of all the Saxon Kingdoms. After this time, East Anglia's influence lessened and the region was frequently under the rule of the Kingdom of Mercia, to the west. It asserted its independence finally in 825 CE only to fall in battle to the invading Danish Vikings in 869, when the famous King Edmund (later Saint Edmund), was killed in a ritualistic manner by the 'Great Heathen Army'. From then on, the Kingdom became part of the Danelaw area of Britain, and Danish East Anglia also included the southern county of Essex. The old kingdom of East Anglia, minus Essex, was absorbed back into a united England for the first time, by King Edward the Elder in 917 CE. The region then became an Earldom under King Knut, consisting of Suffolk and Norfolk, up to and beyond the Norman invasion of 1066. Suffolk and Norfolk later became separate Duchies.

During much of this period and up to this point, the religion of the peoples swapped backwards and forwards between paganism and Christianity, and the area was frequently characterised by its dual faith adherence. King Raedwald is famous for accepting baptism into Christianity, but thereafter keeping two altars at which to worship; one to the Christ and one to the Old Gods of his people. The grave mounds which have been excavated at the world famous site of Sutton Hoo, near Woodbridge in Suffolk, and which are thought to house the remains of King Raedwald, contained items and iconography of both Christian and pagan significance. Edicts and laws were issued by a succession of Kings and Bishops of the region, well into what is thought to be the Christian era, banning such things as tree and well worship, divination by stones and stars, and dressing up as animals and other mythical beasts at certain times of year, to enact ritual plays and dramas. After the Norman Conquest, the region was considered respectably Christian, like the rest of the country, but old habits die hard and much old lore and practice still lingered on.

The Devil's Plantation

Up to the Norman Conquest, the region could be said to be more Anglo-Dane, than Anglo-Saxon by blood, character and culture. Afterwards, during the Middle Ages and later, East Anglia became host to several migrations from the continent of Europe, due to religious and political upheavals across the water. Dutch Protestants, French Huguenots and other refugees all made their way to this part of Britain and made their homes here. Many contributed to the culture of the area and their customs and cultures became absorbed once more into the fabric of life there. The wool trade, a staple of East Anglian economic life for centuries, owed much to its links with the continent and strong trade and cultural ties existed with Flanders, the Netherlands and the Hanseatic states of Northern Germany as well as the Baltic states. During Tudor times, much of the region was staunchly Catholic in nature, avidly supporting Mary Tudor who made a successful bid to claim the throne from her powerbase of Framlingham Castle in Suffolk. Yet only a century later, East Anglia was the scene of the severest witch persecutions under the Puritan fanatic and Witch Hunter General, Matthew Hopkins. At this time also, due to intolerance of their way of worship here, hundreds, if not thousands, of Puritan families left the region and re-settled in New England in America, taking much of the lore and tradition of the region with them, despite their strict Protestant faith. Later on, in the 19th century, Irish immigrants arrived in the west and north of Cambridgeshire and Norfolk, either due to the horrendous famines in their own country or as drovers with the seasonal cattle trade; their traditions were also added to the existing lore of the region, being absorbed into the indigenous magico-religious framework. Thus it can be seen that East Anglia has a cosmopolitan background when it comes to the origins of its lore and magical traditions, deriving as they do from many peoples over a long period of time.

Introduction

However, it is not just the people that go into making up the flavour of the culture and traditions of an area but also, and particularly so in the case of folk-magical traditions, it is the very Land itself which lends its unique character and flavour to the practices of its inhabitants. This is very similar to the French concept of terroir when talking of wine production; that the special characteristics of the geography, the geology, the climate and the very soil itself, all lend themselves to the end product of the produce – in this case the People – of a certain region. East Anglia is bounded on the north and east by the Wash, the Broads and the North Sea, to the south by the River Stour and to the west by the Fens, which once extended almost to Cambridge. This is a readily definable geographical area and was, until very recently, a very isolated part of Britain, cut off from the rest of the country by land and left much to its own devices. Despite its strong trade links with the continent and, strangely, London, contact was mainly by sea or river, because of the impassable marshes and bogs of the undrained Fens to the west and the uncleared Forests of Epping and Hainault to the south, over the River Stour. Within this area, much of the land was relatively flat in comparison to the rest of the country, apart from the East Anglian Heights in the west and north of Norfolk. Much of the land is reclaimed marsh or fen land, providing rich, alluvial soil for agriculture and pasturage for animals; much of the region today remains agricultural in nature and is sometimes called the Bread Basket of Britain, due to its high crop yields. Not for East Anglia the wild and rugged hills and mountains of places like Yorkshire, nor the untamed and dramatic Atlantic coasts of Devon and Cornwall (although the North Sea can be just as threatening when it wants to), but the gently undulating fields and meandering waterways create the predominant character of both the Land and its people. Yet lest you think the people soft and yielding, take note of the underlying geology. Although most of the topsoil is

The Devil's Plantation

either fertile alluvial soil or, in some inland regions, fairly thick clay, beneath this much of East Anglia lies on hard and unyielding chalk, which gives birth to sharp, tough and cutting flint; this too goes into the make-up and character of both the people and its magics.

Today, although communication with the rest of the country and the world is much easier due to modern technology, East Anglia still has no motorways in the interior, few major 'A' roads and is relatively poorly served by the railways. It has no major industrial works, is still mainly agricultural in nature and, until very recently, had no major influx of people from outside the region, let alone from abroad, in the past gradually assimilating drifts of people over a period of time. This is reflected still in the natural suspicion held by the people of outsiders, where someone still needs to have lived in the street or village for 20-30 years before they are not considered an 'incomer' or a 'newcomer'. East Anglians are warm by nature, but you need to get to know them first before they will open up and reveal their genuine characters.

This then is the area of focus of this book; from the Cambridgeshire Fens in the west, to the shifting sands of the Wash in the north; from the crumbling coastlines of Norfolk and Suffolk in the east to the gentle waterways of the Stour on the Essex borders in the south. From this mixture of people and landscape arose a very particular kind of witchcraft and folk-magic, and in the following pages I will attempt to give a feeling of its history, nature and expression.

Nigel Pearson
August 2014.

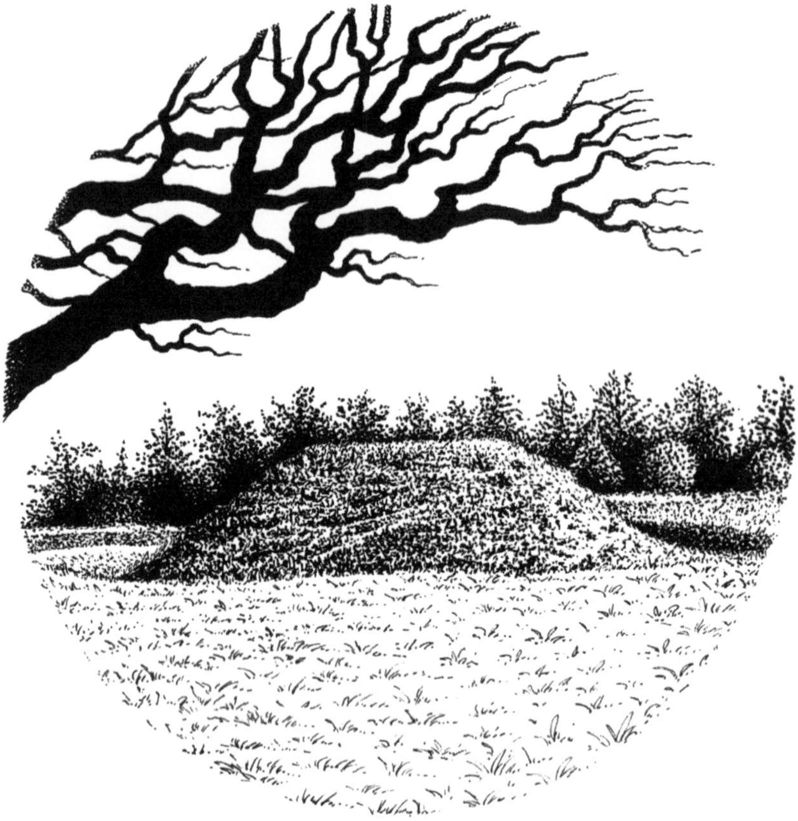

The Living Landscape

It is essentially the quality of the energy in the Land itself that determines the nature of the magic of a place. In East Anglia, this energy is known most often either as 'Spirament', or simply as 'Virtue'. Necessarily, it will vary from place to place; the quality of the virtue in the wet, boggy lands of the west is not the same as that of the sandy heathlands of the eastern coastal regions. Nor is the energy of the rolling pastureland of the inland meadows and fields the same as that of the thick, clay soils of the central uplands. But, as they are all a part of the same geographical and energetic region, they all partake of the same essential quality of East Anglia, be it manifested in subtly different ways.

Echoes of the Ancestors

In one way, this energy is the same in all areas because it is magically composed of the energies of the ancestors; the people who were born, who lived on and worked the Land, who married and gave birth to their own children in turn and died, then to be buried in the soil that they had worked all their lives. They had eaten the produce of the Land on which they lived, rich in the energies of the

The Devil's Plantation

place, contributed their own virtue in turn and then were laid to rest in that very soil, enriching it further. They had considered themselves to be East Anglians and a living part of what it means to be such.

East Anglia is not plentiful in ancient monuments such as stone circles, standing stones or dolmens. What it does have however, are plenty of tumuli, barrows and grave mounds, most of which house, or once housed, the earthly remains of the people who lived there; the ancestors. Even empty and desecrated, these 'houses of the dead' still retain the energy and quality – the Virtue – of the essence of East Anglia. The most famous of these is probably Sutton Hoo; the rich and lavish ship burial of an ancient king, as well as many others spread over a large area containing more than twenty mounds, overlooking the river Deben in Suffolk. Strangely, this area later became used as a place of execution, and gallows were raised on the mounds in later ages. This further enhanced the reputation of the area as a place of the dead and imbued it with eldritch energies that it might not otherwise have possessed. Ancestral and necromantic rites are still carried out in the area of the mounds in secret, to this day, further strengthening the link with the living and the dead, the ancestors, the past and the present. These grave mounds occur all over East Anglia, not just at Sutton Hoo. Places like Snape, Kesgrave, Martlesham, Butley and Midenhall in Suffolk; Belton, Great Bircham, Harpley and Quidenham in Norfolk and Bartlow, Kennett, Stapleford and Whittlesford in Cambridgeshire, to name but a few, all have old tumuli or grave mounds within their bounds. All of these places have legends and lore attached to them, variously describing treasure, giants, sleeping warriors or queens, but all stressing that they are still a living part of the landscape and could revive at any moment, or divulge their secrets and treasure.

The Living Landscape

To my own knowledge, rites concerned with the living virtue of the ancestors and hidden or secret knowledge have taken place on the cliffs at the 'drowned city' of Dunwich, on the Suffolk coast, within the last few years. Dunwich was once the capital of East Anglia, a thriving mediaeval city and Bishopric, before being inundated by the sea in a series of coastal erosions. Little now remains except one street, one church, the ruins of a mediaeval abbey and a few grave stones on the top of the cliff. It is claimed by locals and fishermen, in all seriousness, that the drowned bells of the many churches that once existed in the town, can still be heard ringing during strong sea swells and storms; these portend either great disaster or great good fortune to those that hear them. Human bones often fall from the cliffs onto the beach there – the result of the erosion of the last graveyard – but a few years ago, one of the last grave stones was found to have human bones arranged in patterns before it on the cliff top. There seemed no obvious meaning to these designs and they were mostly ignored as the playfulness of local children or teenagers acting up. However, not more than one hundred yards away, back from the cliff edge, hidden under a close-growing grove of Yew trees next to the abbey walls, were more remarkable designs laid out on the ground. These took the form of mostly concentric circles, made alternately of bone and Yew sticks, laid out in the form of a rough triangle. These circles were hidden from the casual observer and went mostly unnoticed and were not remarked upon, but there was a similarity in pattern between the designs before the grave and under the Yews and they were obviously linked. The site had a long connection with the dead, being partly within the ruins of the old abbey and right on top of All Saints Church graveyard. The Yew tree is also traditionally linked with both death and immortality. No one claimed responsibility for placing these designs and they had disappeared or been removed within a couple of days.

The Devil's Plantation

This modern occurrence of necromantic magic is just a very recent expression of rites that have taken place in ruined churches, graveyards and the approaches to them for centuries. Modern opinion usually states that the reason for this is that most older churches were built on or over the remains of pagan places of worship and that the sites are still used for their connections to the old, pagan magic. This may very well be true, but it is missing an even more important reason. Churches and their environs are chosen as places of magical working because of their liminal nature and their closeness to the spirits of the dead and the ancestors, both of whom are very important to the witch or folk-magical practitioner. Magic workers are attracted to graveyards the whole world over for the aura of power and sanctity that they possess and the ease of access to the Otherworld that may be found there, and the East Anglian witch is no different. Working magically in a place where generations of your forebears have been buried, not only enables the practitioner to tap into an existing wellspring of energy that they may otherwise not be able to access, but also gets the spirits 'on your side', so to speak, and makes the success of your venture much more likely. In East Anglian magical lore, to work where your family have lived, on the very ground that they have worked over the years, adds a great deal of power to your magic, as you are going with the flow of energy, as opposed to working with energies that are in antipathy to you. Many witches carry a piece of stone from the family grave plot, or keep a pot of soil taken from family graves, both to empower their workings and to retain a vital link with those that have gone before. If at all possible, bones from the ancestral graves are also used, but these are, understandably, more difficult to obtain.

Graven Images

In the west of the region, to the south-east of Cambridge, are situated the Gog Magog Hills. They are 240 feet high and situated on their top is the Iron-Age hill fort of Wandlebury. There was once a giant figure cut into the turf there, described by John Layer around 1640 as the 'high and mighty portraiture of a giant which the scholars of Cambridge cut upon the turf or superficies of earth... and not unlikely might call it Gogmagog, which I have seen but it is now of late discontinued'. This giant was last authentically referenced by the Cambridgeshire antiquary William Cole, as being visible when he was a boy around 1724. He states that there used to be many traditions concerning this giant, but that even by his time they had mostly worn away. These traditions stated that Gog and Magog (two giants), lay buried under the hills, that a giant horse was also buried under a nearby hill to the west, and that a golden chariot was buried under the road passing by Wandlebury to the east. Little more was known, other than that games, sports, bull-baiting and wrestling used to take place at various times of year during the 16th and 17th centuries, as Cambridge scholars were banned by the University authorities from attending them.

The earliest tale of the Gog Magog hills that we now possess is told by Gervase of Tilbury in or around 1211, when describing the hill camp of Wandlebury. He states that the top of the hill was a level space surrounded by entrenchments and then goes on to relate an ancient tradition concerning it. He says that if a warrior entered the space at the dead of night, when the moon was brightly shining, and cried out 'Knight to Knight, come forth!' he would immediately be confronted by a strange warrior, armed for combat. The two knights should then charge and try to dismount each other, the one who succeeded in doing so being the winner. This should be done by the challenging knight entering the area alone, although companions may watch from outside the perimeter. Gervase then relates the tale of one Osbert FitzHugh, who made the challenge of the strange knight and came off the winner. As he was leading away the vanquished knight's horse as his prize, the fallen knight cast his lance and wounded Osbert in the thigh, which the victorious knight initially ignored. He took the prize steed back to be admired by his family and servants and it was only when he was taking off his armour that he noticed the wound he had sustained, but which he then scorned. The horse was a magnificent beast, but exceedingly proud and unruly. At cockcrow the next morning, he slipped his reins and fled, vanishing no one knew where and was never seen again. Osbert did have one reminder of his victory on that night however; every year on the same date, his wound, although apparently cured, would re-open and bleed again, only to close once more until the next year. The name of the area where this event took place, Wandlebury, is interesting in this context. It derives from the name of the spirit or demon Wandil, the East Anglian personification of cold and darkness and of an icy winter that threatens never to lose its hold on the Land. A fine patron of a never-healing wound.

Over time, all traces of the hill figures became overgrown and there remained nothing to be seen, but the oral traditions in the area remained, a legacy of the living history of the landscape. In 1954, the late T.C. Lethbridge, experimental archaeologist and sometime dowser, decided to investigate the area in an attempt to see if there was any truth in the local tales of giants, treasure and chariots.

The Living Landscape

Using a combination of methods, both orthodox and non, involving soundings taken with a steel bar and plotted on paper, he obtained the outlines of several figures. They appeared to show that at one time in the distant past, cut into the sides of the hills, had been the images of what he interpreted as an Earth Goddess (Magog) seated astride a horse and leading a chariot, followed by a giant (Gog), both of them preceded by a winged spirit, possibly a solar deity (the figure known as Gog has been identified by some as that very figure of darkness, Wandil, whom the site is named after). They appeared to have the definition of ritual figures, used for worship or other similar rites, whose memories had been kept alive in adulterated form for several millennia. Their exact age was not possible to determine, but that they had become part of the folklore and magic of the area was apparent, particularly in view of the historically attested games and sports that had annually taken place on the site. Unfortunately, Mr. Lethbridge's work has not been continued by other archaeologists and, although he removed the turf on the hill and uncovered the figures, it has been allowed to grow back again and the figures are once more lost to view. They remain, however, as part of the magic and spirit of the place.

Spirits in the Landscape

Also part of the magic and spirit of place, are the beings known as Land Wights. This is a term that is common to most of the country, but in East Anglia, they are known by different and more specific names and types. In Norfolk and north and east Suffolk, the Land Wight is known variously as the Hyter, Hydra, Ikey, Hikey, Hikey Strikey, Hikey Pike, High Sprite, Sprikey, or just the Sprikey Man. These are all looked upon as a type of pixie, goblin, hobgoblin, gnome or demon, although some people see them as a kind of fairy (however these tend to be seen as a specific type of being in their own right and I will look at these later on). They are solitary creatures, and are seen to be essentially benevolent and well disposed towards human beings if treated with respect, and can generally be found in and associated with wooded and grown up areas, rather than in the open fields or meadows. If glimpsed out of the corner of the eye (which is usually the only way they can be seen), they appear to be long and gangly, somewhat twig-like and very swift. On occasion they can appear as shimmering lights in marshy or boggy areas, but again, these are more properly Will O' the Wisps and are described later. Some people have called or likened them to Sand Martins, but this does not stand out in the oral record and is probably a literary allusion to some other, unconnected spirit. The Hikey Sprite will accept offerings such as a bowl of cream, or bread and milk and will create a calm and pleasant atmosphere for the humans in its vicinity. They are sometimes used to frighten unruly or ill-behaved children, much in the way of; 'if you don't stop that the Hikey Sprite will get you', or 'if you go in there/do that then the Spriker will have you'. That aside, they generally ignore or leave humans alone and are rarely glimpsed these days. A variation on this theme is known as the 'little hairy men', who are reputed to live in the Borley Wood/Linton district of Cambridgeshire. Traditionally they scare, frighten or make off with naughty or unruly children. Alternatively, they are known to pelt them with large things 'like apple dumplings', if they are caught out at night, after dark.

Much more badly disposed towards humans are the Yarthkins. These are also solitary creatures, but can be found almost anywhere, particularly on waste ground and uncultivated plots that have 'gone off' or refuse to grow anything productive. The Yarthkin, in East Anglian lore, is particularly inimical to humans and cannot be placated with offerings, however well presented, these actually increasing their antagonism. They can, however, be trapped and removed or disposed of by various means; such is the particular art and practice of various types of Cunning Men

The Living Landscape

in East Anglia. Using such items as red thread, various shaped staves and sticks, blown eggs, runic symbols and talismans, the Yarthkin can be safely disempowered and their influence contained; however this is time consuming and expends a lot of energy and the traps and wards must be renewed at intervals. Much better avoid a Yarthkin altogether.

Also antagonistic towards humankind is the much-dreaded Jack O' Lantern. These Will O' the Wisps frequent any low lying, poorly-drained, boggy or marshy area in East Anglia and also go by the names of Lantern Men, Hob-o'-Lanterns or Jinny Burnt Arses. Said by the Men of Science to be self-igniting flames of marsh gas, the East Anglian native knows better and goes in fear of these wights. The locals know that they are there to lure them off the road and drown them in the watery landscape, in which East Anglia abounds. Nor can the lonely and wary traveller whistle to keep their spirits up as they walk along for it is said that if one man should stand at one end of a field and another at the opposite end and whistle, then the lantern man will always go to the whistler and the other man is safe. This is useful to know, as the lantern man will always try to come up against you and harm or kill you if he is able.

It is equally unwise to mock a Jack O' Lantern by showing him a light or trying to copy him. A Norfolk tale illustrating this goes as follows;

'There was a young fellow coming home one evening and he see the lantern man coming for him and he run! And that run; and he run again; and that run again! Now there was a silly old man lived down there who didn't believe in none of them things and this young fellow he run to his house and say: "O Giles, for heaven's sake let me in – the lantern man's coming". And old Giles he say: "You silly fool, there ain't no such thing as a lantern man". But when he sees the lantern man coming for him, Giles let the young fellow in, and that come for them two, till that was the beginning of a pint pot! And old Giles he thought he would play a trick on the lantern man, so he got a candle and held that out of the window on the end of a pole. And first he held that out right high, and the lantern man he come for that, and he come underneath it. And then he held that out right low, and the lantern man he come up above it. And then he held that out right steady, and the lantern man he come for that and he burst it all to pieces! But they du say, if the lantern man light upon you, the best thing is to throw yourself flat on your face and hold your breath.'

So just you all be warned!

The Good Folk and their Kin

Another class of being altogether is the Fairy. Seen as existing somewhere between the spiritual and the purely natural – of the Land – their lore is richest in Suffolk, where they take on corporeal and visible form most readily. They can be of any height but are most frequently seen as child-sized or smaller, dressed in sandy-coloured clothing and are very shy or wary of humans. There are some recorded instances of them in west Norfolk, most commonly coming from the Irish immigrants during the potato famines of the 19th century. They brought their indigenous fairy beliefs with them and it is from the Irish 'Fir' or 'Fer Sidhe' (man of the hills), that the colloquial term for fairy, 'Ferisher', is thought to come. Some considered them to be petty and spiteful beings, who would readily do humankind down, but others considered them to be helpful, especially with agricultural and household tasks, if they were treated kindly and fairly. During the lambing season, offerings of the first ewes' milk were poured out onto the ground for the fairies who, if denied this, might cause the later lambs to be stillborn. Fairies, the Norfolk housewife learned from her Irish neighbours, could, if annoyed, stop the butter from coming in the churn, or turn the meat in the brine tub sour. When bread dough was put in front of the fire

The Living Landscape

to rise, it could fail to do so if the door was not left open for a fairy to come in and watch over it. The creature had to be rewarded, however, with food left out for it beside the dough. They may interest themselves in man's affairs, by doing him a good turn or, when taking offence at some small incident, leading him into mischief or even danger, or simply laughing at his misadventures.

There are a few accounts of fairy changelings. Fairy children of some growth are occasionally entrusted to human care for a time and then recalled, and humans are now and again kidnapped and carried off to fairyland, never to be seen again. There are also tales of human women being taken to fairyland as midwives and being richly rewarded and returned afterwards. However, if they ever speak out about their experiences, they are sure to be punished in certain ways. For example, a woman who had been taken to fairyland to act as midwife and returned safely, subsequently saw a fairy man when she was at market one day. She approached him and began to speak with him and he, being much taken aback by this, asked her out of which eye she could see him. She indicated the eye and he blew into it sharply. He at once disappeared and she never again saw any of the fair folk, having had the gift taken from her because of her garrulousness. The fairies are generally great enemies of slovenliness and, if the kitchen is tidied before going to bed and the sweepings not taken out, or if the broom is left standing on the floor without being placed standing on its handle, those well-skilled in fairy lore will tell you that the fairies will come and punish the slatternly house keeper. They are fond of singing, dancing in rings, moving hand in hand and playing music together, and are said to ride horses and colts about meadows and fields, much to the farmers' chagrin.

In Suffolk the fairy folk were known as Feriers, Frairies or Pharisees and were most commonly seen or known around the small town of Stowmarket. A few tales will serve to illustrate their nature as known in this county.

The Devil's Plantation

The feriers frequented several houses in Tavern St. in Stowmarket, but never appeared as long as anyone was about. People used to lie hidden to see them and some succeeded. Once in particular by a wood-stack up near the brick-yard, there appeared a large company of them singing, dancing and playing music together. They were very small people, quite little creatures and very merry. But as soon as they saw anybody they all vanished away. In the houses, after the feriers had fled, sparks of fire as bright as stars used to appear under the feet of the people who had disturbed them on going upstairs (this ties in with another name for the fairy folk, that of Peries or Perries, after which the Northern Lights are known in Suffolk – the Perry Dancers).

A Stowmarket woman woke up one night and found that her young baby, who should have been sleeping by her side, had disappeared. Fearing lest the fairies had stolen her, she jumped out of bed and there, at its foot, were some of the little sandy creatures undressing the infant and carefully placing the pins from its clothes head to head on the floor (to negate the magic of the iron that was supposed to keep them at bay). When they saw the mother, they fled laughing through a hole in the floorboards. For a long time after that, the child slept between its parents, pinned by its clothes to the pillows and sheets. Another woman in the town had her child stolen by the feriers, who left a sickly changeling in its place. But the woman looked after the fairy child as if it were her own child and every morning, on getting up, she found some money had been left in her pocket.

Ferishers were thought to ride about at night on horses borrowed from farmers' stables so, to prevent this, care was taken to keep a flint stone with a hole in it (a hagstone), tied to the stable door. However, not only horses were so ridden. In 1832 a farmer in Woodbridge, another Suffolk town, who had a calf to sell, was present when his bailiff was about to bargain with the butcher over the price. The animal was led in and it was obvious that it was very hot.

The Living Landscape

'Oh', exclaimed the butcher, 'the Pharisees have been here and, 'stru's you are alive, have been riding that there poor calf all night.' He then instructed the bailiff to get a stone with a hole in it and hang it in the calves' crib, so that it just cleared the animals' backs when they stood up. This, he declared, would 'brush the Pharisees off the poor beasts when they attempt to gallop 'em round.'

Ralph of Coggeshall was a 12th/13th century Abbot of a Cistercian monastery in Essex and a noted contributor to the Chronicon Anglicanum. He records the tale, known as 'Malekin', the story of a human changeling who took the form of a ghost or Faerie spirit haunting Dagworthy Castle in Suffolk. Malekin, although a house-dweller, performed none of the usual tasks of the house spirit type of faerie, other than entertaining the inhabitants of the castle. She spoke with the voice of a one-year-old child and revealed the following story. As a baby, her mother had gone working in the cornfields and left her sleeping in the shade, as she worked elsewhere. The ever-present and ever-dangerous Good Folk happened to come by and whisked the baby away; unusually, they did not leave one of their own in her place in this case. Malekin was taken away to faerie-land and, having been given the food of the Ferishers, was no longer required to observe the rules and mores of the mortal world. Eventually, she took up her invisible residence in Dagworthy Castle, where she initially frightened the occupants severely; however they soon became used to her ways and came to enjoy the sound of her voice around the castle. She was often heard, but only ever seen once. She revealed her story to a favourite chambermaid who always left food out for her – as is the custom for the Good Folk. In a broad Suffolk accent, she told her tale and said that she had been with the Faeries for seven years, but hoped to regain her mortality when another seven had elapsed. Her apparently humble origins did not stop her either from conversing in Latin with the castle's chaplain and discussing the Holy Scriptures. The chambermaid finally persuaded Malekin to put in an actual, visual appearance, a request with which the spirit complied, but only after getting a promise from the chambermaid that she would neither 'touch her nor try to detain her'. The maid described Malekin as being like a tiny child, dressed all in white linen. It is not recorded whether Malekin ever did regain her mortality, but the provision of normal, human food would have been very important for her, as this would, to some extent, magically nullify the effects of the faerie food she had previously eaten. This is the earliest known written record of a changeling.

Perhaps the most remarkable tale of fairies – and the one which links them most closely with the Land and the life within it – is the story of the Green Children, if indeed fairies they be. This was vouched for by a contemporary historian, one William of Newburgh, and occurred some 800 years ago in the Suffolk village of Woolpit. Some harvesters were gathering in their crop at St. Mary of the Wolfpits (as it was then known), when they suddenly beheld a young boy and girl, standing at the mouth of the wolf-hole or pit, from whence the village derived its name; these holes were always a mysterious sort of place and situated just below the field in which they were working. These children, who were of a normal size otherwise, struck the villagers with astonishment as their skin was tinged of a green colour all over. No one could understand their speech, nor could the children understand what was said to them. They were also clothed in some material of which even the oldest housewife in the village had never seen the like. Weeping bitterly, they were taken to the house of Sir Richard de Caine, the local Lord, where white bread, honey and milk were set before them. But although plainly famished, the children would not touch this or any other food, until some fresh-cut beans were brought into the house. The green food delighted them and by signs they indicated that they must have some. When given some of the beans, they seized

The Living Landscape

upon them and tore open the bean-stalks, instead of the pods, hoping to find food. Not finding any they began to weep copiously again, until being shown how to open the pods they fed upon the beans with great delight and for a long time after would eat nothing else. The boy, who remained 'languid and depressed', died shortly after his arrival in Woolpit, but the girl flourished and being highly intelligent, learned the common language. She also gradually came to have a liking for a normal diet and, with the change, gradually lost her green colouring.

After a while, she was baptised and stayed many years in the service of Sir Richard, 'rather loose and wanton in her conduct', although one version of the tale states that she married a man from King's Lynn and had children, both boys and girls, none of whom were green. Up until the early 1900s some descendants, it is claimed, were still living in the town. She was often asked about the place that she came from and how she and her brother had come to Woolpit. She used to tell her questioners that she came from a place called St. Martins Land, where the people, animals and all that could be seen were green. There was no sun there, only a soft light like that which shines after sunset or twilight, but beyond a broad river there lay a land of light. It was as they were following their green sheep that... 'They came to a certain cave, on entering which they heard a delightful sound of bells; ravished by whose sweetness they were for a long time wandering on through the cavern until they came to its mouth. When they came out of it they were struck senseless by the excessive light of the sun and the unusual temperature of the air; and thus they lay for a long time. Being terrified by the noise of those who came on them, they wished to fly, but they could not find the entrance of the cavern before they were caught.'

Of this strange tale, there has never been a 'rational' explanation, other than that the two green children did, in fact, as they said, come from a Land under the earth.

The Devil's Plantation

As recently as October of 1952, a correspondent to the East Anglian Magazine had this to say on the subject; 'I have heard it said that until quite recently there was a hole in a field beside the Swanton Morley-Bawdeswell road. It was neither an old well nor a drain. It did not appear to have been used by fox, badger or rabbit. Surrounded by coarse clumps of grass and bracken and of unguessed depth, the hole remained a mystery. A whisper spread that it was an entrance to St. Martin's Land where it is always dusk and where the Green Children live. These pixies have always been a constant trouble to the people of East Anglia. The hole was filled!'

At one time, it was believed that a collection of the spirits of a particular area, Land Wights, Ferishers, Hikey Sprites and others, would collect together at night to form what was called the 'Ward'. This was a magical band that protected the village or town from trouble during the dark hours, both internal and external, both spiritual and physical. They would collect at twilight at certain designated places of power around the village, and then travel to their places of 'watch and ward' along special routes that were recognised as such by the local human populace. It was considered unlucky to travel along these routes at night at certain times of year, as they were the special 'property' of the Ward and of other spirits, both great and small, who moved about the Land. This is indicative of the life within the land, the living Virtue and of the seasonal changes in this energy that could be harmful to humans if encountered without proper preparation. Witches and other magic workers were, of course, immune to this prohibition, as they knew and still know how to work with the flow of the Virtue and the beings that are part of it. In some places, it was thought that certain humans, living and dead, also formed part of this protective band and would join in spirit each night with the Ward in defence of their town. These days, however, the Ward is rarely acknowledged and in most areas is in abeyance.

The Living Landscape

🌿 Land Drakes 🌿

Dragons are often associated in many people's minds with the landscape and being representative of the energies contained within it, and East Anglia is not without its own dragon tales as well. This story, which happened in 1405, comes from the Suffolk/Essex border town of Bures St. Mary and is left to us in monkish Latin by John de Trokelowe and Henry de Blandforde. They describe a creature 'vast in body, with a tufted head, saw-like teeth and a very long tail, which did evil by going to and fro among the sheep and killing many'. The bowmen of Richard de Waldergrave, on whose land the dragon lurked, moved out to confront it but the body of the beast turned the arrows aside and they sprang back from its armour, 'as if from stone or iron; and those arrows which fell on the spine of its back glanced off again and sprang away with clangings as if they had struck plates of bronze.' But when the dragon saw that the men were advancing once more, 'it took refuge in the mere and hid among the reeds; nor was it any more seen.'

A fearsome, winged dragon once terrified the inhabitants of Ludham in Norfolk by appearing in the village each night, so that none dared to venture out after darkness had fallen. Each morning, after the drake had returned to its lair, the villagers filled up the entrance with stones and bricks, but these failed to stop the beast from making its nightly sorties. One afternoon, the villagers were horrified on seeing the dragon emerging from its burrow. When it had travelled some way away, a brave, strong man rolled a single round stone into the entrance of the lair, completely stopping it up. After basking in the warm sunshine, the dragon made its way home, only to find its way inside totally blocked. Finding it impossible for it to move the stone it left, lashing its tail in fury and bellowing loudly, over the fields towards the Bishop's palace. There, it passed along the causeway to the ruined Abbey of St. Bene't, where

The Devil's Plantation

it slid under the great archway and disappeared into the vaults underneath. After some time, its former home was filled in and the people of Ludham were never troubled again, the dragon never more appearing.

Finally on this subject, among the MSS in the Library of the Dean and Chapter at Canterbury is the Warden's small, leather-bound book, in which the following story appears; '..... on Friday the 26th September in the year of Our Lord 1449, about the hour of Vespers, two terrible Dragons were seen fighting for about the space of one hour, on two hills, of which one, in Suffolk, is called Kydyndon Hyl and the other in Essex Blacdon Hyl. One was black in colour and the other reddish and spotted. After a long conflict the reddish one obtained the victory over the black, which done, both returned into the hills above named whence they had come, that is to say, each to his own place to the admiration of many beholding them.' Kydyndon Hyl is now known as Killingdon Hill at Kedington on the Suffolk side of the river Stour, whilst Blacdon Hyl, opposite in Essex, is now known as Ballingdon Hall. A mile separates them. On the banks of the Stour, below Killingdon Hill and between it and Ballingdon Hill, is a large marshy meadow, locally known as 'Sharpfight Meadow', probable scene of the battle.

Although this is a very small sample of East Anglian Dragon tales, it is interesting to see how closely each of these beasts is associated with a landscape feature or features; hills, meadows, old ruins, rivers, etc. and how well they bear out the persistent association of them with geomantic energies. In other regions, magical practitioners describe these energies in terms of Serpents, Snakes, 'Worms' and Lizards, but they all contain the same essential import; these animals are the embodiment of the natural, telluric currents that flow through the land and may be made use of by the witch or folk-magician, having sufficient knowledge and expertise. The lay of the land, its character, gentleness or otherwise, contributes to the character of the residing

The Living Landscape

'dragon' and hence the qualities of the energies available there. These are embedded in the old tales and are there as pointers and guides for subsequent practitioners to make use of.

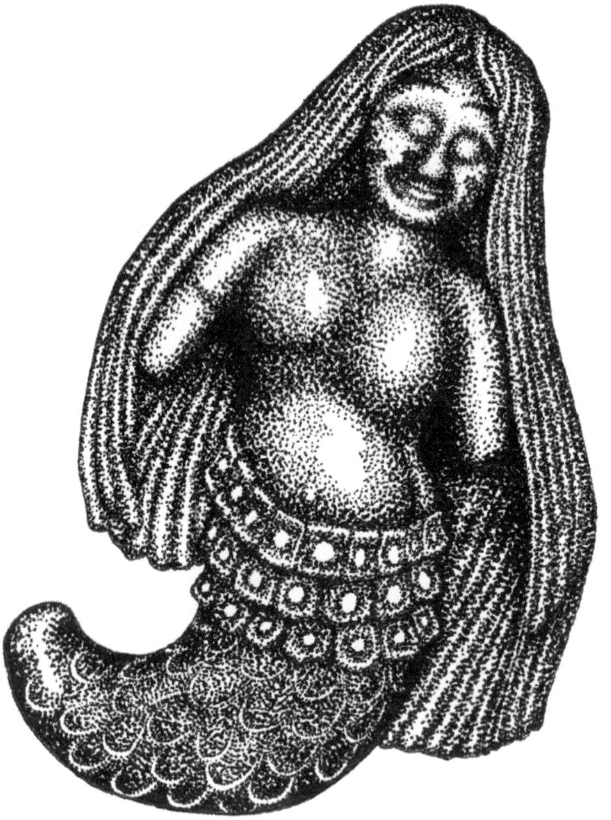

Meremaids, Giants and Spectral Hounds

With East Anglia having such a long coastline, it would be expected that the region abounds in traditions of magic and mystery concerning the denizens of the deep, namely mermaids and their kin. With one notable exception (which I will describe below), this is however not the case. It may be that these tales have now been lost, as there are many church pews and bench-ends carved into the likenesses of mermaids by the mediaeval craftsmen that made them, or it may be that, not having a wild and rocky coastline, these stories never developed as they did in other areas. However, East Anglia does have a tradition of 'land-based' mermaids, continuing the theme of a living landscape and the magic thereof begun in the previous chapter, and these are known as 'Meremaids' or 'Merewives'.

Maids of the Meres

The name Mermaid derives from Old English *mere*, a pool or lake, and it formed the first part of *mere-wif*, 'merewife', the term still preserved in the East Anglian dialect. This is the term applied to Grendel's Dam, or mother, a cannibalistic ogress who lived beneath a lake, described in the Anglo-Saxon classic Beowulf, which many scholars now think was originally written in East Anglia. Like the ogress, the merewives haunted the inland pools, pits and rivers of the inland areas, rather than the seashores, and were thought to pull in anyone who was foolish enough to lean too far over the water. The River Gipping in Suffolk was notorious for containing them, and James Bird (a local man born in Earl Stonham in 1788), wrote in a poem from 1837 about his boyhood in the area and his mother calling out to him;

'Make haste and do your errand. Go not nigh
The River's brink, for there the mermaids lie.
Be home at five!'

The merewives however, mainly lived in pools and pits which, like the lake in Beowulf, were described as bottomless. There were the Meremaid Pits in Fornham All Saints and the well in the village of Rendlesham in the same county, and those in the surrounding districts, which were all reputed to contain meremaids. A correspondent to Robert Chambers *'Book of Days'* (1863-4), writing from Suffolk, informed him that meremaids abounded in the ponds and ditches of his locality; *'I once asked a child what mermaids were, and he was ready with his answer at once, "Them nasty things what crome (hook) you into the water!"'*

It is an old belief that marshland and fenland children were often born with webbed or partially webbed feet (and this is not uncommon in East Anglia in general, even today). Such children, and they were usually girls – so the old belief went – were usually beautiful and were said to be half meremaid and half ferisher; unless their bare feet were seen, they were impossible to tell from normal mortals. They loved to play near meres and dykes, but had a strong homicidal tendency and often tried to push their more normal companions into the pools and drown them. The Cambridgeshire poet J. R. Withers describes much local lore in his verses concerning the countryside around the village of Fordham; in his 1864 poem *'The Pond in the Meadow'*, he writes;

> *And strange were the tales of the pond in the meadow,*
> *And eager we listened with eyes opened wide,*
> *To those tales often told by poor Mary the widow,*
> *Who lived in a cottage the meadow beside.*
> *Play not, my dear boys, near the pond in the meadow,*
> *The mermaid is waiting to pull you beneath;*
> *Climb not for a bird's nest, the bough it may sliver,*
> *And the mermaid will drag you to darkness and death.*

Although sharing their name with the mermaid of classical and heraldic traditions, the merewife is a product of genuine, native tradition, rather than of learned lore. The bugbear that these creatures have become belies the traditional worth and use to which they were put by magical practitioners. As in many cases of native lore, they have been 'demonised' to hide their true value and worth, actually probably by the practitioners themselves, rather than the Church or Authorities. East Anglian magical lore asserts that, like many other openings into the earth, be they on solid ground or not, manmade or natural, they are entrances to the chthonic Other realms and may be entered and journeyed within by those of sufficient skill, knowledge and courage. Like all sorties of this kind, they are not without their dangers and the warnings given of the denizens of the deep may well reflect these actual perils, as well as to scare off dabblers and the merely curious. The merewives, being natives of this Other/ Underworld realm, were the guardians of the thresholds to these realms and the knowledge and powers that could be found and

The Devil's Plantation

developed there. Contact with the merewives could bring about profound changes in the consciousness of the local magical practitioner, if they knew the right techniques, but could bring madness and death to those unprepared and unlearned. It was often to protect the unwary that the tales of danger were started, and to leave the land clear for the local witches to continue to develop their practices undisturbed. The merewife was emblematic of the rich depths of wisdom, magic and knowledge, stored in the Underworld and accessible to the magic-worker. They were and still are, a glyph for the information buried deep in the psyche of all individuals, which may come welling up under the right conditions.

As an adjunct to the tales of the meremaids, it is worth noting a more personal and individual tale of a water-dwelling creature, recorded by the previously mentioned Ralph of Coggeshall, around the turn of the 13th. Century. According to this chronicler, in the reign of King Henry II, some fishermen from the Suffolk coastal town of Orford were hauling in their nets one day when they found they had a most unusual catch. Described by Ralph as a *hominem silvestrem* ('wodewose' or wild man), the being was shaped exactly like a man and was completely nude but extremely hairy, 'in such abundance that it appeared dishevelled and shaggy; his beard particularly was thick and pine-like, and around his chest it was particularly hairy and shaggy.' He was, however, almost completely bald. The fishermen took the man to the Castellan of Orford Castle, Bartholomew de Glanville, who took him in and fed him, initially treating him well. The wild man ate whatever food he was given, but much preferred raw meat and fish, which he would squeeze dry with his hands and consume with relish. He slept on a couch that was provided for him and was generally no trouble, except that he would not or could not speak, remaining quite dumb. The people in the castle did not know if he was human and wondered if he could be an evil spirit inhabiting the body of a drowned sailor. Lacking any evidence from the wild man himself, they hung him up by his feet and tortured him to see if they could get him to speak, but this was apparently unsuccessful, so they desisted and tried another tack. They decided to take the man to mass to see if he was a Christian and whether the solemnity and dignity of the occasion would elicit any response from him. This however failed also, the creature apparently having no interest in the ceremony at all, remaining as mute as ever. The Castellan began to become bored after this, deeming there to be no fun in a 'pet' that only ate and slept. Accordingly, he ordered a portion of the river leading to the sea to be netted off and the creature to be placed therein. In this pen the wild man seemed perfectly happy and his captors began to lose their vigilance in guarding him. Eventually he broke out and swam off to sea, but remarkably, he later returned and stayed another two months, becoming very friendly with the local inhabitants. However, he finally swam away never to return, but the tale has persisted in the area ever since, leading to further stories of encounters with beings from the sea. This tale, and those before, go to show the deep importance, for East Anglians at least, of the desirable but dangerous need for contact with the beings of other realms and places; it almost seems like part of the psyche of the inhabitants of the area.

Herculean Labourers

Giants have always featured in the lore of East Anglia – we have already seen the importance of the Gogmagog hills in this respect – but there are still others that leave their mark in the folkloric record. This is a letter from an unknown correspondent to his brother, dated November 1651;

The Devil's Plantation

'Loving Brother – I thought it worthy my writing to you, what this other day was discovered to many here the like of which few of our predecessors have seen. For here, near the place of your Nativity, at Brockford Bridge, at the end of the street towards Ipswich, by the gravelly way, between the Lands lace (our cosen Rivets) John Vice and another were digging gravell in the Rode, and a little within the earth found the carcase of a Giant (for so I think I may term him) for from top of his skull to the bottom of the bones of his feet was ten foot, and over-thwart his brest, from the ultimate of one shoulder to the other as he lay interred, and before stirring, was four feet. His scull of the bignesse neer of an half bushell, the circumference of one of his thigh bones of the bignesse of a middle-sized woman's wast, the nether jaw bone had in it firmly fixed 16 teeth of an extraordinary bignesse, the other none.

When the finding of this wonder of men was noised abroad, many of the people of the adjacent Townes resorted to see it, and divers out of mere folly, I think, than discretion, broke the skeleton to gain part, or small pieces of bones, to brag they had part of him.

Severall are the opinions of men in judging what time this man lived; some think him to be a Dane, others imagine he might belong to Prince Arthur, but for my part I shall suspend my judgement, and leave it to wiser men; only thus much I think I may say that there hath not lived such a man in England this hundred years: his head lay near a quarter of a yard lower than his feet, and the superfices of the earth was worn down within neer an handfull of his shin bones. He was buried North and South, his head to Ipswich-ward and his feet towards Norwich.

It may be you may say I might have employed my time better than in troubling you with this letter, but I assure you of the truth of this, and the wonder of the thing commanded me to impart thus much unto you.
Your loving brother I.G.'

At Newbourne is a well-known headstone commemorating George Page, the Suffolk Giant, who died on 28th April,

Meremaids, Giants and Spectral Hounds

1870, aged 25 years. It bears the inscription; *'The deceased was exhibited in most of the towns of England, but his best exhibition is with his Blessed redeemer.'* Page stood 7'7" in his stockinged feet.

A massive tomb in East Somerton churchyard, Norfolk, contains the body of Robert Hales, better known as the 'Norfolk Giant'. Hales outgrew everyone in his family, the shortest of whom was six feet, and attained the extraordinary stature of seven feet eight inches; he weighed thirty-three stones. Born in 1820, on his return from Canada, which he visited in 1848, he became the landlord of the 'Craven Head' Inn, in Drury Lane, London, where many visitors were attracted. He was later presented to Queen Victoria and Prince Albert at Buckingham Palace. When he died of tuberculosis in 1863, he was buried alongside his parents.

From the *Ipswich Journal* of 25th August, 1797, comes the following;

> *Sunday, died at Nacton House of Industry, Thos. Smith, aged 37, who before his last illness, which continued upwards of 24 weeks, weighed 21 stones 9 lbs. and although he went drooping (having broke some of his ribs) was still 6'9" high and at his decease his corpse measured 7'2".*

However, all these pale into insignificance against, and may be an attempt to capture and retain the memory of, the exploits of the East Anglian giant, Tom Hickathrift. Although the legends concerning him stretch quite far across East Anglia, the majority of the action in the tales takes place in the far western corner of Norfolk, in a rough triangle bordered by King's Lynn, Wisbech and Downham Market, and more specifically in that area known as 'Marshland Fen'. Upon the western edge of this region is 'The Smeeth', a name that once applied to the whole Marshland (and probably derives from an Old English word meaning 'smooth'). This was, in olden

The Devil's Plantation

days, a fine pastureland about 2 miles or so across and of 1200 acres in extent. Over 30,000 sheep and cattle were grazed here by the 'Seven Towns of Marshland' to whom the plain was common – namely Tilney, Terrington, Clenchwarton, Walpole, West Walton, Walsoken and Emneth. Somewhere in this region of the Marshland, say the legends, was born Tom Hickathrift, 'in the reign before William the Conqueror', the son of a poor labourer also called Thomas Hickathrift. His father died not long after Tom was born, and his poor old mother was forced to work day and night to support him, since he was very lazy, and ate a huge amount, 'for he was in height', says one story, 'when he was but ten years of age, about eight feet, and in thickness five feet, and his hand was like unto a shoulder of mutton; and in all parts from top to toe, he was like unto a monster, and yet his great strength was not known'. He had a giant's appetite too, as the rhyme goes;

> *'He ate a cow and a calf,*
> *An ox and a half,*
> *The church and the steeple,*
> *And then all the people,*
> *And still had not enough.'*

Although there are many tales concerning Tom, the earliest – and main ones – occur in a book by John Weever called, *'Ancient Funerall Monuments'*, dated 1631. Both tales feature the cart wheel and axle that Tom used as weapons and for which he is best remembered. The first tale is called 'How Tom showed his Strength and slew the Giant'.

Feeling sorry for his poor, widowed mother having to keep such a lazy and gluttonous son, a local farmer said she could have two bundles of straw for nothing, as long as she got someone to collect it. Tom's mother obtained a thick cart rope and, after much pleading, managed to get her son

Meremaids, Giants and Spectral Hounds

to agree to go and collect the straw. When he got to the farm, the farmer told Tom he could have as much as he could carry, so Tom laid the rope on the ground and piled up as much straw as would have filled a whole wagon, tied up the bundle and easily carried it home. The farmer was much dismayed at loosing so much straw, but would not go back on his word, so decided to do something about the next load. He hid two large stones, both weighing a hundredweight apiece, in the straw stack and waited for Tom to return. When Tom came back, he laid out his rope as before, piled up the straw again, including the two stones without even noticing them, tied up his bundle and walked away as easily as he had done the first time. On the way home, the stones both fell out at intervals with a thump and Tom thought they were loads of corn that had been badly cleaned from the stalks, resolving to tell the farmer about it later. When he arrived back home and his mother saw the huge amount of free straw that she had acquired, she could hardly believe her luck; she was soon boasting to all and sundry of how her son had carried such great loads and what a fine man he was. After this, Tom was rarely idle again, as people came from far and wide to employ a man who had the strength and could do the work of three or four grown men. Amongst those seeking his services, was a brewer from King's Lynn, who asked Tom to carry beer for him from Lynn to Wisbech. Tom agreed to this and the brewer showed him the way that he must drive the dray carrying the beer, avoiding the area known as the Smeeth. This area was then controlled by a fearsome Ogre or Giant, who killed anyone who dared to put a foot on what he considered to be his property. Tom

The Devil's Plantation

began his job and journeyed along the roundabout way prescribed by the brewer, but soon became tired of this, deciding that if he went across the Smeeth, he could cut his journey in half. So one day, Tom set off right across the Smeeth. But no sooner had he begun his journey across this land, than the giant came rushing out of his cave-fortress home, roaring and shouting, challenging him to a fight and threatening to dash his brains out with his huge club. 'Do you not see how many heads hang upon yonder tree that have offended my law! But thy head shall hang higher than all the rest for an example'. To which Tom then gave the classic riposte 'A turd in your teeth for your news, for you shall not find me like one of them'. Enraged, the giant returned to his cave to fetch his club, whilst Tom climbed down from his dray, took off a cart wheel and the axle-tree and held them before him as his own club and shield. When the giant returned, there began a mighty battle; Tom eventually beat the twelve-foot high ogre into the ground and sliced off his head. After this deed Tom became the hero of the Marshland, and was henceforth known to all as 'Master' Hickathrift (a formerly distinct title that lost its significance in the 17th century). Tom went into the ogre's cave and found it filled with gold and silver and jewels of every size and colour; all the riches the ogre had taken from those he had killed. From that day on, Tom became very rich and all the people were able to come and go across the Smeeth as they liked, without fear of the ogre anymore.

The second tale concerning Tom goes as follows and shows Tom as the defender of those in conflict with authority. A rich and powerful Lord lived in Tilney and was a great thorn in the side of the locals, as he insisted that the common ground on which they grazed their cattle actually belonged to him. One day the Lord went so far as to round up all the cattle that were on the common and drive them into his own yards. He then rode to the nearby village and announced to the people that unless they renounced all

Meremaids, Giants and Spectral Hounds

claim to the land, they would never see their beasts again. This situation would obviously cause great hardship to the locals and made them very angry. They swore that they would never give up the land and vowed to get their cattle back, even if it meant fighting for them. The next day they armed themselves with knives, pitchforks, hoes, rakes and anything else they could lay their hands on and marched on the Lord's house, broke down the gates and marched up the drive. However, they found the Lord waiting for them, with all his armed retainers, as one of the Lord's servants had overheard the plan the previous day and had forewarned the Lord. There began a most ferocious battle, with the villagers definitely getting the worst of it, being armed only with farm implements, whereas the Lord and his retainers were fully armed with swords and shields. The villagers were pushed back, off the Lord's property and onto the disputed land of the Smeeth, and it was looking very bad for them when Tom Hickathrift, who lived nearby, drove onto the scene in the large wagon he used as a coach, because of his size. Although a giant, Tom had learned his lessons in the past and had given up his lazy and gluttonous ways, and had become a kind and caring man. He had heard something of the misfortunes of the villagers in the past, and could now see that they were in deep trouble and could do with some help. He therefore leaped down from his wagon and reached for his club, which he usually kept with him. However, on this morning, he had forgotten it and had left it lying on his kitchen table. Without a second thought, he heaved up his wagon, removed one of the wheels and the axle-tree, as he had done before, and stood ready armed for battle. Holding the wheel before him, he waded into the battle, whirling the axle-tree over his head like a flail and laying about him at the Lord's men for all he was worth, until they were all lying dead or senseless on the ground. He then spied the Lord, who was standing at the back of the combat, well out of the way and challenged him to a fight, man to man. The Lord, who was really a big

The Devil's Plantation

bully and a coward at heart, fell on his knees at Tom's feet and begged the giant for mercy. Standing over him with his 'shield and club', as if about to crush the life out of him, Tom agreed to spare the Lord, on condition that he give up all claim to the disputed land, return the villagers' cattle and never trouble them again. The Lord readily swore to the conditions, if only Tom would let him go. So Tom promised to do so and afterwards the villagers received all their cattle back and were never troubled by the Lord again.

Apart from John Weever's book, chronicling the actions of Tom Hickathrift, there were many chapbooks written in later days of his exploits and deeds, including the tale of how he won a wager by a drinking contest, kicked a huge stone like a football right into a neighbouring parish, and how he made friends with a travelling tinker who helped him put down a rebellion; most of these tales include the use by Tom of the cartwheel and axle-tree as weapons. Many places in the Wisbech area are pointed out as showing traces of Tom's existence; there are his own grave, the stone that he kicked, the ogre's mound or grave, 'Hickathrift's candlesticks' (actually the broken shafts of old preaching crosses) and the various parts of a stone coffin said to be Tom's and of a large size. All of these pieces have been put together by various researchers in the past and various theories have been advanced as to who Tom Hickathrift actually was, if indeed he ever existed as a living man at all. One of the most recent, based on extensive research, both field and literary, concludes that he was originally – or at least based on the memory of – Sir Frederick de Tilney, 'a man of more than ordinary strength and stature, and had his chief residence at Boston. He attended King Richard I, anno 1190, into the Holy Land, was with him at the siege of Acon, where he is said to have performed prodigies of valour, and was there knighted for his services...'[1]

---

1. Thompson, Pishey, *'History & Antiquities of Boston'*, Longman & Co., 1856, pp.373-5.

Meremaids, Giants and Spectral Hounds

However, there are still lingering doubts over this and for many local people – and certainly those with an interest in the sanctity of the land and its lore – Tom Hickathrift is more than the memory of a Norman knight. Embedded in his story are many echoes of times long past, further back even than the Norman Conquest and of the remains of what may be some half-forgotten lore. T.C. Lethbridge, the antiquarian, mentioned in the previous chapter in connection with the Gogmagog hills, maintained that Hickathrift is the remains of a deity that was once worshipped by the Iron Age Iceni tribe, indigenous to the area in question. His ideas on this subject have been mostly ridiculed by scholars, both amateur and professional alike, because of the many supposed errors in his research and conclusions. However, despite the admittedly erratic nature of both his methods and conclusions, they may be missing the point, and Lethbridge is far from alone in his conclusions. Despite extensive research, no one knows the origin of the name 'Hickathrift'; it has just not been possible to trace it, etymologically or otherwise. It is entirely possible, despite all claims to the contrary, that it is indeed a survival of the 'Iceni' name. Indeed, in the region in question and further afield in both Norfolk and Suffolk, remains of this very word are acknowledged to exist in certain place and dwelling names; the Icknield Way, Icklingham village, Ixworth, Hickling village and Broad, to name but a few; a number of them have been kept alive in Anglo-Saxon names, migrated from the original British tongue.

Another example of the longevity of language, custom and tradition, is the occurrence of ancient 'counting words', used by shepherds in both Norfolk and Suffolk, to count their sheep. One such example from Suffolk goes as follows; Hant, Tant, Tethery, Futhery, Fant (5); Sarny, Darny, Dorny, Downy, Dick (10); Hain-dick, Tain-dick, Tuthery-dick, Futhery-dick, Jigger (15); Hain-jigger, Tain-jigger, Tuther-jigger, Futher-jigger, Full Score. The West

Norfolk Shepherd counted his sheep to the chant of; Ina, Tina, Tether, Wether, Pink; Hater, Slater, Sara, Dara, Dick. Both of these examples have been acknowledged linguistically to be remnants of the speech of Iron Age Britain – so-called 'Celtic Language' – which have survived for over two millennia. It is therefore not inconceivable that Tom Hickathrift is indeed a survival of the Iron Age tribes of the area. This attests both to the tenacity of place/name and folk-memory, but also the tenacity of the underlying beliefs that keep them alive. When dealing with the powers of the land, it is unwise for academia to discount anything.

Dark and Demon Dogs

Haunting the coastline from the Wash to the Deben and beyond, and inland along the Peddars Way into the Brecklands, on marshland roads and mudflats, through the Fens and into the Broads, pads the ancient terror known as Black Shuck. For many hundreds of years the legend of the ghostly black hound has been kept alive and is probably the best known of all East Anglian spectres, still appearing to people today. He is typically seen as a huge, great, black shaggy hound, with blazing red eyes and dragging rattling chains behind him, instilling terror into all he comes upon and considered a portent of impending death or doom by most. Although generally called Black Shuck, he is known by many other names too; the Galleytrot, Old Scarfe, Owd Rugman, Shug Monkey and the Hateful Thing being some, although some form of Shuck or Shuggy is most common. Nor is he always a large black hound, appearing as anything from the size of a Labrador (shrinking into a cat!), a white rabbit in Thetford, to a calf or a donkey and even a monkey on a few occasions. Sometimes he was invisible, only his fierce breath, padding feet, fearful howls or the clanking of his chains giving evidence of his presence. Sometimes he could be seen without his head, but always with his glowing eyes appearing in the middle of where his head should be. One tale from Garveston in Norfolk goes;

> 'They du speak of a dog that walks regular. They call him Skeff and his eyes are as big as saucers and blaze wi' fire. He is fair as big as a small wee pony and his coat is all skeffy-like, a shaggy coat across, like an old sheep. He has a lane, and a place out of which he come, and he vanish when he hev gone far enough.'

Another informant from the village of Clopton, Suffolk, reported, 'a thing with two saucer eyes', on the road to Woolpit. It would not move out of his way but grew larger and larger as it breathed: 'I shall want you within a week'. The man died the next day.

One Christmas day in the middle of the 19th. Century, Black Shuck pushed against a small, blind boy who was standing on Thetford Bridge with his older sister. The little boy plaintively asked his sister to send the big dog away, but his sister assured him that there was no dog anywhere near them. However, the terrified boy insisted that there was, and that it was trying to push him into the water to drown him. The sister then felt the poor boy being carried away from her; she realised then that what he could feel, and she could not see, must be the terrible Black Shuck that she had heard so much about. Just as her little brother was about to be pushed into the water, she dragged him back from the edge and, hand-in-hand, they rushed off back to their waiting parents at home.

Villagers in the Waveney Valley round about Geldeston call it the 'Hateful Thing', or the 'Churchyard or Hell-beast'. One old village woman claimed that she saw it one night on the road between Gillingham and Geldeston. She tells the story in the following words;

'It was after I had been promised to Josh that I saw the Hateful Thing. We met Mrs S. and she started to walk with us. I heard something like a dog running pit-pat-pit-pat-pit-pat. "I wonder what that dog wants", I said to Mrs S. I was walking between Josh and Mrs S. and I lay hold on Mrs S's. arm and she say "It's in front of us; look, there it be." Just in front was what looked like a big, black dog; but it wasn't a dog at all; it was the Hateful Thing and it betokened some great misfortune. It kept on until we came to the churchyard, when it went right through the wall and we saw it no more'.

In Norfolk, Neatishead Lane, near Barton Broad, is a favourite walk of Shuck, as is the cliff path from Beeston, near Sheringham to Overstrand. This recalls the old adjuration in the legend of St. Margaret;

Still be though still,
Poorest of all, stern one,
Nor shalt thou, Old Shuck,
Moot with me no more.
But fly, sorrowful thing,
Out of mine eyesight,
And dive thither where thou man
May damage no more.

A more humorous tale involves the grounding of Noah's Ark on Mulbarton Common, south of Norwich. Scoffers had better not go to Mulbarton. When one village elder was heckled on the point, he replied with some heat;

'Thass trew! Trew as I stand here. Where else could it ha' grounded? Aren't this the highest bit o' ground for miles around? When Ole Nick see the Ark he got inter a poont (punt), an' curled his tail up under the thwart and come rowin' around jest as Noah had opened the winder to let the dove in. And Nick sings out: "Mornin' Cap'n Noah. Nice mornin'

Meremaids, Giants and Spectral Hounds

arter the rain". But ole Noah he sees Nick's tail a-curled up under the thwart an' he sings out: "I know you. You're Owd Shuck! You goo to Hell". And bangs the winder down'.

However, perhaps the most famous accounts of the legend are to be found in *'Holinshed's Chronicle'*, an ambitious history of England which was updated to include contemporary events, and a pamphlet entitled *'A Straunge and Terrible Wunder'* written by the Rev. Abraham Fleming, Rector of St. Pancras Church. Both accounts were published in 1577, shortly after the events recorded therein. According to Holinshed's Chronicle;

> 'On Sundaie the fourth of August (1577), between the houres of none and ten of the clocke in the forenone whilest the minister was reading the second lesson in the Parish church of Bliborough (Blythburgh), a towne in Suffolke, a strange and terrible tempest of lightening and thunder strake through the wall of the same church into the ground almost a yard deepe, drave downe all the people on that side above twentie persons, then venting the wall up to the venstre, cleft the doore, and returning to the steeple, rent the timber, brake the chimes, and fled towards Bongie (Bungay), a towne six miles off. The people that were stricken downe were found groueling more than halfe an houre after.........". At Bungay the storm "wroong in sunder the wiers and wheels of the clocks, slue two men which sat in the belfrie, when the other were at the procession or suffrages and scorched an other which hardlie escaped.'

However, Fleming gives the account as starting in Bungay church and includes the infamous Black Shuck;

> 'Sunday, being the fourth of this August, in ye yeer of our Lord 1577, to the amazing and singular astonishment of the present beholders, and absent hearers, at a certain towne called Bungay, not past tenne miles distant from the citie of

Norwiche, there fell from heaven an exceeding great and terrible tempest sodein and violent............ There were assembled at the same season, to hear divine service and common prayer, according to order, in the parish church (St. Mary's) of the said towne of Bungay, the people thereabouts inhabiting, who were witnesses of the straungeness, the rarenesse and sodenesse of the storm, consisting of rain violently falling, fearful flashes of lightning and terrible cracks of thunder, which came with such unwonted force and power, that to the perceiving of the people.....the church did as it were quake and stagger, which struck into the hearts of those that were present, such a sore and sodain feare, that they were in a manner robbed of their right wits.

Immediately hereupon, there appeared in a most horrible similitude and likenesse to the congregation then and there present, a dog as they might discern it, of a black colour; at the sight whereof, together with the feareful flashes of fire which then were seene, moved such admiration in the minds of the assemblie that they thought doomes day was already come.

This black dog, or the divel in such a likenesse (God he knoweth al who worketh all), running all along down the body of the church with great swiftnesse, and incredible haste, among the people, in a visible fourm and shape, passed between two persons, as they were kneeling upon their knees, and occupied in prayer as it seemed, wrung the necks of them bothe in one instant clene backward, in somuch that even at a moment where they kneeled, they strangely died.'

After reflecting somewhat on the wrath of God, he continues;

'There was at ye same time another wonder wrought; for the same black dog, still continuing and remaining in one and the selfsame shape, passing by another man of the congregation in the church, gave him such a gripe on the back, that therewith all he was presently withdrawen together and strunk up, as it were a piece of lither scorched in a hot fire; or as the mouth of

a purse or bag, drawen together with a string. The man albeit he was in so straunge a taking, dyed not, but as it is thought is yet alive; whiche thing is mervalous in the eyes of men, and offereth much matter of amasing the minde.

Meanwhile, the Clerk of the church, who had gone outside to clean the guttering, was thrown to the ground during a violent clap of thunder; and at the same time, the wires and wheels of the church clock were *'wrung in sunder and broken in pieces.'* Inside the church, the Curate exhorted to prayer and *'comforted the people'* until the frightening manifestation of the black hound had passed away, leaving behind it marks on the stones and church door *'which are marvellously renten and torne, ye marks as it were of his clawes or talans.'*

According to Fleming, next, on the same morning, in the church of *Blythburgh*, about twelve miles from Bungay;

'the like thing entred, in the same shape and similitude, where, placing himself upon a maine balke or beam, whereon same ye Rood did stand, sodainly he gave a swinge downe through ye church, and there also, as before, slew two men and a lad & burned the hand of another person that was there among the rest of the company, of whom divers was blasted. This mischief thus wrought, he flew with wonderful force to no little feare of the assembly, out of the church in a hideous and hellish likeness.'

The marks of his talons, burned into the inside of the north door of the church, can still be seen today.

Interestingly, archaeologists have recently discovered the skeleton of a massive dog that would have stood 7 feet tall on its hind legs, in the ruins of Leiston Abbey in Suffolk, close to both Bungay and Blythburgh. The remains of the massive dog, which is estimated to have weighed 200 pounds, were found just a few miles from the two churches where Black Shuck killed the worshippers. It

The Devil's Plantation

appears to have been buried in a shallow grave at precisely the same time as Shuck is said to have been on the loose in this instance.

Coming forward in time, there is a legend of a black dog too, at Blickling Hall, Norfolk. In the 19th century, alterations on the Hall were being made by Lord and Lady Lothian, by the demolition of some partitions in order to form a dining-room;

> 'I wish these young people would not pull down the partitions', said an old woman in the village to the local clergyman. 'Why so?' 'Oh, because of the dog. Don't you know that when A. was fishing in the lake, he caught an enormous fish and that, when it was landed, a great black dog came out of its mouth? They never could get rid of that dog, who kept going round and round in circles inside the house, till they sent for a wise man from London, who opposed the straight lines of the partitions to the lines of the circles and so quieted the dog. But if these young people pull down the partitions, they will let the dog loose again, and there's not a wise man in all London could lay that dog now'.

This tale is interesting in that it links the occurrence or appearance of the hound with a practical knowledge of geomantic function and is the only tale told of its kind, as far as I am aware. It also links the Black Dog with the liminal area of the lake, which, as we have seen earlier in the chapter, is a gateway to the Other/Underworlds, guarded by supernatural beings; it is possible that the Black Dog may be another one of these guardian entities.

The common name for the black hound, Shuck, is generally considered to derive from the Old English *scucca* or *sceocca*, which means a devil/the Devil, a demon or a goblin (the 'sc' in OE being pronounced as 'sh'). There is also the likelihood that it comes from the East Anglian dialect word 'Shucky', meaning shaggy or hairy, a marked characteristic of most descriptions of the Hound. The first known use of the term comes from the Norfolk Chronicle or Gazette, in 1805, in an account by the Rev. E.S. Taylor of Martham as follows;

> *'Shuck the Dog-fiend: This phantom I have heard many persons in East Norfolk, and even Cambridgeshire, describe as having seen as a black shaggy dog, with fiery eyes, and of immense size, and who visits churchyards at midnight.'*

However, the term was obviously already in use beforehand, but for how long beforehand, no one knows. In regards to the appearance of the phantom in, at or near to churchyards and graveyards, there is another old tradition that is worth noting here. It was customary in years gone by, to bury a black dog in any new graveyard, before any other burials took place. The dog was intended to act as a guardian for the dead who were laid to rest there, and to protect the entrance to the Otherworld, ensuring that none came out – or went in – that were not supposed to. This practice goes back many millennia and is still rumoured to continue today in some areas; the dog is said to be buried in the North, or North-East of the graveyard, the traditional direction of the Dead and the Underworld.

Attempts to explain the origins and nature of the Black Hound have been many, some prosaic and some fantastical. He is said to be the memory of one of Odin's battle hounds, brought over by the Viking raiders in the 9th century. Whilst this may sound appealing, Odin did not have any war or battle hounds, but was accompanied by two wolves, a description never applied to Shuck. It is possible that he is the remains of a 'fetch beast', conjured by the Norse shamans to clear the pathways for their invasions, but there is no remaining evidence for this, however attractive; but the pathways theme is pertinent and I will come back to that in a moment. In the Anglo-Saxon classic, 'Beowulf', previously referred to in the

The Devil's Plantation

case of Grendel's Dam and the Merewives, the monster Grendel himself is termed a 'scucca' and referred to as master of the fens and moors, some of the very places said to be haunted by Black Shuck in more modern times. He is also linked in popular imagination with the Devil and witchcraft, considered to be the Devil in animal form. Whilst there *are* recorded cases of the Devil appearing in dog or hound form in Suffolk, the descriptions of Shuck's appearances does not seem to fit any of these. He is often linked with Churches and graveyards, as we have seen, as well as crossroads, being described as coming from, passing over or into, or finishing his perambulations at one or the other; this also links in with the fact that the most recorded instances of sightings/encounters of the hound are on paths, roads, trackways, etc. as mentioned above.

It is these latter aspects of the Black Hound that I think give us the biggest clue to his nature and function; this is either as a guardian of the 'ghost roads' – the energetic and spectral pathways across the Land that guide the spirits of the dead on their way, or lead the spirits of living witches and magical practitioners to locations of power or gatherings of their kind – or as a 'psychopomp', guiding the deceased on their last journeys to the Otherworld. It has often been remarked that Black Shuck is nearly always seen walking/padding along or beside a path or trackway and that his presence either heralds or initiates a death or near death experience (sometimes also averting disaster if it is not the person's time to die). It seems highly likely that this Hound is a product of the Living Landscape, given form and function, and imbued with the energy to guard/guide those souls in need over the liminal point between life and death that we all must pass at some point. That he is given such a form by tradition and local culture only goes to show a living tradition stretching back hundreds, if not thousands, of years, as dogs and hounds have been seen as guardians of the gates of the Underworld for millennia, particularly and especially by the succeeding cultures that have inhabited East Anglia and the rest of these Isles. That he is feared, seen as a/the Devil, shunned and reviled, is only indicative of the lack of understanding of most people of the natural Laws and Ways of the Land and their separation from them.

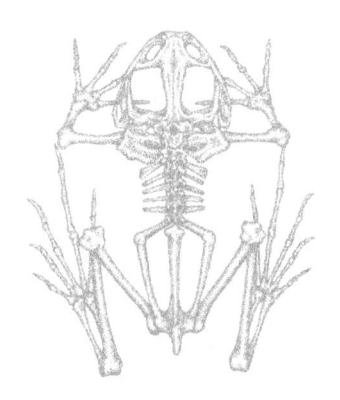

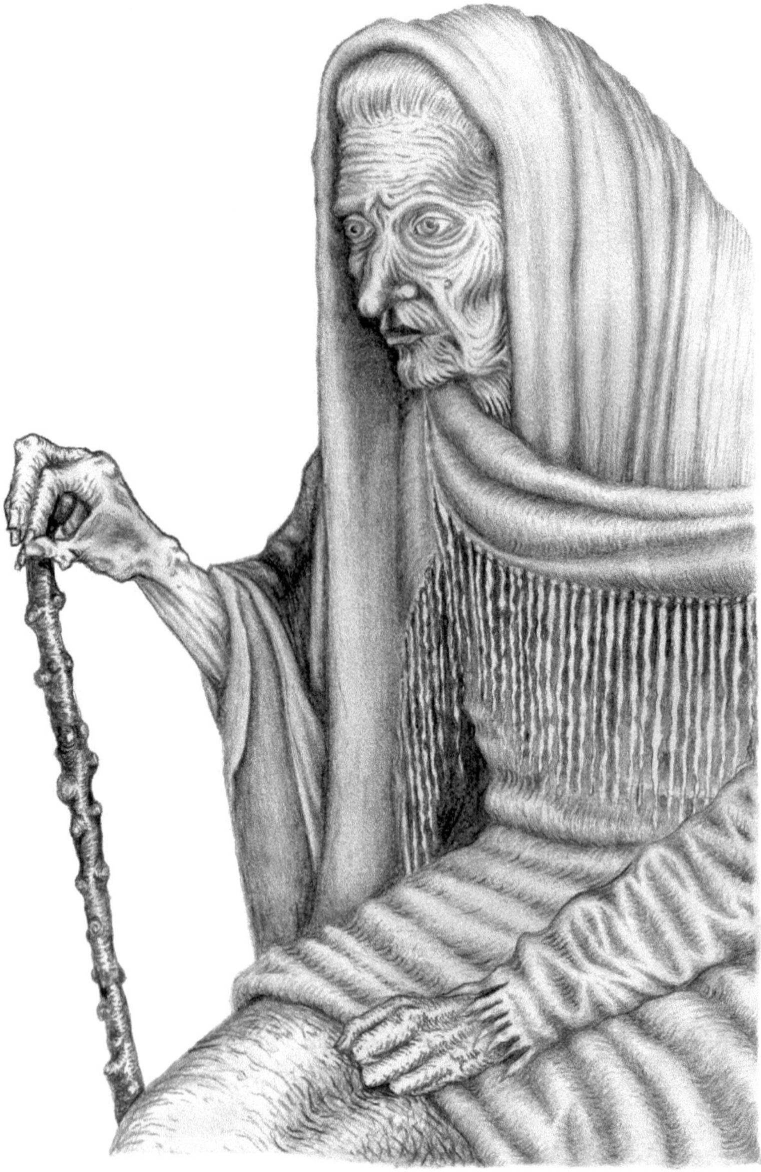

Characters of Craft

Witch Country

East Anglia has been known as 'witch country' for many years; indeed it is known as the witch country, due to the many recorded instances, both ancient and recent, of its colourful, magical practitioners. This does not necessarily imply that there were more magical folk in East Anglia than anywhere else (although the number of persecutions would seem to bear this out), but that there was, and is, a perceived 'differentness' about the witches and cunning folk who lived in this part of the country. They are seen as something slightly 'other', possessing maybe a little more unusual knowledge than your average magic worker. These magical folk were mostly country people (although they numbered the gentry and folk of other classes amongst themselves as well), who had a knowledge of the practical applications of the natural energies of the places that they lived in, of the magical properties of the animals and plants in their areas and, sometimes, of the spells and rituals to be found in the grimoires and magical books of the more educated townsfolk. They were often downtrodden and marginalised, living on the edges of society and often shunned for their knowledge and practices. They were often notably rebellious souls, who kicked against the traces of what was then accepted as normal in society. Conversely, some were well known and accepted members of their locality, much sought after and respected for their knowledge and abilities; they could often help their neighbours when more orthodox methods and practitioners failed them. They used whatever came to hand for their purposes and this included psalms and prayers of the dominant, Christian, religion of the day. Their knowledge was generally handed down orally from one practitioner to the other (although there are the tales of various hand-written 'Black Books', such as 'The Devil's Plantation' and 'The Secret Granary'), and no one knows how old this knowledge was; it may have been 'inspired' the day before yesterday, or it may contain elements that were hundreds of years old, even pre-Christian in origin. To the magical practitioner, it did not matter where it came from, it only mattered that it worked. If a piece of old heathen lore that had come from Saxon or Danish wise men or women still worked, then it was used; indeed, there is a strong thread of dual-faith observance that runs through the whole of East Anglian magical lore, however faint. If a piece of the consecrated host from Mass cured the gout, then it was used. Indeed it could easily be seen by anybody that cared to look, that the saints and prayers, the rites, relics and rituals of the (Catholic) Church could cause miracles to happen, so these were incorporated into magical practice also.

Dual Faith

For a long period of time, Christianity and folk magic/witchcraft existed alongside each other without causing any friction; it was only after the Reformation that serious problems for magical practitioners arose, especially in East Anglia. Before this time, 'magic' was used by the Church itself under many guises and before looking at some individual magical practitioners of more recent times, I would like to give an example of one such practice by the Church, carried out during the Middle Ages, that has all the hallmarks of a magical rite. An article in the Suffolk Chronicle of 20th October, 1810, goes thus;

Extraordinary Custom Formerly Practised by the Monks of Bury St. Edmunds, Suffolk

The religious fathers of this monastery had propagated an opinion, that if any married woman that had no children and wished to become a mother, would but come with a white bull to the shrine of St. Edmund, and make her offerings and vows, she should presently after obtain her desire; and as it was usual to institute processions, to give great dignity and solemnity to the ceremony, it was thought necessary to have a very public one on this important occasion, and for this purpose, a white bull was provided, elegantly adorned with garlands of flowers, ribbons, etc., which being led by one of the monks, the petitioning lady at the same time following him, and often stroking his milk-white side, the procession thus proceeded through Churchgate and Guildhall streets, and along the Cook-Row down to the great West-gate of the abbey, attended by the monks singing, accompanied with a prodigious concourse of people, forming a very numerous cavalcade. – The Bull being dismissed, the lady entered the church, advanced to St. Edmund's shrine, said her prayers, made her offerings at his altar, kissing the stone, and entreating with tears, the blessing of a child, she then returned from the abbey with full assurance of speedy success. This custom had gained so much credit in many parts of the world, that not only many eminent women of this country had recourse to it, but even several ladies belonging to foreign parts. But as it would be very inconvenient for those distant ladies to come in person to perform these ceremonies, it was pronounced to be equally efficacious for them, if they caused to be offered by any other means, one of these wonder working animals at St. Edmund's shrine. A copy of a deed was formerly, and probably at the present time is preserved in the Augmentation

Office, to the following effect; That John Swaffham, sacrist of the monastery of St. Edmund's Bury, certifies to all Christian people, that on the 2nd June, 1474, three religious persons of the city of Ghent, came and offered, as has been accustomed of old time, in the presence of several reputable people, at the shrine of the blessed king, virgin, and martyr, St. Edmund, to the honour of God, and of the said glorious martyr, one white bull, for the accomplishment of the longing of a certain noble lady.'

This appears to be a magical rite, with sacrifices, by any other name.

Coming forward in time, just post-Reformation, we can see that, although rooted in (Catholic) Christian theology, such practices had now become most suspect. The following comes from a book, published in 1562, by Dr. William Bullein, entitled; 'Defence against all sickness, sornes, and woundes that dooe daily assaulte mankinde.' Dr. Bullein was rector of Blaxhall in Suffolk, before going to London, where he took up medicine and made his name as a surgeon. He writes;

'I dyd know wythin these few years a false Witch called M(other) Line, in a town of Suffolk called Perham (Parham), which with a payre of Eben beades and certain charmes, had no small resort of foolish women when their children were syck. To thys lame Witch they resorted to have the Fairie charmed and the Spyute coniured away: through the prayers and the Ebene beads which she sayd came from the Holy Land and were sanctified at Rome. Through whom many goodly cures have been don, but my chaunce was to burn ye sayd beads. Oh! That damnable witches be suffered to lieu unpunished and so many blessed men burned: witches be more hurtful in this realm (Suffolk) than either quarten, pox or pestilence. I knew in a towne called Kelshall (Kelsale), in Suffolk, a Witch whose name was M(other) Didge, who with certain Aue Maries upon her Eben Beads and a wax Candle, used this Charme folowyng

for S. Anthonies fyre, having the sicke body before her, holding up her Hande saying: "there came two Angels out of the North east, one brought fyre, the other brought frost, out fyre and in frost. In nomine patris, etc." I could rehearse an C of sutch knackes of these holy gossips, the fyre take them all, for they be God's enemyes.'

So purely by the use of consecrated beads – a rosary – and prayers from the Catholic liturgy a woman was now declared a witch in the newly Protestant England – even when, *'Through whom many goodly cures have been don.'*

On a lighter and slightly more humorous note, some of the traditions in Norfolk are worth mentioning here. It seemed that witches in North-West Norfolk played a real part in the lives of ordinary folk there from the 14th century onwards. Oral traditions passed on from one generation to another insist again and again that an aged woman living alone was sure to be a witch, well-versed in the black arts and other tricks of the trade, which enabled them as co-partners of the Devil to play on the fears – and incredulity – of the local folk.

One of the supposedly witch-ridden places was Castle Rising. Here, in 1614, the Earl of Northampton founded Trinity Hospital, where twelve poor widows or spinsters could live out their lives together, receiving a dole of six shillings a week. A governess was also provided to watch over them. The Earl thought that by keeping the old women together and providing for them, that they would forsake the devil and all his works and settle down and become good Christian folks. Besides coals and medical attendance they were provided with suitable clothing; this, amongst other things, consisted of a tall, black, cone-shaped hat and a long, black cape. Little did the Earl think that by choosing this apparel he would be setting the pattern for traditional witch-dress for centuries to come! Nor did he take into consideration what would be the end result of keeping twelve old women, well-versed in the magical arts,

The Devil's Plantation

housed under one roof. Apparently as soon as they were settled in and comfortable, they set about holding coven meetings at midnight, to the scandal of the governess set over them. Oral tradition relates that, in due course, the magical influence of this original twelve spread out over the vicinity, and not only were new covens formed in Castle Rising itself, but they also appeared in the nearby villages as well! Tradition, however, is silent on the actions of the Earl concerning this turn of events; perhaps he gave up and just let them get on with it!

❦ *Witchfinder General* ❦

Before continuing, brief mention must be made here of the notorious, so-called 'Witchfinder General', Matthew Hopkins. I do not wish to give this vile man and his accomplices space, much less credence, but the harm and terror that they caused to presumed witches of the Eastern Counties in the 1640s cannot be overlooked in a work of this kind.

Hopkins is reputed to have been the son of John (or James), Hopkins, vicar of Wenham in Suffolk and was a failed lawyer, practising sometime in Ipswich, Suffolk, then Manningtree in Essex. It was there, in 1644, that Hopkins, along with his assistants John Stearne and Mary (Goody) Phillips, began his infamous career. English law, as Hopkins well knew, forbade torture as a means of extracting a confession, but Hopkins pushed the definition of torture to its limit. It was in Manningtree that he first accused a poor, aged, one-legged woman named Elizabeth Clarke of being a witch, and suggested that she was the leader of a local coven that met on Friday nights and offered up sacrifices to the Devil. Upon examination, a third teat was discovered on her body, but it subsequently took three days and nights of continuous 'walking', to exhaust her to the point where she was prepared to confess to possessing five imps in the

Characters of Craft

forms of cats and dogs, which she suckled from her extra teats (which were of a certainty only warts or other wens). As part of her confession, she implicated five other women, saying they were her chief confederates. In their turn, these women, when apprehended and 'questioned', gave the names of yet more poor unfortunates. Of those arrested, four died in prison before their trial and up to nineteen may subsequently have been hanged. Their confessions, though they may sound improbable to us today, became the standard fare of witch trials for the next year or so. Imps and familiars were reputed to have been given names such as Pyewacket, Elemanzer and Grizzel Greedigutt, names which Hopkins stated 'no mortal could invent'.

The success of this trial and others in the same area, led Hopkins and his associates to tour the counties of Suffolk, Norfolk and Cambridgeshire, Huntingdonshire and Bedfordshire, seeking out suspected witches for large sums of money. Sure in the belief that all witches bore on their bodies, in the form of extra teats, the marks which proved that they suckled their devil-given imps, Hopkins had the naked bodies of his victims thoroughly and roughly searched by his assistants for the incriminating evidence. To discover the places on their bodies on which the Devil had set his mark, places which were believed to be insensible to pain, he had his victims 'pricked' with long, pointed blades (some of which retracted into the handles to ensure that they felt no pain). To encourage the witches to confess their crimes, he had them 'tortured' by starvation and prevented from sleeping by having them walked up and down a room for days and nights on end – which, technically, was not torture under the law. Until forbidden to do so, he had many of them ducked or 'swum' in a pond or local river to see if they floated, which proved their guilt. He employed other 'watchers' to keep the accused men and women under constant surveillance, so that the existence of their imps could be proven, and arranged that a small hole be made in the door for the creatures to enter by. In case the imps should 'come in less discernible shape, they that watch are taught to be ever and anon sweeping the room, and if they see any spiders or flies to kill them. And if they cannot kill them, then they may be sure they are her imps.' Moving across the Puritan Parliament-supporting heartland, he forced confessions from those he had been paid to find and bring to trial; many were hanged, many others died in gaol from old age, disease or as a result of their experiences at his hands and those of his assistants.

By 1646 however, the tide of opinion was turning against Hopkins for his violent and costly actions. Amongst others, the Rev. John Gaule, vicar of Great Staughton in Huntingdonshire, published his *'Select Cases of Conscience touching Witches and Witchcraft'*. Whilst not denying the very existence of witchcraft, he complained 'Who is this man who takes upon himself to be the giver of life or death? He could do no more harm if he were himself the servant of Satan. Hopkins' "signs" mean that... every old woman, with a wrinkled face, a furry brow, a hairy lip, a gobber tooth, a squint eye, a squeaking voice or a scolding tongue... having a ragged coat on her back, a scull-cap on her head, a spindle in her hand and a dog or cat by her side, is not only suspected but pronounced for a witch'. He also exposed the methods of torture used by Hopkins for extracting his confessions – the searching, the enforced walking, the pricking and the constant watching.

Other criticisms followed from Essex and, most especially, from Norfolk, where Hopkins was charged not only with cruelty but with enriching himself at the country's expense. He answered these attacks in his pamphlet, *'The Discovery of Witches'*, published in 1647, in which he attempted to justify his methods and in which he denied demanding more than twenty shillings of any town. (In fact this was always his initial estimate of his and his assistants' expenses; the actual fees that he eventually charged after apprehending the so-called witches usually amounted to many pounds in every town he visited). His self-appointed mission of ridding England

Characters of Craft

of all her witches, however, was coming to an end. In that same year, faced with mounting hostility and ill health, he retired from public life. What happened to him after this has long been a subject of intense speculation. It has been a popular – if somewhat wishful – belief, that he himself was swum as a witch and found wanting. A contemporary poem from *'Hudibras'* by Samuel Butler, appearing to describe Hopkins, gives support to this rumour, as lines from the poem concluded; *'Who after prov'd himself a witch, and made a rod for his own breech.'* However, it is much more likely that, suffering from tuberculosis, Hopkins returned to Mistley near Manningtree, where it all began, and died in the August of 1647. So ended the short, but cruel career, of the Witchfinder General.

❋ Mother Lakeland ❋

In 1645, one of the more notable witch trials took place in Ipswich, Suffolk. Similar methods to those used by Hopkins were employed to extract a confession from Mother (Mary) Lakeland, probably the most famous of the Suffolk witches. This case is interesting for a number of reasons. Firstly, it was known that Mother Lakeland had been 'in business' for many years, selling potions, love charms, enchantments and remedies to the people of Ipswich, quite openly and without prosecution; all the normal work of a witch or folk-magician, to whom the general populace were used to going in times of trouble. Secondly, in her 'confession' (following), it was stressed that she was a 'professor of religion', a devout Christian, although she had served the Devil for nearly twenty years and had never been required to renounce her beliefs. This smacks strongly of a dual-faith allegiance, the one faith not troubling the beliefs of the other, in the eyes of Mother Lakeland at least. Finally, Mother Lakeland was, unusually, burned to death, rather than being hanged – which was the normal method of execution for witches in England, post-Reformation – because she was convicted of killing her husband. In English law, this was considered to be petty-treason and, along with grand-treason (killing the Monarch), was punishable with death by burning. Had she not been convicted of killing her husband, she would have hanged like any other witch. The details are given in an old tract entitled *'The Laws against Witchcraft and Conjurations'* and goes as follows.

The Confessions of Mother Lakeland, of Ipswich, who was arraigned and condemned for a witch, and suffered death by burning, at Ipswich, in Suffolk, on Tuesday, the 9th September, 1645.

The said Mother Lakeland hath been a Professor of Religion, a constant hearer of the Word for these many years, and yet a Witch (as she confessed) for the space of near twenty years. The Devil came to her first, between sleeping and waking, and spake to her in a hollow voice, telling her that if she would serve him she would want for nothing. After often solicitation, she consented to him; then he stroke his claw (as she confessed) into her hands, and with her blood wrote the covenants. (Now the subtilty of Sathan is to be observed, in that he did not press her to deny God and Christ, as he useth to do others; because she was a professour, and might have lost all his hold by pressing her too far). Then he furnished her with three imps, two little dogs, and a mole (as she confessed), which she employed in her services. Her husband she bewitched (as she confessed), whereby he lay in great misery for a time, and at last dyed. Then she sent one of her dogs to Mr. Lawrence, in Ipswich, to torment him and take away his life; she sent one of them also to his child, to torment it, and take away the life of it, which was done upon them both; and all this (as she confessed) was because he asked her for twelve shillings that she owed him, and for no other cause.

She further confessed, that she sent her mole to a maid of one Mrs. Jennings in Ipswich, to torment her and take away her life, which was done accordingly, and this for no other cause but for that the said maid would not lend her a needle that she desired to borrow of her, and was earnest with her for a shilling which she owed the said maid.

Then she further confessed, she sent one of her imps to one Mr. Beale, in Ipswich, who had formerly been a suitor to her grandchild; and because he would not have her, she sent and burnt a new ship, that had never been at sea, that he was to go master of; and sent also to torment him and take away his life; but he is yet living, but in very great misery, and it is vainly conceived by the doctors and chirurgeons that have him in hand that he consumes and rots, and that half of his body is rotten upon him as he is living.

Severall other things she did, for all which she was by law condemned to die, and in particular to be burnt to death, because she was the death of her husband (as she confessed), which death she suffered accordingly.

But since her death, there is one thing that is very remarkable, and to be taken notice of: That upon the very day that she was burned, a bunch of flesh, something after the form of a dog, that grew upon the thigh of the said Mr. Beale, ever since the time that she first sent her imp to him, being very hard, but could never be made to break by all the means that could be used, break of itself without any means using. And another sore that at the same time she sent her imp to him rose upon the side of his belly, in the form of a fistula, which ran and could not be braked for all the means that could be used, presently also began to heale, and that there is great hopes that he will suddenly recover again, for his sores heale apace, and he doth recover his strength. He was in this misery for the space of a yeare and a halfe, and was forced to go with his head and his knees together, his misery was so great.

Old Winter

Moving forward in time we come across a man renowned as being a wizard, called 'Old Winter'. Winter lived and plied his trade in Ipswich, Suffolk and was the most famous wizard in the whole county. He took up his trade in 1744, the previous cunning man that he had been apprenticed to having then just died. He soon acquired a name as a 'thief-taker', due to his expertise at seeking out and meting out his own form of justice to those who preyed on and stole from their neighbours. According to local tradition, it began in the following manner. Old Winter (then a young man), was walking home up Fore Street one night, when he spied someone digging in one of the small gardens of the houses there. Winter knew the old couple who lived there and that they had no living kin, but the digger seemed to be young and vigorous and was helping himself to a whole pile of cabbages. It was night time and dark, so it was difficult to tell who it was, so Winter waved his hand and the thief was frozen to the spot, unable to move. Winter carried on back home and went to bed. The next morning he was up early and back at the old couple's garden, where the thief was still frozen to the same place, a crowd now gathered round him, eyeing him and the pile of vegetables beside him with amazement. With another wave of his hand, Winter removed the holding charm and the thief was released, only to be taken away by the authorities for his attempted crime. Winter's reputation was made and he was in demand all over the county.

Some time later, the following tale was told about him. This version is quoted from *'History of Stowmarket'*, by the Rev. A. Hollingsworth, printed in 1844.

> *The most famous man in these parts as a wizard was Old Winter of Ipswich. My father was in early life apprentice to him and after that was servant to Major Whyte who lived in Stowupland at Sheepgate Hall. A farmer lost some blocks of wood from his yard and consulted Winter about the thief. By mutual arrangement Winter spent the night at the farmer's house, and set the latter to watch, telling him not to speak to anybody he saw. About twelve a labourer living near came into the wood-yard and hoisted a block on his shoulder. He left the*

yard and entered the meadow, out of which lay a style into his own garden. And when he got into the field he could neither find the style nor leave the field. And round and round the field he had to march with the heavy block on his shoulder, affrighted, yet not able to stop walking, until ready to die with exhaustion, the farmer and Winter watching him from the window, until from pure compassion Winter went up to him, spoke, dissolved the charm, and relieved him from his load.

Winter continued in this way for many years, until he finally decided to retire to Aldeburgh, a town on the coast some thirty miles distant from Ipswich. We are given a clue as to how he may have achieved his remarkable successes by a piece in another book of local history. This final tale of Old Winter is taken from *'Some Materials for the History of Wherstead'*, by the Rev. F.B. Zincke, published in 1887.

A Wizard's Familiars

Over forty years ago the occupier of a farm of about 400 acres, and who was also a churchwarden, told me that in his younger days – he was then about sixty-five – on his entering the room of a wizard with whom he was acquainted (and he a church warden?), the wizard's name was Winter and he resided in Aldborough: the name of the man and his place of residence were given in the belief that they were all but unanswerable vouchers for the truth of the story – he saw on the table before the wizard some half-dozen imps. They were black, the colour of the white man's devil. In form and size they were something between rats and bats, the most mischievous and hideous of English animals. They were twittering to the wizard: they could not be allowed human voice. As soon as my informant entered the room they were ordered to vanish: the mysteries of iniquity must not be exhibited to honest men. They obeyed this order by gliding down to the floor: they could not have the same modes of locomotion as God's creatures. They then vanished through the floor: solid substances, impermeable to God's creatures, were permeable to them. I take it for granted that the narrator had seen all this.

The Devil's Plantation

Jabez Few

Not all wizards or cunning men had serious intent in using their familiars. Jabez Few, who lived in Willingham, Cambs. and died in the 1920s, kept some white rats which the villagers there knew as his imps. He loved to play all manner of practical jokes with them, especially if it meant scaring or alarming the locals. He once took them to the local pub, the Brewer's Arms, and the people in the bar there swore they could hear them running up and down the stairs; however, when the door at the bottom of the staircase was opened, there was no sign of anything at all. Another tale is told locally of his antics and their results, indicating the continued knowledge of local witchcraft and how to deal with unwanted occurrences of it.

One day Jabez put one of his imps in Connie Todd's bedroom and it couldn't get out, so someone said to old man Dudley – it was his house that Connie lodged in – 'You must get a big tom-cat and he'll get it out'. So Dudley shut a big, ginger tom in the room. Presently there was a terrific noise of fighting and when the door was opened there was fur all over the floor and the cat was flying up and down the curtains. But that imp was still somewhere about and it just couldn't be got rid of.

Then somebody else told old Dudley he'd have to get a stone jar, put some clippings from a horse's hoof in it and the legs of a toad, then put the bottle on the fire, and if it didn't break then the spell would. So Dudley got the jar all ready and was just going to put it on the fire when someone called at the house. So he had to put off trying to break the spell. He told his visitor what he was going to do and called Jabez every name under the sun for getting that imp into the house. 'I'll shoot him one day', he declared. Jabez must have heard what he said, for about twenty minutes later he came up to the house, gave a loud whistle and the imp came out as meek as anything.

Characters of Craft

As an adjunct to the above, the following was published in *'The East Anglian'*, for 1869 and is self-explanatory.

> *A Plan for Discovering and Punishing a Witch*
> *When you have good reason to believe that you have been bewitched, get a frying pan; pull a hair out of your head, and lay it in the pan; cut one of your fingers and let some of your blood fall on the hair. Then hold the pan over the fire until the blood begins to boil and bubble. You may then expect the witch to come and knock at your door three times, wanting to borrow something, and hoping to make you talk. But you must hold your peace. If you utter a word, you will still be more bewitched: if you refuse to speak, you will so work upon the witches' blood as to cause her death; and then you will be set free (Information obtained in a cottage not far from Beccles towards the end of last year).*

This last charm above, and variants on it, is a fairly standard way of removing a charm from oneself and getting back at the person who set it in the first place. It relies on the fact that there is now a link existing between you and the witch (as s/he presumably took something of yours to create the link in the first place), and you can get back at them by using the same link. The stricture on silence is essential as, if a word is spoken, the counter charm will be broken and the counter magic re-bound back onto the sender.

Tilly Baldrey

A witch of a different kind was Tilly Baldrey, who practised her craft in Huntingtoft in Norfolk, in the 19th century. She was known as a 'Toadswoman', meaning someone who had successfully gone through the ritual needed to acquire the famed Toad Bone, and something I will go into in more detail in a later chapter. The possession of this bone gave the owner power over animals and humans both, and was much used in East Anglia, most notably by the Society of Horsemen but also, and originally, by witches and folk-magical practitioners too (it is likely that Old Winter also possessed the bone, because of his strong power over the actions of thieves). The following story relates both the power possessed by Tilly and an accomplice, but also relates back to the previous charm above, concerning the need for silence when breaking the hold of the witch.

Tilly and her compatriot, Sue Isbill, had fallen out with the farmer from whom they were used to getting their milk each day.

> *'You on't come to mine no more for the milk'* [said the farmer, as related by his grandson], *'du yew goo and get your milk off o' someone else who'll put up wi' your ways.'*
> *'So Tilly and old Sue they bewitched the milk in my grandfather's dairy, and he couldn't git the butter to come – that blossomed every time. They borrowed other churns, but 'twern't no mander o' use, and at last, one Sa'day market day, my grandfather he went to the wise man at Norwich and told him how the butter was sp'ilt and how they couldn't never keep the cows in the shuds at night: they'd be tied up to staples every night and of a mornin' they'd be runnin' out abroad all over the midders.*
> *Well, the wise man he thought and he thought. "Ha' you tied up the churns wi' ropes?" he say. My grandfather he say yis, they'd tried everything; so the wise man told'm something and took his money, and my grandfather come hoom.*
> *Next-day-mornin' they barred up all the doors and shutters same as the wise man told 'em to, 'cause he said them old witches they'd come that day and try to get in, but they mustn't let 'em. My grandfather said he'd shoot the old mawthers, but the wise man he said he mustn't dew nawthin' tu 'em nor yet spack to 'em. So they come and they rattlcked at the doors an' they hallered and they blarred till they was right dumb, but they weren't let come in n' yet spoken tu, so that brooke the charm, and that there butter come as right as could be after that.'*

Characters of Craft

Tilly fared better on another occasion however. Her husband, 'Dola', had run away with a woman from another village, Neoma Cason – *'a nice lookin' mawther at that time of day she was an' all; a lot of difference to pore old Tilly'* – and Tilly was determined to have her revenge;

> *'Howsomedever when Tilly knowed they was gone to together she never did a hand's turn to interfere with them tew, but she brought Dola hoom from Thistlefield sixteen miles wi' her charms. That was the masterpiece that was. She only sat there in her keepin' room and said her charms, and Dola he come hoom backwards the whool way...*
>
> *Tilly fair rightsided pore old Dola when he came hoom like that, and he's got a gret lock o' hair what Neoma Cason give him. Tilly she got that off of him time he was comin' tu... and she frizzled that over fire and seft the ashes, and Neoma she fared to pine away to nawthin' along o' that lock o' her hair bein' 'stroyed.*
>
> *So Neoma went to the wise man. He telled her that was old Tilly that was bewitchin' of her, and she must git them ashes away from Tilly, don't she'd go right inter a decline. But that fared as though the witch was stronger an' what the wise man was, 'cause Neoma couldn't niver get over Tilly's troshel* [threshold], *them charms of hers was so po'orful; so Neoma she died in a decline same as the wise man said, and Tilly she went to the funeral and hulled* [threw], *them ashes into Neoma's grave.'*

So beware a Toadswoman scorned!

🌿 Using the 'Eye' 🌿

Another Norfolk woman who was determined to get her revenge for a slight done to her was old Mother Staselton, who had the reputation of possessing the 'evil eye'. This is an eye-witness account, recorded at the time;

The Devil's Plantation

'She wur an ill-favoured old woman, sure enough, and she wore a scarlet cloak [This was one of the ceremonial garments denoting the status of the witch]. *But there were many who would come and see her. Not common folk alone, ye know, but some in carriages would drive up to her door; and some who were that ashamed of being known to do it that they would come secretly by night. They would ask her all sorts o' questions and she would have an answer for all. Well, one day my uncle was out walking with a friend, and he see her a-coming – but a long way off. She wur at such a distance that he couldn't ha' heard what a' said, but you understand that the red cloak wur conspicuous. So he says to his friend: "Here comes that old devil", and when she come up to him she say: "Ow, aye, here come that old devil, and take care that you do not get your neck broken before next week." So the verra next day, he walked a long way off on business… and when he come back he got a ride wi' a friend on a load o' coals. Now he wur a-sitting on the back, and his friend was on the front. She wur an old woman, ye know; and he just turned his head to luk down the road after some cattle that were a-coming, when all of a sudden the cart turned right over, and the coals went a-flying over the road, and my uncle and the old woman went a-flying into the hedge, and the horse came down into a heap.*

Yes, for certain sure that wur the witch, and when it happened to one of one's own, one knows all about it, and that it wur the truth sure enough. It's ill meddling wi' witches.'

And never a truer word was spoken!

At about the same time, also in Norfolk, lived a woman named Mrs Mullinger of Monk Soham, who was also reputed to have the evil eye. She was held in great fear as, if she was ever crossed or took a dislike to anyone, she would look 'sideways' at their pigs or other livestock and they would invariably fall ill and die. Her 'Eye' was so strong that it would even pass through walls too. If she was sat at home by her fire and was in an evil temper, her neighbour on the

Characters of Craft

other side of the party wall would never be able to get his fire lit or to burn well.

The Eye was also used some time before this, in North Walsham, again in Norfolk. It was used by an unnamed old man, who had nearly been knocked down by a team of horses that were being driven by a local farmer. The next day, as the farmer was working in his fields, he pulled out his watch to see the time. He saw that it was 11 o'clock in the morning, the same time as the incident with the old man the previous day, when he had glared at him so queerly. Instantly he began to feel dizzy, nauseous and light-headed. He was aware of nothing else, until he came to much later, to find himself in his own bed, where he had been carried by his workmen when they had discovered him. Exactly the same thing happened on the following two days, at exactly the same time. He consulted a local 'doctor', who informed him that he was suffering from epilepsy and gave him some 'black medicine'. He was instructed to take this at exactly five minutes to eleven the next morning, after having made the sign of the cross over it. The farmer went home and did as he was instructed and never had another attack again – but he was very careful driving his team of horses around town after that.

In this instance, the unnamed old man was evidently seen as a wizard of some kind, so the farmer consulted a local 'doctor', who was presumably a cunning man of some sort. The clue is given in the fact that it was 'black medicine' that he was given to drink – as opposed to some named remedy – and told to make the sign of the cross over it before drinking it at a very specific time. No medical doctor would give such instructions in that day and age.

❦ A Little Learning ❦

The fact that the person giving aid in this case was termed 'doctor' is interesting, as some male witches or cunning men

The Devil's Plantation

did have some learning, or at least liked to pretend that they did, and sometimes used books of magic as a source of their remedies and spells. The title 'doctor' may be indicative of the locals appreciating his knowledge and giving him the honorific as a result. Such an educated cunning man, also hailing from Norfolk, in East Dereham, was named Claypole, as recorded by Dr. A. Jessop, in one of his East Anglian volumes of lore. He states that the coroner for East Dereham was conducting an inquest in the 1880s on a woman who had been found dead at home, in her own bed. He was told by her husband, giving evidence, that she had been found wearing some written charms around her neck, which the woman had bought from Claypole herself. The coroner, not being of a magical frame of mind, returned the charms to the cunning man himself, with dire threats of prosecution for fraud, if he did not pay back to the husband the money which the dead woman had paid him for them. Some years later, the coroner bumped into a young man who had been apprenticed to Claypole and learned that he had lost his future trade through the actions of the coroner. Apparently, Claypole had been so frightened by the threats given by the coroner that he had decided to give up his trade and get rid of his magical books and manuscripts. The then apprentice had been asked to aid his master in destroying his precious volumes, but, as he regretfully told the coroner;

> 'Master, says I, I ain't a-goin' to touch them sort o' things, not if it's ever so. I don't mind digging the hole but I never heard tell of them Zode Jacks doing no one no good. So he ups wi' his grit books and we digged a hole, big as a pit that wor, and he set them in right careful.'

So ended that particular line of Master and apprentice in the Cunning trade, and lost forever are the valuable books of magic and lore that could have told us so much about the magic practiced in that place at that time.

Some say that one of Claypole's books was his copy of *'The Secret Granary'*. This is possibly a version of *'The Devil's*

Plantation', or vice versa, but we will now never know. The Secret Granary is said to still be in use by some East Anglian witches today, but each version is different, as it is not a coherent tradition.

There seems to have been a tradition of literary magic in that area of Norfolk, as another Cunning Man, Mr. Rix of Shipdham, not far from East Dereham, was also known to have used magical books in his work in the late 1800s and was known locally as a 'planet reader'; presumably some form of astrologer. On one occasion he was consulted by a simple shepherd from Tottington, who said some of his sheep had been stolen. He knew this to be true, as when he counted his flock's tails, he had more tails than bodies. Rix, a canny man and an excellent problem solver, consulted his charts and books, charged the shepherd 20 shillings, gave him some tobacco and told him to go home. The shepherd was instructed that when he got there, he was to smoke the tobacco in silence and speak to no one, but that he must use sign language if he was to communicate. Then, also in silence, he was to re-count both his flock's tails and bodies. The shepherd duly followed these instructions to the letter and, when he had finished counting, found that his missing sheep had returned, as he had the same number of tails as bodies now! I'm going to resist the obvious comments, both about planet readers and Norfolk shepherds!

Daddy Witch

One of the most famous of all Cambridgeshire witches was known as 'Daddy Witch' of Horseheath. It might at first seem that her name implied a certain ambiguity in her gender, but this is not so, as she was definitely a woman and acted accordingly. The name, or more correctly, 'title', 'Daddy', is a local form of the name for the Devil or Horned God and denoted that the woman in question was one of his adherents or devotees.

The Devil's Plantation

Miss Catherine Parsons read out a lecture to the Cambridge Antiquarian Society on the 1st of February, 1915, entitled *'Notes on Cambridgeshire Witchcraft'*, based on information she had collected from local people in and around the area of Horseheath. She collected further material which is recorded in a manuscript dated 1952, but which has never been published. She admitted to 'considerable difficulty' in collecting the beliefs which still remained, 'owing to the dread, even to this day, of offending the parish witch, to whom everybody must be extremely courteous.' It is from her that we now have most of our information on the witchcraft of that time and place.

In her lecture she initially states; 'In Horseheath witchcraft is by no means a lost art. In this parish we have ghosts as real as ever they were, superstition is rife, the wise woman is fresh in our memory, we have our folklore, certain interesting customs, and cures for almost every ill. The parishioners tell us that there always were witches, and that there always will be, because they are mentioned in the Book. Unfortunately it is the biblical references to demonopathy which seem to make this phase of superstition hard to die. One is told that the chief difference between a witch and an ordinary woman is, that if the latter wishes her neighbour misfortune, her wish has no effect, but the same wish in the mind of the witch has effect, because the witch is believed to be in league with the devil, she having made a contract to sell her soul to him in return for the power to do evil.'

Parsons then goes on to give accounts of various types of supposed witchcraft curses and charms, tales of imps and counter charms and then turns to the subject of the witches themselves. She says; 'The earliest witch remembered by my fellow parishioners at Horseheath, went by the name of Daddy Witch. It is said she was an ancient bony creature, half clothed in rags, who lived in a hut by the sheep-pond in Garret's Close, and that she gained much of her knowledge from a book called *The Devil's Plantation*. When Daddy Witch died (1860), her body was buried in the middle of the road, which leads from Horseheath to Horseheath Green, just where the road passes the close opposite the sheep-pond. Her grave is marked by the dryness of the road, said to be caused by the heat of her body.'

A Horseheath woman recorded in 1935 in the Women's Institute Scrapbook that, 'to have good luck you must nod your head nine times before passing over the grave.' In July of that year a fire spreading along the road stopped when it reached the grave, turned and went over the fields. So it would appear that Daddy Witch's powers did not die with her, but remain in the area.

Parsons goes on to record that; 'Daddy Witch in her prime would be amongst the many witches and wizards who flocked for miles around Horseheath to attend the frolic and dances held at midnight in lonely fields by the master witch of the neighbourhood, ... and that witches and wizards returning in the early hours of the morning were seen to be in a terrible state of perspiration.' This dancing seems to be a popular activity of Cambridgeshire witches, and holds a meaning that is not well understood anymore, as Parsons further records; 'As for dancing, all men, young and old, were eager to dance at Horseheath fair with a witch, who, it is remembered, danced the hornpipe better than any man or woman for miles around.'

Try to Remember...

A curious thing recorded by Catherine Parsons is as follows; 'We hear that the witch from the neighbouring parish of Withersfield was often seen by Horseheath people riding through the air to attend these revels [above], upon a hurdle.' This may have been a Cambridgeshire peculiarity, as it accords with the memories recorded of the witch Bet Cross, from Longstanton in Cambs. who was active in the late 1800s. A woman who used to run errands for her as a girl recorded the following in 1921;

'Then there was that business with young X. He was walking down the lane by the church one Sunday afternoon, and there he saw Bet Cross ridin' on a hardle. I don't rightly know which way up the hardle was, but there she was, and young X he said to her: "Ah, Bet Cross I see ye. I'll tell on ye. Yer a-riding on a hardle." And Bet Cross she give 'im a queer look and she says: "Young man", she says, "you can tell on it when you think on it." And the funny thing was that it went right out of 'is 'ead, and he never did tell on it till 'e 'eard the bell goin' out for 'er death, and that wasn't for years. And when 'e 'eard the bell 'e said: "Why, if that isn't for old Bet Cross that I met ridin' on a hardle. Funny thing, I never thought to tell on it till now.'

The blocking of memory also seems to be a common feature of witchcraft in this area, as some witches seem to have been unwilling that anyone who saw them should be able to recall the fact for a given period of time; sometimes they were even unwilling that those who consulted them should remember what was told them. So when an Ely man saw a witch drifting down the river Cam (on a hurdle?), she shouted out a warning of a dire calamity that would happen to him, unless he told some of his friends. However, when he was in the company of his friends, he was unable to recall what the calamity was that the witch had told him about, and a short while afterwards, he died. At another time, when another Ely man consulted a local witch, she gave him the information that he was looking for, but added that he wouldn't be able to recall it until he had heard the bells of Great St. Mary's Church in Cambridge peal three times.

By Royal Appointment

When the then Prince of Wales bought the estate of Sandringham, in Norfolk, in 1863, there were known to be several wise women living in the vicinity; these folk he had cleared out of their homes. He also pulled down the old cottages and replaced them with more modern dwellings, to house the estate workers. However, one old woman was allowed to remain, in the nearby village of Flitcham. Even the newly appointed agent to the Prince of Wales dared not turn her out, for not only was she reputed to have the power of cursing, or the evil eye, but she was also known to have a vast knowledge of herbal cures when all other remedies had failed. She would wander miles in search of a certain herb that she required and lots of folk sought her aid when they needed either a starter or a stopper in times of distress.

As the years passed by, the health of the Prince of Wales began to deteriorate, due to his hectic 'social life' and love of good living; in 1880 he finally broke down and was confined to his bed. He was very ill for a considerable time and nothing seemed able to get him back on his feet again. Much distressed at this situation, the Princess of Wales, Princess Alexandra sent for her sister-in-law, the Grand Duchess Olga of Russia. Both ladies feared that ordinary medical efforts had failed, and both agreed that another opinion should be sought; also that the only way to get the Prince back on his feet, was to use the Danish belief in the supernatural, combined with the Russian inherited faith in sorcery and black magic. Accordingly, discreet inquiries down the social scale revealed the fact that some of the kitchen staff had good cause to be grateful to an old woman, a supposed witch living at Flitcham, for getting them out of a muddle that single women were not then supposed to have gotten themselves into.

In due course, the old woman was commanded to appear before the Princess, who suggested that perhaps the old woman knew of some remedies that would help the Prince to recover. The wise woman replied; 'I can give you a bottle of wine which I have made myself. Give the Prince three glasses a day, and within three days – unless he is in the Undertaker's hands – he will be sitting up in bed.' Four days later, a groom from the royal stables brought the old woman

The Devil's Plantation

the news that the Prince of Wales was getting better; also, would she give him three more bottles of wine to take back. He then handed her a purse, which she discovered upon opening it later, was full of gold coins. The folk tale ends here, but there is a follow-up to the story.

Some fifty years later, a local folklorist was in the area of Flitcham and, having heard the tale, thought he'd make enquiries about it in the local pub. The landlord of the Bell Inn, it turned out, was familiar with the story, but told the enquirer that the old woman concerned had been dead for years; however, if he felt like buying the old chap over by the fire a pint or two, then he might learn a bit more about it. Introductions having been made and drinks having been purchased, the old chap began to open up on the subject.

'I was only a young man when she was about, but my mother and she were real old cronies. Few people called in a doctor when they were queer; they all went to the old gal instead. I still remember what her brew of rue tea was like; it was nothing less than liquid gunpowder and everyone said it was so powerful it would shift a traction engine. She had a lot of cures in her house, some in jars; others in bottles. She used to make a lot of home-brewed wine, which she never drank herself; gin was her tipple. One day, when she was a bit tiddly, she showed my mother a handful of gold coins. She boasted they were given to her by the Princess of Wales, in return for supplying bottles of her special mandrake root wine when the Prince of Wales was very ill. The old gal also supplied the gentry with this wine; it being a well-known fact that it was just the stuff to supply a much wanted energy.'

Spying on the Witches

W.H. Barret, who was a Cambridgeshire folklorist and avid collector of tales from the Fenland region in the 20th century, had many stories to tell of the witchcraft in that

Characters of Craft

area. He recorded that the fear of witchcraft was rife in the Fens between Litttleport and Ely and in Brandon Creek until the early years of the 1900s. Some of the old women who did not mind acquiring a reputation for practising witchcraft added to their incomes by preying on the fears of their neighbours. One old woman from Brandon Creek in the late 1800s, was in the habit of placing little mounds of silt on people's doorsteps overnight; everyone knew that the soil most probably came from freshly dug graves in the churchyards, on higher ground, away from the peaty areas of the Fens. The next morning, the woman would arrive at the house, puffing and blowing as though she'd just run a long way, and swearing that she'd seen the Devil placing the soil on the doorstep. She promised that if the householder were to hand over a few pence, then with her charms she would avert the evil power placed on the property and placate the 'Old 'Un'. The householder was usually only too happy to hand over a few pence and avoid the disaster that was sure to follow otherwise.

Although there are many tales *about* witches, it is often very difficult to find out exactly what their practices were in the past; so much material has either been lost, destroyed or is hidden and kept secret from prying eyes. It is therefore all the more remarkable that W.H. Barrett has recorded a tale from his grandmother, which happened to her husband as a young man, concerning an actual meeting of a group of witches. Her husband was employed as a millwright and it was in about 1850 that the following events took place.

The young man was working on a mill near Prickwillow, on a desolate site near the river Lark. He spent the week in the millman's derelict cottage, sleeping in the loft and only returning home at weekends to get more food for the following week. One night, having had his supper, he climbed the ladder to the loft and went to sleep. Sometime during the night, he was awakened from his sleep by noises in the room below him. He crept forward to the trap door in the floor of the loft and, quietly and gently, lifted it an

The Devil's Plantation

inch or two and peered down. Below him, he saw two old women about to light a fire in the hearth with bits and pieces of wood he had discarded from his work. Intrigued, he said nothing, but lay down and watched what was happening. Soon he saw the cottage door open and, from the light of the fire on the hearth as it now blazed up, saw four more old women enter the cottage, one of whom was a woman he recognised from his own village.

All of the women had brought a rush basket with them, full of food and drink, and they were soon sitting on the floor, in front of the fire, sharing out the fare and tucking in. After they had finished eating, they continued to sit in a circle by the fire and carried on a conversation in hushed whispers. By this time it was beginning to get rather warm, so the old women all began to discard their long cloaks, to reveal that they had very little on underneath them. Around the bare leg of one of the women, the millwright saw a garter of plaited horsehair, which she was proudly showing off. Another of the women then proudly displayed her own pair of garters, which she declared were made of viper skin. A third woman, not to be outdone it seemed, pointed to her breasts, which were covered with a garment made from ferret skin and then yet a fourth stood up to demonstrate that she was wearing a chemise made entirely out of lambskin.

At this point, the millwright accidentally knocked the open trapdoor which fell with a loud bang, startling the women below. With loud shrieks, they grabbed at their cloaks and baskets and fled the cottage, out into the darkness of the night. The next morning, the millwright found that one of the rush baskets and one of the black cloaks had been left behind, so he took these with him when he went back home. The following Saturday he delivered these to the old woman whom he had recognised, who lived in Brandon Creek and was reputed to be the local witch by all the villagers. 'Here you are', he said to her, 'these were left behind by you or your pals the other night in the millman's cottage down in Prickwillow Fen.' The old woman grabbed the cloak and basket from him and spat directly in his face, telling him that as surely as he lived by making windmills, it would be a windmill that would see him off. This did actually happen some years later; as he was working at repairing a mill, the top collapsed and crushed him to death.

Monica English

Moving into the 20th century, we come across an enigmatic figure, known as Monica English. She was born Monica Mary Barnes on the 8th of January 1920, at Harrow in Middx. She also went by the name of Mary English and was an accomplished artist, as well as being an 'old-style' witch. In the 1950s and 60s, Monica lived at Gayton, near Kings Lynn in Norfolk, and it is here that she came into contact with a traditional witch coven, and subsequently became a member. Michael Howard writes in his book on modern Traditional Witches, *'The Children of Cain'*, that he first became aware of her in 1967, via a book written by Cottie Burland, a one-time porter at the British Museum. The book was entitled *'The Magical Arts'* and in it was published a charcoal drawing of the Greek god Pan, attributed to an artist called Monica English. Some time later, Howard attended a talk given by Cottie Burland at the annual Quest conference in London, organised by Marian Green.

In this talk, Burland mentioned Monica English and gave some details of the coven she said she belonged to in rural Norfolk. They used little ritual and met in each other's houses to dance in a circle and raise the power. The male leader of the group stood in the middle of the dancing coven and projected or directed the energy that was raised by the group. At the end of the meeting they had a shared meal of 'cakes and wine' to ground themselves before leaving. The last 'Master' of the coven had been a Roman Catholic and had died some years before. The coven was apparently made up of landed gentry and agricultural workers, which is fairly common for a rural, traditional witch group. The members who were the ordinary folk were not keen on having anything to do with other witches, and were rather annoyed that Monica English had apparently joined a modern group, as they did not think that the members of the modern Wiccan movement were real witches. Burland said in the talk that English had made the rather wild and unsubstantiated claim that her coven had been founded in Saxon times and had continued to practice in an unbroken line in Norfolk ever since. That was all that was publicly heard or known of Monica English, until the publication in 1998, of the autobiography of Lois Bourne, entitled *'Dancing with Witches'*.

Lois Bourne was a member of the coven founded in Brickett Wood, Hertfordshire, by Gerald Gardner, the originator of the modern pagan religion known as Wicca. Bourne had been a member of the coven in the late 1950s and, after Gardner's death in 1964, had briefly served as its High Priestess. This was the coven that Monica English had joined and which had so angered the rural members of her original Norfolk coven. In 1959 Bourne says that English was aged about forty and she describes her as 'the aristocratic witch'. She had honey-coloured wavy hair, grey-green eyes like a cat, long tapering fingers and spoke with a cultured voice. She also exuded a 'strong sexual attraction' and the male members of the Brickett Wood coven, including Gardner himself, were fascinated by her. When she danced skyclad (naked), during some of the coven's rituals and made wild, vocal calls, Bourne says that owls came from miles around to sit on the roof of the meeting place and answer her. Strange shapes and shadowy forms also appeared in the working circle in response to her calls; when asked about this by Bourne, English apparently just laughed and said that it was 'real witchcraft'.

Characters of Craft

Lois Bourne and Monica English became friends and they sometimes met socially together, along with Cottie Burland. Bourne visited English at her manor house at Gayton and it was there that English revealed that she secretly belonged to a local coven, with 'an unbroken tradition of over two hundred years'. She had apparently discovered the coven after moving to the area in 1953 or 54 and English told Bourne that she had been ordered to join Gardner's coven, to find out if it was a threat to the older, traditional ways; her parent coven had become concerned over Gardner's love of publicity and were worried that it was bringing the Craft into disrepute. Bourne was eventually asked by English to join the Norfolk coven and, after a couple of refusals, she finally agreed; she was inducted into the group at All Hallows of 1964, just after Gerald Gardner had died. Bourne's recollections of the coven were very different to those of Cottie Burland, and she makes it sound all rather grand, rather than the more down to earth and rural affair previously described.

At the time of Lois Bourne's induction, Monica English was the Magistra (Mistress, or female leader), of the group and she was assisted by a man known as 'Bertram', who acted as the Magister. Although they were the outward leaders of the group, there was an elderly couple known as the 'Lord' and the 'Lady', who were the real power behind the throne. Bourne says that the group had over thirty members in it, but that not everyone attended every meeting; however, everyone was expected to attend the four Grand Sabbats of the year. The group was geared towards celebrating the round of the rural and agricultural year and, whilst there was a Goddess who was acknowledged, the prime deity worshipped was the Horned God and it was he that had the ultimate power.

Michael Howard says that another source of information, who wished to remain anonymous, had told him that horses were an important totem animal to the group and that they worshipped the Iron Age horse goddess, Epona. Howard's source claimed that when the coven met out of doors, the members rode on horses to the meeting and the animals were then included in the rites that followed. According to this source, the children of the original members of the group still keep it going today.

Lois Bourne wrote that, weather permitting, meetings were held in the grounds of a large country house, in local woods, and at a spring in the vicinity, near the village where Monica English lived. If the weather was too inclement, the coven met in a large barn built on farmland belonging to one of the members. The rituals indoors were presided over by the Lord and Lady mentioned previously, who sat on chairs on a raised platform, overlooking the rites themselves. Unlike the wilder nature of the rituals at Brickett Wood, the rites of the Norfolk coven were much gentler and quieter, often being conducted in complete silence and there was also a lot of meditation involved. When Bourne was inducted, she was informed that; 'Silence is the ultimate and final initiation. The Gods are silent. Everything comes out of silence. The true bliss of experience is without words.' Monica English and her husband moved away from Norfolk in the latter part of the 1960s, to Yorkshire, and it was there that she eventually died in 1979.

Today's Characters

The characters of the Craft of today, are mostly unknown outside of their immediate associates, and generally desire to stay that way. It must be understood here that I am referring purely to the older style, Traditional Craft, as opposed to the modern, pagan traditions, developed and made popular since the 1950s and 60s. Gone are the days of the local village witch, who plies his or her trade within the local society and bounds of the neighbourhood; the days when everyone knew where to go to get help, but kept quiet about other 'goings on', for fear of getting on

Characters of Craft

the wrong side of the operators. Nowadays, new ways have come in and are much more public, the older style characters and practitioners preferring to take much more of a back seat and keep quiet about their Craft. However, a few whispers do still surface here and there and the word is passed on to those who need to know.

It is rumoured that there is still a coven in rural Norfolk, who venerate the old gods of the Angles and the Danes; they hold the Norse god Loki to be sacred and their rites still include the worship of Woden and Freyja. Their rites are said to be quite 'primitive' and not for the faint-hearted.

I have been informed of a couple of Crafters who are known as the 'Hermits of Mole End' and who live in mid Norfolk. They have an exquisite garden with a dynamic mixture of native and exotic plants, and part of it is almost like a colourful forest. They have a tiny Circle in the garden which is used for magic in a very gentle and simple way. They live a very simple life with no car, no central heating (a wood fire only), no fridge, no TV, no computer, no mobile phone, no washing machine. They are contactable only by Royal Mail or astral message. They believe that it is important to pass on traditional techniques so that they are not lost, and contacted my informant, a fellow Crafter, to that end. I was passed a message to convey their philosophy and vision;

> 'In East Anglian magic we stitch the fabric of our lives into the landscape. The plough stitches the pattern onto the land and the fishing nets weave a pattern into the sea. A lot of East Anglian magic is about human life and the landscape. The relationship becomes more personal because it isn't a product of other people. It is very much between the worlds. You own it in your imagination.'

Another informant, who is a very experienced magical practitioner and born East Anglian, provided me with the following details about his knowledge of old-style Craft in the area;

The Devil's Plantation

'There was a well-respected senior witch from Walsingham, Norfolk at the initial meeting of the Pagan Front (later Pagan Federation) in the late 1960s. I believe that both she and another lady from Kings Lynn area were from a pre-Gardnerian line. I also caught a whiff of something 'old' going on in Castle Acre in Norfolk, but nothing I could give any detail on.

There is the odd one exception: back in the 1980s when I was taking my first practical steps in a Pagan path, I came in contact with a middle-aged couple in the Thetford area. They told me they were the sole remnants of a group going back a very long time. They had been the youngest couple, and the rest had died. I worked with them several times over about 6 months, before they retired to a place far away. They never made any great claims, and some of their practices would have been considered post Gardnerian. However, most of their work was very simple and did not involve any tools except for a stang – they primarily worshipped a Lord, but a Lady also. The couple were very kind to me, but also needed something from me in return. I promised I would never reveal their names, and had no contact with them after they moved away. There was no initiation or hierarchy, and they were very suspicious of using stuff from books. I cannot tell you much more about the Thetford couple: they certainly believed that they came from a long line of local witches – I cannot tell whether it was true or not, but I believed them. They cast a circle deosilwise and closed it widdershins. They acknowledged 'powers' in the quarters but were clear that they were inviting, not summoning. They went out on a full moon, but occasionally used dark moon for specific magic. They could summon a mist very effectively to cloak their presence (something I regrettably never learnt the secret of). They had a knowledge of herbs, and used them for both healing and once for ill wishing a neighbour who was giving them trouble. They burnt them with an invocation that time. As a married couple they used sex magic to raise power for specific magic. They did not call it Drawing Down the Moon, but simply "her getting the Goddess in her".'

Characters of Craft

I have personally had contact with two groups who work on the Suffolk/Norfolk borders, and claim to have pre-Gardnerian origins. One of them derived their knowledge from a group based in Yorkshire (who I know), who derived their knowledge from a family tradition based in Sussex; however, my contact in this instance said that the Sussex group hailed from a family line that originally came from Framlingham in Suffolk, so all they were doing was bringing the tradition back home. The other group claims an ancient lineage, worshipping the Witch Mother and Witch Father, the true parents of witchcraft and the first deities of all. They work primarily outside, whenever possible, using few tools and a minimum of ritual. Metal is anathema to their rites, although silver and gold are permitted to be worn, but not used as tools. They do use a stang and some other farm implements, honour the four directions and may work within or without a circle, depending upon the occasion.

In south-east Suffolk there is a tradition that is primarily Horned God honouring, although a primal goddess is also acknowledged. The emphasis is on gaining knowledge, both of themselves and of the Otherworlds, and using that knowledge to develop power; the power is used primarily to further their knowledge, but also for practical spell-working and healing. Herbs and plants are used and a practical approach is encouraged; rites are simple and worked mostly in silence, as practitioners tend to work alone and large group gatherings are not encouraged, although they share a group ethos and practice.

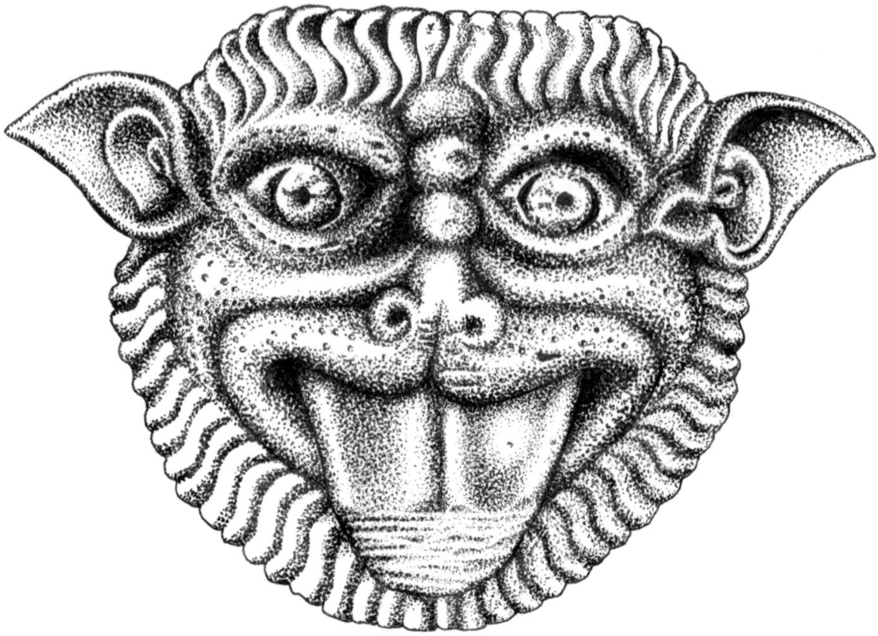

Speak of the Devil...

❦ ...And He Will Appear! ❦

There is a general prohibition on using the term 'the Devil', and the further into East Anglia you go, the more this taboo is observed, other names being used instead. It is generally supposed that this is because, like the title of this chapter, if you speak the name of the great demon, then he will appear to carry you off. This, however, does not hold true universally, and there are plenty of tales and legends, particularly connected with buildings and places in the landscape that bear his name. There may be several reasons for this and I will examine some of those later on, but for now I would like to relate some examples of the Devil appearing in the East Anglian folkloric record, to give an idea of how He was generally perceived.

❦ The Devil in Cambridgeshire ❦

Stretching for seven miles between Reach and Woodditton in Cambridgeshire, close to the border with Suffolk, the Devil's Dyke is a well-preserved and probably Anglo Saxon bank and ditch earthwork that blocked a land corridor between marshy fen and dense woodland. Initially referred

The Devil's Plantation

to by the Anglo-Saxons simply as 'the Ditch', in the Middle Ages it was known as the Great Ditch, Reach Ditch or St. Edmund's Dyke. It was only in post-medieval times that the name Devil's Dyke became attached to it. It first appears in the Latin form *Daemonis fossam*, in 1574, being given the English translation Devils-dike in 1594. Legend tells that the Devil arrived at a wedding at Reach Church, but the guests naturally turned him away as he had not been invited. He fled the church in anger, his huge flaming tail scoring a groove in the earth, forming the dyke. As with most such monumental works, some have believed that it was created by giants, but the legend mentioned is consistent with the old tradition of the Devil as a builder.

Also in Cambridgeshire, the Stone Cross in March – or the base of it that remains – sits at the corner of The Avenue and Causeway Close, possibly marking the site of an ancient market in the original village. Legend says that the townsfolk wanted to build a new church nearer the market place, although they already had one, St. Wendreda's, but on the other side of the river in the old town. These plans did not go down very well with the Devil, as he considered that the Fens and the surrounding areas belonged to himself and his minions, so every night he came and tore down what had been built the day before. The cross was erected to try and drive the Devil away – it succeeded, but the church was still never built. This legend was still remembered and told by the inhabitants of March in the early 20th century when it was collected and other legends about the Stone Cross were also current among local children. It was said to have been a resting point for the body of an unnamed queen, who was being transported over a great distance to her burial place. Also, children were told that if they walked twelve times around the topmost step of the cross base, they would hear the Devil 'sharpening his knives'.

When the people of Thriplow decided to build their church in the hollow in which the village lies, the Devil moved all the stones to the top of the hill, close to the

Speak of the Devil...

site of a large, Bronze Age burial mound. Unwilling to face the task of bringing them all down again, only to find them possibly moved to the top of the hill once more, the builders gave in and built the church where it now stands, overlooking the village. Similarly, in Cottenham, the church now stands at one end of the village. Tradition states that it was once decided to rebuild it nearer to the middle, for convenience sake, but that, night after night, the stones were removed by the Devil to the old site, so there it stayed.

In the village of Tydd St. Giles, the current tower at St. Giles Church stands about fifteen metres away from the main church, where it was rebuilt in the 1880s, probably to give a sounder footing in an unstable area. The original tower had fallen a hundred years earlier, but the story given is that although the people tried to attach it to the church, the Devil kept moving it away. A variation on this tale states that the Devil couldn't abide the sound of the bells, so it was he who pushed over the tower originally. The idea of the Devil and his minions not being able to bear the sound of Church, or indeed any blessed bell, is very strong in East Anglia. Small hand bells are used in some forms of magical working and play a large part in exorcisms and cleansings of places, not just by the official clergy, but by magical practitioners in general.

Suffolk's Stones

Turning now to Suffolk, the church of St. Botolph at Iken (the site of the original Ikenho), on its promontory projecting above the lower surrounding marshland, is believed to stand on the site of a 7th century minster; this is reputed to be the first Christian mission site in East Anglia (see Chapter 8 for more on St. Botolph and his ministry). When Botolph first arrived, he had to cast out the Devil, various marsh demons and monsters that infested the area, as they had for centuries claimed the higher ground as 'sacred' to themselves; because of this he became renowned for his sanctity and power. However, things went a bit further than usual in this instance of exorcism, as the Old One, having no intention of leaving his home territory, put up a great fight. Apparently there were deaths, reported ghosts, and the tale of materials for the building of the minster being moved mysteriously at night, before the Devil was finally vanquished. This particular site would seem to have been used and hallowed by previous faiths, hence the supernatural activity there and the aura of sanctity; perhaps the very reason that St. Botolph was given the site for his minster in the first place.

One of the very few well-known stones of Suffolk stands in St. Mary's churchyard, in Bungay. Known by various names – the Druid's Stone, Devil's Stone or Giant's Grave – it is locally reputed to have been the scene of ancient Druid rituals. Apart from being rather rough and mossy, it could initially be mistaken for just another gravestone; however it is actually an embedded, granite glacial erratic, 60cm x 30cm x 76cm high. In the early 1920s it was referred to as a 'fallen monolith' and was re-erected on its original site in around 1925. One theory proposed it had been taken from the ruins of Bungay Castle for use as a headstone. The legend of the Druid's Stone says that after having danced about it, or knocked upon it, twelve times, young girls would place their ears against the stone to hear the answers to their questions or wishes. Another version states that children would dance around it seven times on a certain day of the year, then wait for the Devil to appear. A local writer said in 1934 that 'some consider it to be a Ley or Direction Stone...'.

On the subject of stones, in the Suffolk village of Middleton, opposite the road from Vale Farm, near Fordley Hall, there was once a huge boulder where children were in the habit of placing pins in the various cracks and holes, running round it as fast as they could, then putting their ears against it in the

Speak of the Devil...

hope of hearing the Devil speak. This tradition was further enhanced, as the stone was reputed to be the meeting place of the local witches, although this obviously did not deter the local children. Underneath it there was said to be buried a hoard of treasure that no one could retrieve, as the stone was immovable. A local farmer once attached a team of horses to it, but failed to dislodge it.

In September 1930, a Mr. Claude Morley reported the discovery by himself at Wenhaston (Suffolk), of a 'mammillated erratic stone of 44 inches high x 33 broad and 21 deep (1.1m x 1m x 53cm), of the stratum of the celebrated Hartest Stone'. This 'hitherto-unrecorded rock' was found deep within a wooded copse that obscured a clay pit in Chapel Field, just south of Mill Heath. He believed this to be the 'final remnant' of St. Bartholomew's Chapel, which once existed not far away. However, the stone had been known about locally for many years prior to this 'discovery' and there were already legends attached to it. One of these held that it was thought to be a 'Druid Stone'. Another, stronger, local tradition held that it was known as the Devil's Stone, and the hollow in which it sits as the Devil's Pit, a gathering place for local folk-magic practitioners in the past. The rock is definitely a glacial erratic, not a former part of the fabric of a medieval chapel, and was possibly exposed during excavations at the clay pit many years ago. Indeed, the stone and pit are recorded as eminent features of local legend and have been for some time.

The church of St. Peter in the small Suffolk village of Westleton is a little church of about 1300, with no bell-tower as it fell through natural causes in 1776; it does however have a small brick bell-cote erected on the west end to house the single bell. Local tradition states that the Devil lives below a small grating at the base of the wall, just to the right of the priest's door. In front of the grating is the Witch's Stone, a simple, toppled 14th century gravestone, flush with the ground. Legend says that grass will never grow over it. For generations local

The Devil's Plantation

children have practiced the following custom here; first place a handkerchief or piece of straw in the grating, then using the Stone as your base, run round the church either three or seven times anticlockwise, but never look at the grating till the end. Back at the Stone, either the object will have vanished, or you'll hear the Devil rattling his iron chains below the grating (this smacks very much of a downgraded or dimly remembered self-initiation rite, as in the case of the Devil's stone in Bungay, above, but more on that subject later). To the north-west of the same parish is a road known as 'Devil's Lane', which may have gained its name from the activities of smugglers, who were said to have used a 'Jack O' Lantern' to frighten people into staying indoors. However, it may well be an 18th century enclosure road as it borders an area once marked on maps as 'Devel's Field'; this is possibly another of the ubiquitous plots of land known as the Devil's Plantation and left fallow for the Old 'Un.

At the nearby village of Wangford, running three times round a particularly large and magnificent oak tree in the graveyard of St. Peter & St. Paul's Church was said to be a sure way to summon the Devil. At Syleham, the isolated church of St. Mary stands at the end of a long causeway next to the river Waveney. The Devil is locally reported to have stopped it being built in its intended location, by removing each night the stones that had been laid at its original site. This church is interesting in that it is thought to be one of the places of an ancient way-mark stone, incorporated into the building; it would originally have stood out and have been an obvious feature of the landscape, visible over a long distance. Finally in Suffolk, in St. Michael's churchyard at Oulton (which is reportedly frequented by Ferishers on certain days of the year) is a large glacial, granite stone 1.4m x 1.2m x 76cm high. This was dredged up from the bed of Lake Lothing in the 19th century, during excavations for the new Lowestoft harbour. On the reverse of the stone is a planed surface, inscribed

Speak of the Devil...

with the words 'George Edwards; C.E. - J.P; 1804-1893'. Edwards, who was engineer in charge of the operations, wished the boulder to be placed upon his grave; but since the date of his death, a few local legends have gathered round it. Firstly, it is said that placing one's ear against the stone at any time of day or night will cause the listener to hear the church bells. And secondly, and more important in this instance, running round the stone three times will cause the Devil to appear. Could this be another local meeting place for magic workers?

Norfolk's Hills and Hollows

Moving north into the county of Norfolk, we come across more encounters with the Old One. At Beechamwell, the Devil is credited with making the round barrow called Hangour Hill, by scraping the earth from his spade after digging out the Saxon Bichamditch or Devil's Ditch. Beneath the mound is said to be hidden a pair of silver gates; where these gates lead, nobody knows, but they are reputed to be the entrance to a great marvel and a wonder. In addition there is a strange legend here, which is possibly the remnant of 19th century antiquarian musings, but is interesting in that it contains one of the few references to named, pagan deities in East Anglian lore. The ruins of All Saints Church are said to be haunted by the appearances of the goddess Diana and her hunting hounds. This possibly developed from the idea that there were once thought to be temples to the sun (Bel), and to the goddesses Diana and Venus at, respectively, Beechamwell, and the nearby hamlets of Caldecot and Shingham. The plantations around these areas were supposed to be haunted by a pack of spectral hounds known as 'Bel's dogs' (although there is, unfortunately, no evidence that these temples once existed).

Part of Mossymere Wood lies within Corpusty parish, and within it on the southern side towards Saxthorpe is

The Devil's Plantation

an eighteen metre depression known as the Devil's Dish. In 1717, human remains and 'relics' were found here, but instead of being taken to the local church and buried in the graveyard, they were reburied where they were found. This was believed to have incurred the anger of the Christian God which is why, on July 23rd that year, several large oak trees were seen to sink into the earth there, with water bubbling up around them. After the oaks had disappeared, the water drained away, and thus the Devil's Dish was born, the Old One having claimed the remains as his own.

At East Wreatham, there is a stretch of water known as Langmere. This is a single, small lake, one of many such meres throughout the Brecklands, but when the water level falls, the little island in it becomes connected to the shore by a narrow isthmus. It was said locally, that any shepherd or cattleman who drove his animals onto the island would suffer misfortune or ill. The water was believed to be the domain of the Devil, and none would ever dare to hunt fowl or fish there.

At Ludham, there are large, earthen mounds known as the Devil's Hills and, according to local lore, there are two versions of how they originally got there. The first story goes that the Devil dug a deep pit at Hall Farm, Neatishead, and carried away a large load of gravel in his wheelbarrow, for purposes unknown. The barrow overturned and spilled some of its load at Irstead, forming Bunker Hill, and again by the banks of the River Ant (whose bed ever since has been gravelly), creating two mounds called the Great and Little Reedhams. Finally the barrow broke down completely at Ludham, where he kicked the barrow in exasperation, yelling 'How!', thus forming windmill-topped How Hill. He then stamped angrily on the ground, the earth opened up beneath him and he jumped in and disappeared. The second version of the story says that the Devil dropped a load of gravel at a place in the River Ant called Irstead Shoals. The cart toppled again at Ludham, making him howl with rage, resulting in Howle Hill. Totally fed up,

Speak of the Devil...

he dumped the last load, along with the wheelbarrow, at the place where the ruins of St. Benet's Abbey now stand. 'And it's a queer thing', say the locals when asked about the stories, 'but all the places are in a dead straight line, and they're the only spots for miles around where you'll find gravel underfoot!'

It is very interesting and pertinent to note here that Howe when derived from the Old Norse: haugr means hill, knoll, or mound and may refer to a tumulus, or barrow. However when derived from Old English: hol it can refer to a hollow or dell. East Anglia was well within the boundaries of the old Danelaw area, and so either derivation is possible.

On the boundary of Moulton St. Mary and Cantley parishes was a 'cavernous hollow' known as the Callow (or Caller) Pit, which in elder times was used as a hiding-place by smugglers and outlaws. It is said that by night the ghost of a headless horseman rides around it before galloping off to Callow Spong a mile away and vanishing. Although the water was very dark, locals often talked about dragging out the iron chest of money that could be seen just below the surface. One night, two men from Southwood decided that they would actually try this, and managed to hook the iron ring on the end of the chest. After hours of labouring with its great weight it finally came to the surface, and one of them cried out; 'We've got it now, and not even the Devil himself shall have it!' At once, a cloud of evil-smelling vapour surrounded the pool, a long, muscular, black arm erupted from the water, grabbed the chest with claw-like fingers, and a fierce tug of war ensued. The Devil proved too strong, and he dragged the chest back into the water, never to be seen again; the men were left with only the iron ring from the end of the chest as a reward for all their labours.

At Thetford, close to the Suffolk border, Castle Hill at 80 feet high is one of the tallest Norman mottes in the country, and is almost certainly built over much earlier earthworks. It is said that when the early 12th century

The Devil's Plantation

Cluniac priory founded here by Roger Bigod was ruined after the Reformation, six silver bells (one version says seven) were taken from the priory church and hidden beneath the mound for safe keeping. Another account says they were bells of solid gold. Also, a story is told how a king once owned a magnificent castle on the site of the hill, but when his enemies landed in strength, he buried not only his treasure but his entire castle beneath tons of earth, forming the huge mound we see today. Local legend states that Castle Hill was made by the Devil, which is corroborated by the story that a muddy pool in the moat north of Castle Hill's ramparts is called Devil's Hole; walking round the pool, seven times, at midnight will conjure up the Devil to visible appearance, whence you may then make a request of Him.

At Tunstall, a few miles from Great Yarmouth, village tradition states that a fierce fire happened at St. Peter and St. Paul's church many years ago, leaving the tower and nave in ruins, only the chancel being left to be used for services. After the fire, local lore says the parson and one of his churchwardens argued about who should take possession of the church bells, which had survived the fire unscathed. However, whilst they were arguing, the Devil popped up and snatched the bells away (breaking the taboo on being able to stay in their presence), and scampered off towards the marshes. 'Stop, in the name of God!' cried the parson. 'Curse thee!' cried the Devil, dug a deep hole and leapt in down to his own domain, and it filled with water after him, becoming Hell Hole. 'The spot where this took place is now a boggy pool of water, called Hell Hole; and an adjoining clump of Alder trees is called Hell Carr. In summer time, a succession of bubbles – doubtless caused by marsh gas – keep constantly appearing on the surface. Those who believe in the tradition, find this circumstance a strong confirmation. For, as it is the entrance to the bottomless pit, the bells must be descending still; and the bubbles

Speak of the Devil...

would necessarily be caused by the bells sinking in the water' (*Notes and Queries*, 1853). Harking back to mediaeval ideas, this story has elements in common with that told at Southwood, where the black arm that emerged from the Callow Pit (above), also belonged to the Devil.

Finally in Norfolk, the miles-long Fossditch or Fendyke is said to have been created by the Devil dragging his foot along the ground, and later, in scraping off his boot, the clod of soil fell to form Thetford Castle earthworks. This further strengthens His association with the Castle and emphasises the huge size of the actual earthworks there.

Liminality

I admit that the previous sections are, necessarily, a small selection of the available traditions and lore concerning the Devil in East Anglia; I have, however, endeavoured to ensure that they are a representative selection of the type and kind of legends found in the region. It can be seen from these that the vast majority can be split into roughly two kinds of traditions; those concerning churches and other kinds of buildings and those concerning the landscape or features therein.

These two types of tradition, however, both have something very significant in common, something that is very pertinent to folk magic and witchcraft in East Anglia; they both deal with places of liminality, borders or lines (leys?), where one world or universe comes into contact with another and there is the possibility of a crossover, or information exchange between them. This is finely illustrated in the nature of a church building, which necessarily straddles two worlds and may also be built on or over a previously sacred place or area. Tradition states that much magical practice took place either in the church itself, or else in the graveyard/cemetery or in the surroundings. Liminality is further illustrated by

The Devil's Plantation

the meres, ponds, lakes, banks, ditches, barrows, hills and other types of earthworks described above, all of which partake of the nature of 'borderlands' or crossover places where unusual events may take place.

There is also the added feature that some of them deal in buried, lost or forgotten 'treasure', or the entrance to other worlds, beneath or alongside our own. The 'treasure' often refers to hidden, secret or lost knowledge, rather than actual material wealth, and the otherworlds as the realms where this information may be found or rediscovered. These latter are major features in all types of folk magic or witchcraft, contrary to the impression that the Church would normally like to give to them.

❦ Cunning and Mighty is His Nature ❦

Continuing with this theme and its connections with the concept of the Devil, it can be seen from the examples given above that this being of folk lore is not generally thought of, or feared as, the great anti-Christ and principle of ultimate evil that he is normally portrayed as being. So how is the Devil viewed in East Anglian lore and magic and who, exactly, is he perceived to be by the practitioners that call upon him?

In a magical context, i.e. in the view of the witches and folk magicians, he was seen as a being that was against the accepted norms of society. He was firmly linked to ideas of mayhem, civil disobedience, lack of good citizenship

Speak of the Devil...

and ruthlessness. He was cunning in executing his will and desires and in achieving his ends. He was a being characterised by his lust for pleasure and the good things in life and, significantly, for his knowledge of arcane secrets and power over the things of this world – his magical knowledge and ability were things that normal society, and in particular the Church, deemed dangerous, forbidden and not to be indulged in.

Witchcraft was associated with the Devil mainly because he was the symbol of opposition, 'evil', but opposition to whatever was the norm and, hence, frightening to most people. This aspect would have appealed greatly to the class of people who called on Him, who were mostly from the common folk of the working classes, who laboured in the fields for little reward and who were subject to the whims and fancies of the Church and State. Indeed, we have seen in the previous chapter that many of the witches of this region exemplified the very traits I have just ascribed to the Devil himself. Those folk of the Gentry or learned classes who called on him, were likely to do so for slightly different reasons to their less well-educated, but no less intelligent, cousins. It would likely be the Devil's knowledge, abilities and power that they were seeking to understand, to further their own knowledge and abilities in these areas; and maybe kick over the traces a bit as well.

In this being, are we here speaking of or describing a pre-existing, pagan deity, dimly remembered through the passage of the years? Or a conflation of one or more of these with the Biblical Prince of the Fallen Angels? This is somewhat difficult to determine. Certainly he was never addressed by any of the known historical, pagan names or titles, such as Cernunnos, Calirius, Belenos, Taranis, or any of the other deities that were known in East Anglia from antiquity (with the one exception of the coven, previously noted, that still, apparently, worships the old Norse gods, Loki, Woden & Freyja). Nor does he appear to be viewed as such by those who worked with him.

The Devil's Plantation

He is given various names or titles – as some are clearly descriptive; Old Harry (West Norfolk), Old Scratch, Old Ragusan, Daddy, Sam, Him, Bargus, the Old Lad and Old Horny. The possible origin of some of these names in pagan deities is obscured by the taboo of never actually saying the name of a deity, but using an epithet instead, although this cannot be discounted. As we see in the title of this chapter 'speak of the Devil and he will appear', applies equally to deities of all types. But different districts had different levels of prohibition, hence the varieties of names that do appear, each clouding the issue. What can be said is that he was conceived of as a being of great power, subtlety, knowledge and ability, who was – mostly – on the side of the underdog and was willing to aid and abet those people who were outside the norms, or on the edges of, society. He is a spirit of nature representing such in all its moods, including its expression in human nature. Such activities as sexual promiscuity, Sabbath breaking, gambling, becoming intoxicated, adolescent brawling and gossiping, to name but a few, might come under this heading. In this guise he is the natural continuation of the spirit of some of the more anarchic ancient gods of course. I contrast this entity with the Old Testament Devil, who on the instructions of God goes out to tempt and is not himself the spirit of anything other than Divine Will. This Devil and the tendency he represents was representative of an anti-moralistic strain of thought in the Folk Culture. In the Suffolk Folk Songs there is occasionally a reference to the Flash Girls and Flash Boys; this reflects a sub culture of anti-moralism and excess. Whether that equals anti Christianity or just plain secularism is open to debate. That he was, in fact, also considered by some to be similar to, or a close associate of, the Biblical Satan upon occasion cannot be denied, but this was unusual and not the norm. That he was also pictured as bearing horns or antlers, cloven hooves and carrying a pitchfork upon occasion can also not be denied, but that these in themselves betokened a Satanic origin cannot be upheld, as all these attributes also belonged to pre-existent deities as well.

He could be called upon for his aid in a variety of manners, or invoked during various forms of 'self-initiation' (some of which I will look at later), which he was willing to give under certain circumstances and usually for an exacted price. This gave the witch and their initiator an extremely close and very strong bond, almost preternaturally sexual in nature. The witch appreciated the vast immensity of the being with which they were involved; the fact that he embodied, empowered and to some extent partook of, the nature of the Land around them. He could be fiercely wild and savage at times, gentle and playful at others. Never to be fully trusted, he could, and would, test and terrify in equal measure; but he would also teach, empower and expand the mind and the abilities of the witch beyond the accepted and measurable norms.

Men in Black

Further to the spiritual, or non-material, being of the Devil, there were those physical persons who sometimes personated or represented him in various manners to his adherents, sometimes confusing the historical record in the process. Although far from a common practice in East Anglia, as most magical practitioners were solitary, we have seen in the previous chapter that they did upon occasion meet up to engage in dancing and feasting, or to discuss various matters, both magical and mundane. Sometimes at these gatherings, there was a man (as it seems always to have been a man), who appeared to the attendees as the embodiment of the Devil himself.

He was invariably addressed as the Devil (or the local name used), was dressed all in black, frequently cloaked and either masked or wearing a cover over his head upon which he typically wore either sheep or goat horns. Very occasionally

The Devil's Plantation

he would appear in dog or hound form, but there is little descriptive evidence for this. He was often crippled or lamed (or appeared to be so), harking back to the attributes ascribed to some of the 'Sacred Kings' of antiquity; and was generally very secretive, few people knowing his real identity in the locality.

He was said to possibly have connections with either the aristocracy or local gentry, alternatively to have links with the Gypsy or Romany community in the area ('where there are gypsies, there you will find witches' is an old country saying). This may possibly indicate a link with the magic and lore of the Horsemen and their Society, as Romany horsemen were known to have been brought into this area to train local people in their detailed knowledge of the horse and its magic. Alternatively, this may indicate a mix of magical cultures and a swapping of knowledge; it was known that during the times of greatest persecution, witches on the run often found a sympathetic haven with the other outcasts of society, the Romany gypsys. That there would inevitably have been an exchange of magical knowledge can pretty much be taken for granted, and that members of both cultures would be welcome at the magical meetings of the other would seem to be highly likely in that case, both benefitting from the information and experience gained.

The Devil's representative generally convened any larger meetings in the area, at places like remote crossroads, deep pits that were unused or abandoned (such as old chalk or flint minings), secluded woodlands, or barns on private and isolated property. Occasionally fields or meadows were used, often with the knowledge or agreement of the local farmer, who may join in with the festivities at the end of the meeting. His role appears as that of co-ordinator of events and as a link with the Otherworlds, standing in place of the Devil in the meetings. He would engage in sexual practice with members (in some rare cases with both males and females, despite the taboos

Speak of the Devil...

of the time concerning homosexuality, demonstrating the antinomian role of the Devil and the disregard for social norms); dispense charms and herbal knowledge and perform divinations for people. He would appear to be the local 'priest' of the Devil, the Magister or 'Master Witch', functioning in much the same role for his flock as his Church equivalent.

In addition to his role as 'master of ceremonies', he could also tour the countryside and minister to *'His'* devotees, or seek out likely candidates for inclusion in the rites and practices. It is sometimes confusing in the historical record whether the spiritual or the physical Devil is intended (and, indeed, they do seem to be somewhat changeable), but there are several descriptions of a 'Black Man' or a 'Man in Black' (the terms are ambiguous, sometimes confusing and not a little contradictory), appearing to people and offering them pacts or bargains. These pacts sometimes came in the form of imps or familiars, which needed to be signed for in a big book, whereupon the Black Man disappeared and the witch could then perform marvellous feats with their new charges. An article appeared in the Sunday Chronicle in 1928, concerning the village of Horseheath in Cambridgeshire. A black man (sic) called on Mother Redcap (a generic name for a country witch), in the village one day and, 'produced a book and asked her to sign her name in it. The woman signed the book, and the mysterious stranger told her she would be the mistress of five imps who would carry out her orders. Shortly afterwards the woman was seen out accompanied by a rat, a cat, a toad, a ferret and a mouse. Everybody believed she was a witch and many people visited her to obtain cures.' She was, in fact, believed to be the successor to the (in)famous Daddy Witch, as already described above.

At Loddon in Norfolk, in the 19th century, the local witch lay dying and told her daughter that she must follow in her trade after her, as she had been bound to

The Devil's Plantation

the Devil as a child. The girl refused, but shortly after her mother died, a mysterious stranger (in black), arrived in the village. He enquired after the dead witch and called at her house, 'made love to the girl' and then took her away. But he was no ordinary man, the villagers were sure, but the Devil, to whom the girl had been bound by her witch mother.

Further confusing the issue somewhat, is the use of the term 'Devil' to describe the 'leader' of one of the many secret societies that existed in East Anglia, historically and, in some cases, up until the present time. These societies included The Horseman's Word, The Millers Fraternity and the Confraternity of the Plough, all valuable and essential trades in a place such as East Anglia. The Devil of these societies in such cases describes a person performing a role and a function, rather than an entity or a title in itself. This person, who took on the role, would be present at initiations into the society, cloaked and horned in some way as to represent the personage to the initiate, and would customarily administer the oath and passwords to the new member. He would give certain aspects of knowledge of the particular trade involved and demand reparation if any of the rules were broken. It is likely that the question; *'Have you seen the Devil?'* sometimes used in country greetings on initial meetings with a stranger, is a type of watchword to tell if the newcomer is an initiated member of one of the societies. If the wrong answer is given, then the stranger is not a 'brother'. Likewise, part of the questioning to an already initiated member for gaining admittance to a meeting, would be; *'Who told you to come here?'* The correct answer to gain admittance would be; *'The Devil.'* That the Church misinterpreted these practices and assumed that all members of local fraternities were devil-worshippers, shows the lack of understanding that it had of its flock and their indigenous beliefs and practices. However, due to the clandestine nature of these activities and the close-

Speak of the Devil...

knit societies in which they existed, it would be unusual to think that a member of one society would not probably also be a member of another similar one, exoteric or esoteric.

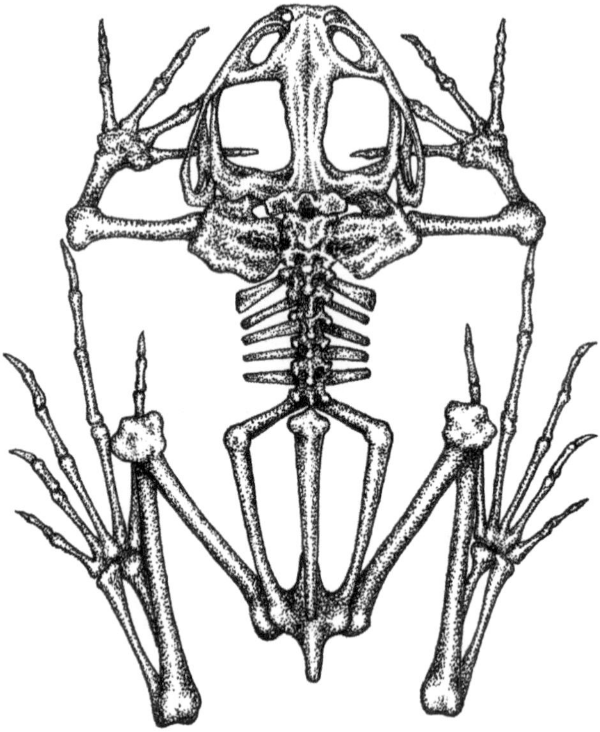

Witch Ways

Very few of the actual techniques of the old witches of East Anglia have been recorded, most having been passed on only orally and rarely committed to writing. The few recorded instances from different practitioners bear little resemblance to each other and it seems that most witches had their own ways of doing things, rather than belonging to an organised 'society'. However, there are a few instances where witch practices seem to coincide, and one of these is the manner, or manners, of 'initiation' or achieving the power to work their magic. Contrary to modern, pagan expressions of witchcraft (or Wicca as it is more generally called), historical and Traditional Craft does draw its power from the being sometimes known as 'the Devil'. We have looked at this being in the last chapter and seen how he is viewed within this tradition of magic and lore, so there is no need to suspect or imply pacts with the Satanic powers here, although a pact of a kind is indeed what is made. What was, and is, intended here (as these techniques are continued in the present day), is a real and coherent link with a powerful being, who both is and represents in his own being, a source of energy and connection with the Otherworlds previously discussed. Indeed, we have seen that some of the practices performed at some of the sites associated with him may be truncated or half-forgotten rites of initiation to him and/or in his name. That these techniques also necessarily imply a form of spiritual and/or magical change within the witch practicing the rite should also be understood; indeed the subsequent use and expression of the power gained in these rites would be impossible without it.

Circles of Might

One of the known methods for calling the Devil is by the use of the magic circle. In some instances, this may well have been borrowed by the rural witches from some forms of classical magic, as printed books of ceremonial and ritual magic were readily available from the 18th century onwards, but the circle has been known and used as a magical device from time out of mind. Again, we have seen in the last chapter how 'games' of circling stones, etc. at certain places were – however much in fun – originally intended to call him up. For initiatory purposes, the method employed was to create one of these circles on the ground in a pre-selected place of power or sanctity within the landscape, often already associated with the Devil, as in the previous chapter. The circle was marked physically on the ground in some manner, usually with powdered chalk, soot, flour or sand, and the witch would stand inside it and recite a form of words that would call the Devil. In keeping with the antinomian nature of the Devil and to create the right magico-spiritual conditions within the witch, the Christian Lord's Prayer was often used, recited backwards. Other forms of chanted formulae were also used, containing words of power, such as 'Abracadabra' and 'Calabar'. It must be remembered in this context, that the witch was not deliberately trying to make a pact with evil, but 'kicking over the traces' of the society in which they lived. Anything that went against the societal norms was viewed as shocking, but also therefore, powerful and

Witch Ways

was utilised in a magical context to add energy to any practical rite. There was no intention to try to destroy the Church – indeed, most witches went to Church because they had to, and would consider themselves Christians – but to go against the grain would be a powerful and in this context, magical, thing to do.

Catherine Parsons, in her lecture previously referred to (see Chpt. 3), concerning the witchcraft in and around Horseheath in Cambridgeshire, says;

> '*a circle is drawn on the ground, with perhaps a piece of chalk ... the Lord's prayer is said backwards, and the Devil suddenly appears within the circle, perhaps in the form of a cockerel, but all kinds of things are said to suddenly spring out of the ground.*' Parsons says further that; '*the Devil usually appeared ... in the form of an animal, such as a rat, mouse or toad.*' Also; '*And if the person standing within the circle becomes so frightened that he steps out of the circle, we are told the Devil would fly away with him.*'

In the 1960s at Castle Acre, in Norfolk, a circle was discovered and photographed before it was destroyed. The circle was made of soot, being barely 3 feet across and clearly being intended for the use of a single individual, perhaps in some such rite as described above. Other circles were also found in the area around Kings Lynn at that period. It is worth noting here that circles had other uses too. To find a circle marked outside, or around, one's property was/is cause for alarm. It is a sure sign that magic had been practiced and, if the operator had not informed the owner of the property beforehand, it was certain that the working had not been for the owner's benefit. The circle had been deliberately left to let the subject know that a spell had been placed on either them, or their property.

Drawing the circle creates an artificial and temporary sacred area in which to work. Creating the circle in an already empowered, liminal area, noted for its association with the Devil, increases the chances of the operation being successful. It also increases the effect on the psyche of the witch involved in the rite, again increasing the likelihood that they will come away from the operation profoundly changed. Whether the appearance of the creatures mentioned above happens in actuality, or within the sphere of perception of the witch alone, matters not a jot; that they appear and are apprehensible to the witch means that the rite has succeeded and the pact achieved.

Toads and Bones

There are a few other known methods of solo witch initiation, such as night-long vigils in sacred places, fasting and prayer, or a combination of all of them, very similar to Christian methods of achieving unity with the divine, but with an obviously different purpose. However, there is one other method that was and still is employed to create a witch that is considered to be more powerful than any other, and that is the use of the Toad Bone rite. This practice is fairly well known within the folklore of the area, but is most often associated with the rites of the Society of the Horseman's Word and its own methods of initiation and horse control. It is rarely associated with the creation of a witch, although it has been used in East Anglia for many years, probably many centuries, outside and alongside that of the Horsemen and their practices; indeed, it was known and used in this area long before the advent of the Horsemen. That some people may have been members of both 'organisations' and that there has been cross-fertilisation in use and methods over the years is certainly possible, if not actually probable given the nature of the culture of the region, but it remains a fact that the use of the Toad Bone rite within the workings of the East Anglian witch has been generally overlooked or ignored. The rite is of ancient provenance, being recorded by Pliny the Elder in his Natural History as early as 77 CE, although different versions of it are known from places as far apart as India, Egypt and Germany in the ancient world. Variations of the rite are given in some of the Anglo-Saxon herbals and, in more modern times, it has been practiced in both Africa and the southern United States, using cat's bones instead of toad's, with the same effect.

In East Anglia, the rite is sometimes alternatively known as 'Going to the River', being descriptive of the practice itself, and as 'The Waters of the Moon'; this latter name has been recorded from only one source, in *The Pattern Under the Plough*, by George Ewart Evans. However, as this is one of the fullest descriptions available, I shall here give it as it was recorded. The informant was an old Horseman from Wortwell, Norfolk, named Albert Love, who was born in 1886 and worked with horses all his life. He is unusual in that he powders the bone, whereas it was normally dried and kept about the person.

> *'Well, the toads that we used for this are actually in the Yarmouth area in and around Fritton. We get these toads alive and bring them home. They have a ring around their neck and are what they call walking toads* [the Natterjack toad, Bufo calamita]. *We bring them home, kill them, and put them on a whitethorn bush. They are there for twenty four hours till they dry. Then we bury the toad in an ant-hill; and*

The Devil's Plantation

> it's there for a full month, 'till the moon is at the full. Then you get it out; and it's only a skeleton. You take it down to a running stream when the moon is at the full. You watch it carefully, particular not to take your eyes off it. There's a certain bone, a little crotch bone it is, it leaves the rest of the skeleton and floats uphill against the stream. Well, you take that out of the stream, take it home, bake it, powder it and put it in a box; and you use oils with it the same as you do the milch. While you are watching these bones in the water, you must on no consideration take your eyes off it. Do [if you do], you will lose all power. That's where you get your power from for messing about with horses, just keeping your eyes on that particular bone. But when you are watching it and these bones are parting, you'll hear all the trees and all the noises that you can imagine, even as if buildings were falling down or a traction engine is running over you. But you still mustn't take your eyes off, because that's where you lose your power. Of course, the noises must be something to do with the Devil's work in the middle of the night.'

This description, as I have said, was given by a horseman and therefore would not focus on quite the same aspects as would a witch. Here is another description given by the 'King of the Norfolk Poachers' from *I Walked By Night*, edited by Lilias Rider Haggard; this rite was given to the narrator by his own grandmother, who was well versed in local magic and spellcraft, and was quite evidently the local wise-woman. The account would appear to date from around 1850 and is unusual in that, of the recorded accounts that we have, it specifically uses the term 'Witch craft'.

> 'There was one charm she told me of wich was practiced wen any one wanted to get command over there fellow Creaturs. Those that wished to cast the spell must serch until they found a walking toad. It was a toad with a yellow ring round its neck, I have never seen one of them but I have been told

they can be found in some parts of the Cuntry. Wen they had found the toad they must put it in a perforated box, and bury it in a Black Ant's nest. Wen the Ants have eaten all the flesh away from the bones it must be taken up, and the person casting the spell must carry the bones to the edge of a running stream the midnight of Saint Mark's Night [April 25th], and throw them in the water. All will sink but one single bone and that one will swim up stream. When they have taken out the bone the Devell would give them power of Witch craft, and they could use that Power over both Man and Animiles.'

We have already encountered Tilly Baldrey of Huntingtoft in a previous chapter, but here is a description of how she achieved her remarkable powers from *Eastern Counties Magazine*, 1901;

'You ketch a hoppin' toad and carry that in your bowsom till that's rotted right away to the backboon. Then you take and hold that over runnin' water at midnight till the Devil he come to you and pull you over the water, and then you be a witch and you kin dew all mander of badness to people and hev power over them.'

A further description is related from just over the border in Lincolnshire, concerning the gaining of witchcraft power. After you have de-fleshed the toad, you must;

'Take the bones and go down to a good stream of runnin' water at midnight an' throw the bones i' the stream. All the bones but one will go down stream, an' that one as wont go downstream is the breast-bone. Now, you must get 'old of this 'ere bone afore the Devil gets it, an' if you get it an' keep it allus by you – in your pocket or wear it – then you can witch; as well as that, you'll be safe from bein' witched yourself.'

The Devil's Plantation

The reference above to the Devil getting hold of the bone before the witch refers to an aspect of the rite which normally comes later, although there are regional variations. To complete the rite, the witch would go to either a barn or a graveyard/cemetery for either three or five consecutive nights and keep vigil. On the last night the Devil will come and demand a pact with the witch. If the witch refuses to make a formal pact, then the Devil will demand blood in return for favours and services rendered. This may safely be given, but the witch must at all times remain in control of the situation; i.e. they must become the Devil's master (The Devil may try to trick the bone off the witch, or otherwise fight/wrestle for it). If the Devil refuses to obey, the witch may strike out at him, or a sign representing him, with a 'gad' or ceremonial wand. This wand is in effect the visible sign of the witches' status as a Toadwitch and is recognised as such within the rural environment. It is a natural wooden wand, around which honeysuckle, clematis or another creeper has wound, creating a spiral effect in the wood. After the successful completion of the rite, the practitioner is a fully empowered (Toad) Witch and has control over animals, people and various aspects of nature and is able to summon supernatural aid when needed. To gauge whether it is likely that the prospective witch 'has the power' and is likely to succeed at the rite, there is a way that they can assess this beforehand. The 'postulant' has to gather the spores of the bracken plant (known as 'fernseed'), from a piece of uncultivated land – the ubiquitous 'Devil's Plantation' – at the stroke of midnight. If a thunderstorm should suddenly break out as the seed is being picked, then the Toad rite is likely to succeed; fernseed is associated with lightning in the local lore and its appearance betokens a blessing on the operation.

I will recap the whole rite and add salient points not explicit or described in the foregoing narratives. Using this rite to become a witch, one must obtain a toad or frog (areas vary in the specifics) and, if it is alive, it must be killed and dried out; this can be done by hanging it on a Blackthorn bush (the animal does not have to be alive first, there are examples of dead ones being used as well). It must next be left on or buried in an anthill, until all the flesh has been stripped from it and only the skeleton remains. This is usually done from one full moon to the next. All the bones must be collected and taken to a (north-south flowing) stream, at midnight, on the night of the full moon, where the moon can be seen reflected in the water (St. Mark's and St. John's Eves are sometimes specified as preferable as well). The bones must be cast onto the surface of the water and watched exceedingly carefully, until one bone detaches itself from the others and appears to float upstream. This bone must be taken and kept safe. It is imperative to the successful performance of the operation, that the aspirant does not take their eyes off the bones for an instant, no matter what disturbances, noises or interruptions may manifest themselves. To do so is instant failure. Hearing a rushing wind or a storm is said to signify success however and the witch is thereafter able to see the wind. To complete the rite, the aspirant must keep vigil for a number of nights (3 or 5), in either a barn or a graveyard, depending on their magical orientation, having the toad bone with them at all times. On the final night, the Devil (or representation), will come and attempt to get the bone away from the aspirant, but must be mastered and made to obey the witch. A pact may be made, or be implicit in the success of the operation (i.e. the witch retains the bone and denies it to the Devil), endowing the witch with newfound abilities and insights.

It must now be stated that this rite has always been known to have its attendant risks. Firstly, it should never be attempted before and until certain signs and omens have appeared to the aspirant witch. These signs may appear in nature, or in dreams or by other means, but must be seen first before making the attempt at the rite. Apart from the harm that may occur by failing in the attempt, the successful completion of the operation brings with it its own complications. The toad witch may experience various mental infirmities, which can include hallucinations, delusions and paranoia. They may believe that they are being followed or being watched, or may think that there are strange things hiding in the house or climbing the stairs. The rite opens the mind of the witch up to very powerful and sometimes quite primaeval and chaotic forces, and it is only a magician of the strongest mental capacity that can control these energies. The bone itself was sometimes considered to lose its power as it aged and, if the witch wished to retain their own powers, a new bone had to be prepared and the old one discarded, with all the concomitant risks of repeating the ritual. An old Toadsman was once asked what to do to attain his remarkable powers of control over animals and people; the reply was, 'Don't, for if you do, you will never rest.' An early and possibly violent death is to be expected. It is up to the individual to weigh the risks and decide whether it is worth it for the benefits attained.

On the surface of it, the Toad Bone Rite seems to be a piece of horrendous and even blasphemous magic. The killing and dismemberment of the toad seems cruel in the extreme (although a dead toad can also be used), but it must be remembered that this rite did not arise from a culture tuned to our delicate, modern sensibilities, but from one that was full of poverty, starvation and often hand-to-mouth existence. Within the relevant folklore, the toad (and its cousin the frog), is an embodiment of all that is evil, bad and poisonous within the natural world, and is therefore an excellent vehicle for the aspirant to identify with in this rite and surpass or overcome in its successful completion. It would also seem to parallel the death, entombment and resurrection of Jesus, but in a perverted and inverted manner, thereby making a pact with the 'powers of darkness'. However, this is to miss the whole point of the rite. The aspiring witch identifies themselves with the death and dismemberment of the toad and it is themselves, or rather their 'lower', mundane self or mentality that dies. What arises out of the rite, by the one-pointed focus at the river and the claiming of the special bone, the overcoming of all disturbances and terrifying illusions and the subsequent, successful battle with the Devil, is a reborn, awakened and empowered magical practitioner. The witch has undergone their own death and rebirth ritual, complete with the harrying of hell and has emerged having a greater capacity for understanding and utilising the hidden aspects and powers of the natural world. It depends on their strength of mind and character as to how they then cope with their new insights and abilities, and it takes a strong mind to do this.

Toads in Magic

As well as being used in the rite as described above, the toad/frog has been employed in other magical practices in East Anglia for many a year. An East Anglian dialect word for bewitching, charming, cursing or placing a spell of any kind on a person or animal is 'tudding', i.e. 'putting the toad on' someone. Anyone who had the nickname of 'Tuddy' was always treated with the greatest of respect and caution.

If someone wished to acquire the power of the evil eye, they had to catch nine, live toads, string them all together on one line and leave them to die. They then had to be buried in the ground. After this, the witches' eye would become malignant, bestowing the power to overlook, bind, curse and even kill someone, just as the toads had been bound and killed and placed in the ground. Actually putting the toad on someone, involves catching a live toad and burying it in a specific place in the road near where the victim lives. The toad must be buried using a three-pronged fork and left to die; as the toad wastes and perishes so too will the victim. Another way of putting the toad on someone is to place live toads up the chimney, naming the victim and the curse as you do so. As the creatures waste away in the heat of the fire, so the victim is also consumed. If the toads shriek or cry out, it is a sure sign that the spell has been successfully cast; however, if they burst and fall down the chimney, then the spell is removed. Toads were also used for apotropaic reasons as well as cursing. A Suffolk method of protecting your house from lightning is to put four toads – called Hedge Toads - into terracotta flower pots and to bury them at the four corners – one in each – of your garden. The toads form a kind of magical grid, which will prevent the lightning from striking your property.

Toads were used in healing practices too. Catherine Parsons describes how whooping cough was treated in Horseheath, by rubbing the sufferer's palm with a live toad or frog. The animal was immediately buried alive and, as it wasted and rotted away, so too would the cough. A sufferer from warts had to catch a live toad, place it in a bag and hang it up somewhere where they would walk past it every day. The warts would be transferred to the toad and the sufferer would be freed of them. Swallowing live toads and frogs was a cure for weakness and consumption, whilst another cure for whooping cough involved holding the head of a frog or toad in the mouth for a few moments. A wise-woman's 'cure' for breast cancer used to be practiced using a toad in the Fens of Cambridgeshire. A live toad was obtained and the warts on its back were rubbed vigorously; this caused them to expand and give out a liquid toxin, not fatal to humans. The toad was then rubbed on the tumour until it ceased to give out the venom, whereupon it was placed back where it had been found and left to live. It is now thought that the toads natural toxin, may have had an anti-cancerous effect on the malignant tumour, as reports of success with this technique were not uncommon.

Finally in this batrachian section, a technique that employs the toad's attributes and reputation as a leaper between worlds, a liminal being, able to pass from one reality to another and thereby carry messages or bring about change. The witch needs to catch a toad and kill it, or find an already dead one; the latter is preferable in this case, the more perfect the condition the better. The toad is buried in a container of salt for 6 moons and allowed to dry out completely. For the next 6 moons, it is rubbed with a specific mixture of oils; this is done three times, once every 2 moons, leaving the oils to sink in and act as a preservative, leaving it to dry out each time. Lastly, the toad is cured in the smoke of a particular kind of incense at full moon. It is then wrapped in black cloth and put away in a dark place, until the moon changes. At the new moon, it is brought out and enchanted, such that it becomes a vehicle for the witches' will; this makes it capable of taking the wishes of the witch into the Otherworld, there to await manifestation, or else to carry the witch themselves into the other realms, for the purposes of seeking knowledge and magical power. The toad is kept secure in a wooden box when not being used, only being brought out during the hours of darkness. Wishes are written on small slips of paper, and placed inside the box with an incantation and left there until they come to fruition.

With the Help of the Dead

Continuing with the theme of the Otherworld, it was a long established tradition that witches worked with beings that lived there and also visited them there on occasion. In East Anglian witchcraft it was completely accepted that the two worlds of 'here' and 'there' shared an association far closer and less mystical than theologians claimed, and that the exalted 'Heaven' and the abysmal 'Hell' of theology, while suitable for maintaining discipline over unenlightened devouts, only existed in the theological imagination; this was, nevertheless powerfully influential, particularly so when a Church, or the entire faith, became wealthy and militant. But as a matter of fact, East Anglian witchcraft recognised that between 'This Place' and the 'Other Place', there was a definite affinity and, far from existing totally and distantly apart, they were very close; close enough for it to be seen from day to day, that an overlapping existed. Since the requirements of many spells made it essential that all manner of pathways to manifestation were investigated and acted upon, the means for communicating with that Other Place became a life's work for many witches. As previously mentioned, East Anglia is not well endowed with stone circles or other such monuments, but there are many burial mounds and these were well used, along with the many remote graveyards and cemeteries in the region.

A method of contacting the spirits of the deceased, or to work with your own ancestors, is as follows. The witch must go either to a burial mound or the grave of their family deceased, on the night of the dark moon. They must take with them food and drink which was particularly liked by the deceased, if known, otherwise the best that they could afford. A gift of pure, local honey, smeared on the ground or grave is especially valued. They must approach the place from the west, at midnight, and place the food and drink on the ground. The witch must then make a small cut in their left hand and, whilst the blood drips directly onto the grave or the mound, call upon the spirit of the being they wish to communicate with, three times. After this they must sit down and share out the food, as if they were having a meal with the deceased, telling them what they wish to know, find out, or have the spirits do for them. Finally, they must then go to sleep on the mound or beside the grave and, if they have been successful in their operation, the spirits will come to them in their sleep and tell them what they need to know. At dawn, the witch must wake and clear all away and go home, but leaving the food offerings, without turning round or looking back.

Another method of working with the dead and foreseeing the future with their help can be done using the following method. You must obtain a human shin bone and remove the marrow from the middle. Replace this with tallow and a wick made from twining together strips taken from the shroud of a corpse or the cords used to bind it, so that you have a kind of lamp or candle. Compound an incense made of linseed, fleabane seed, roots of parsley and violets. Go to the burial mound or gravesite and light the incense, calling on the spirits to help you foresee that which you wish to know. Light the candle and walk three times widdershins around the mound or grave in total silence, but holding in mind what you wish to know. Return to the smoking incense and gaze deeply into the fumes. If the spirits are with you, then you will see your answer. Leave offerings of food and drink in thanks for their help. Visions might also be seen by using a pail full of water or a candle flame and gazing into them after having called on the spirits for help.

A witch could use the power of the dead in other ways too. Images could be made of someone, for good or ill, by mixing together quantities of wax, herbs and corpse dust. By adding a little of their own blood to the mix, the witch could call upon the spirits to aid their work. Here is a charm contributed to *'The Suffolk Garland'* in 1818, by a Mrs Cobbold of Holy Wells, Ipswich. It was found amongst the papers of Thomas Colson, a fisherman who lived at St. Clements in Ipswich, who was drowned in October 1811. He was known by the nickname of 'Robinson Crusoe' and had quite a considerable reputation as a magic worker of some power. The note was written in his own handwriting;

The Devil's Plantation

> *A Charm – to make a young woman*
> *seem to be in love with a young man.*
> Take new wax, and the powder of a dead man, make an image with the face downwards and in the likeness of the person you wish to have; make it in the ouers of mars and in the new of the mone; under the left arm-poke place a Swaler's hart and a liver under the rite; you must have a new needal and a new thread; the Sprits name must be menchened, his Sine and his Character.
>
> I take this opportunity to inform my friends that about 16 yeares ago this Charm was put in practice by sum willians of Witches at Needham-Markett, William Studd been one of them; and they have put me to much torment and lamed me many times, they own to me that they make use of part of the bones of Mrs Wilkerson of Felixstow, she that suffered at Rushmere sum yeares ago; this is sartainly true, and I am ready to give it on oth if required. – Thos. Colson.

The article in the Suffolk Garland goes on to give a description of Thomas Coulson and his death;

> He was a firm believer in the evil agency of wizards and witchcraft. On this subject he was by no means uninformed; and a frequent perusal of the Daemonology of ... K. James I, ... soon confirmed his belief in these absurd opinions. He appeared also to have read "Glanvil's Saducismus Triumphans" with considerable attention ... His mind was so haunted with the dreams of charms and enchantments, as to fancy that he was continually under the influence of the mischievous tormentors. His arms and legs, nay, almost all his whole body, was encircled with the bones of horses, rings, amulets and characts, verses, words, etc; as spells and charms to protect him against their evil machinations. On different parts of his boat was to be seen the "horse shoe nailed", that most effective antidote against the power of witches. When conversing with him, he would describe to you that he saw them

hovering about his person, and endeavouring, by all their arts, to punish and torment him ... However powerful and effective his charms might be to protect him from the agency of evil spirits, they did not prove sufficiently operative against the dangers of storm and tempest. For being unfortunately being driven on the Ooze by a violent storm on the 3rd October, 1811, he was seen and earnestly importuned to quit his crazy vessel; but relying on the efficacy of his charms, he obstinately refused; ... And poor Robinson sunk to rise no more.'

This extract is interesting if for no other reason than the light it sheds on the practices and types of magic used by a working witch/wizard himself, at the beginning of the 19th century.

Healing was also available by calling on the help of the dead. If someone had a bleeding or cancerous tumour, then they could apply the cure of the Dead Hand. The witch had to find a corpse (usually of a person who had been hanged or died from violence) of the opposite sex to the patient. The hand was detached from the corpse and the sufferer's tumour was stroked with it, all the time the witch calling on the spirit of the dead person to aid in the operation. The hand was then buried and, as it rotted away, so would the tumour. This cure was also used for 'swelled throat' or goitre. Dried and powdered human remains were also mixed with water and herbs and given to the patient to drink, for various ailments, whilst the help of the dead was petitioned. A thread, usually red, that had been tied round the neck of a corpse could be used to stop nose bleeds or other haemorrhages, by tying it round the affected body part and moss or mould that had been found growing on a human skull was considered particularly effective. It too was dried and powdered and given to the patient to drink, for complaints as varied as sterility to miscarriage.

Working with Familiars

Having passed through the various trials of initiation and the Otherealms, the witch would normally find themselves in command of one or more familiars, or as they were generally known in East Anglia, Imps or Impets. These were either given to the witch at the time of their initiation by the Devil to seal the pact, or arrived a short time afterwards, either brought by the Devil Himself, or by one of His earthly servitors. Sometimes imps were passed on by other witches in the family and, unless you could get rid of them to someone else, you were thereby made a witch yourself, whether you wanted to be one or not. The imps were the outward and visible sign to all that the person was indeed a witch and, moreover, had the power to control and use them, for either good or ill. To outsiders, the imps appeared to be nothing more than small, domestic pets or wild animals that had been tamed. These included creatures such as cats, dogs, mice, rats, bats, toads/frogs, ferrets and sometimes hares. To the witch, however, they were something more.

Not very many witches were ever dedicated to causing harm exclusively – as may be thought. The majority of witches sought power and, having once obtained it, could hardly dedicate their lives to a daily or weekly curse for a very basic reason; total evil was as unlikely as total good. Therefore, what the witch sought when seeking supernatural aid was an ally in the performance of their craft, an adjunct to their power, and an opportunity to strengthen their vocation; this was sometimes beneficial and sometimes not, but which was rarely exclusively negative. These imps, therefore, were their magical servitors, not quite of this world and definitely having access to the Otherealms. They were also their eyes and ears in this world, in places that they could not get to easily. They carried charms and spells that were difficult for the witch to deliver personally and occasionally served as a form in which the magic worker could project their spirit, or

Above: Ancient Yew grove, on the cliffs at the ancient town of Dunwich. A site of recent necromantic rites.

Left: One of the remaining gravestones, with human bones, on the cliffs at Dunwich.

Above: Grave mound at the Anglo-Saxon burial site of Sutton Hoo, in Suffolk. Considered to be the place where Raedwald, King of East Anglia, was buried. Rites to the Ancestors are said to still take place here.

Leftt: Wooden carving of a Meremaid set into the plaster wall of a mediaeval building in Ipswich.

Above: The interior of the north door of Blythburgh Church, Suffolk; scene of a visitation from Black Shuck.

Right. Close-up of the church door, showing scorch marks left by Black Shuck.

Above: Weather vane of Black Shuck in the town square, Bungay, Suffolk.
Left: Tapestry panel, depicting the Black Dog, St. Mary's Church, Bungay.

Facing: The Devil's Stone, also known as the Druid's Stone, outside the Church of St. Mary in Bungay, Suffolk (above), and the Devil's Stone, outside the Priest's door, at the Church of St. Andrew, Westleton, Suffolk.

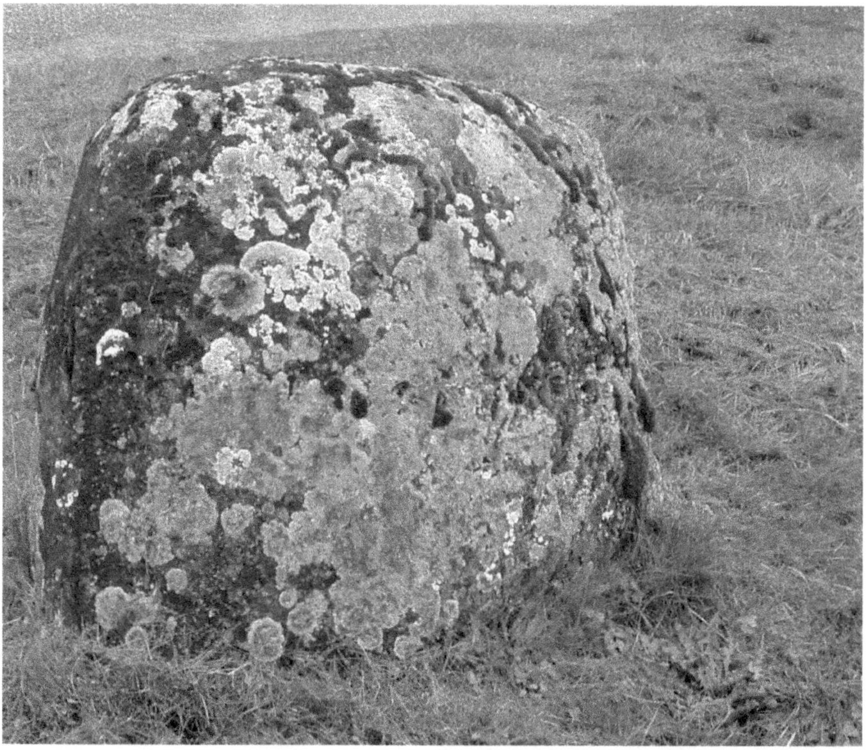

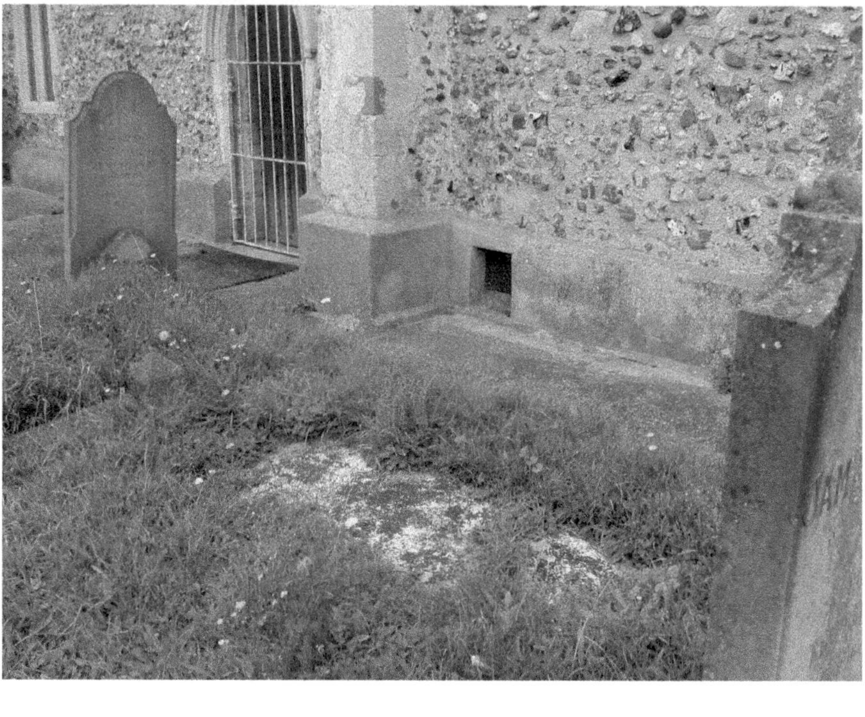

Left: A string of protective Hagstones, hung up outside a cottage in Suffolk.

Facing above: A collection of Belemnites and fossilised Sea Urchins, also known as Thunderbolts and Frairy Loaves, respectively. These stones are used as protective and luck bringing charms in East Anglian magic.

Facing below: A selection of older and more modern Horse Brasses from the author's collection. These are used both as protective charms and as a divination tool.

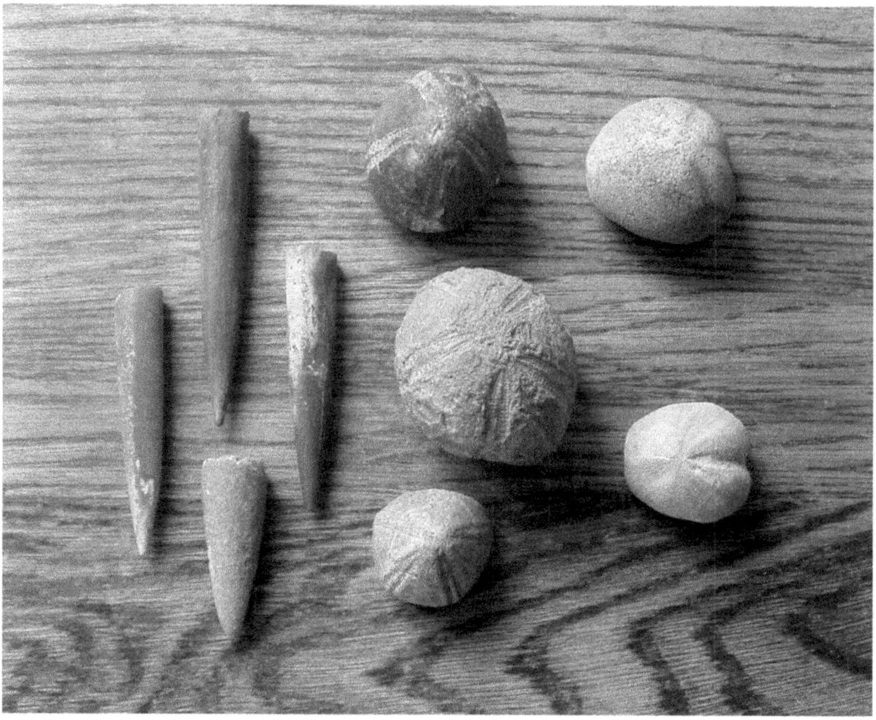

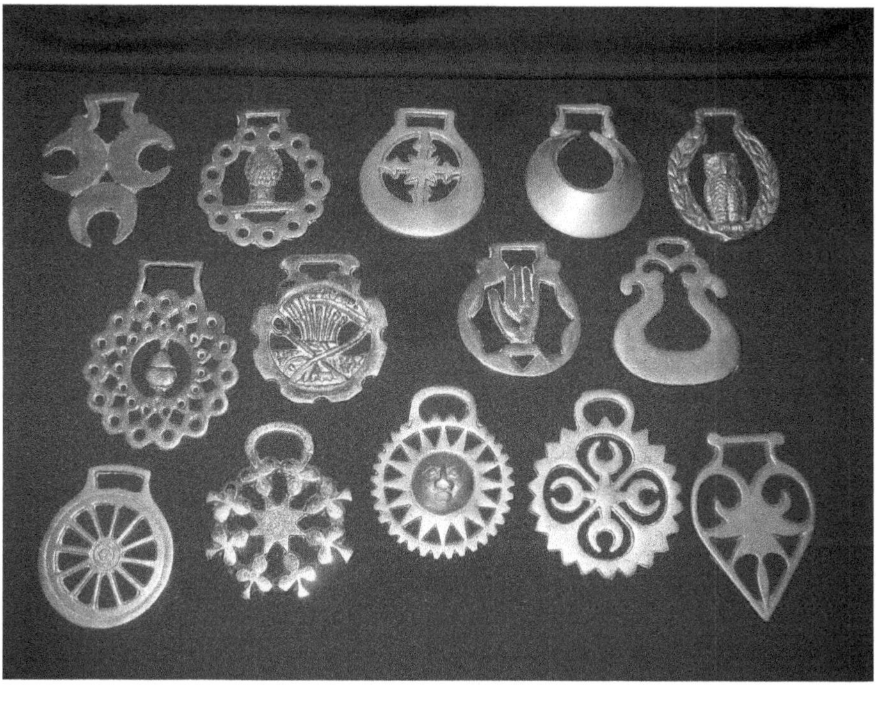

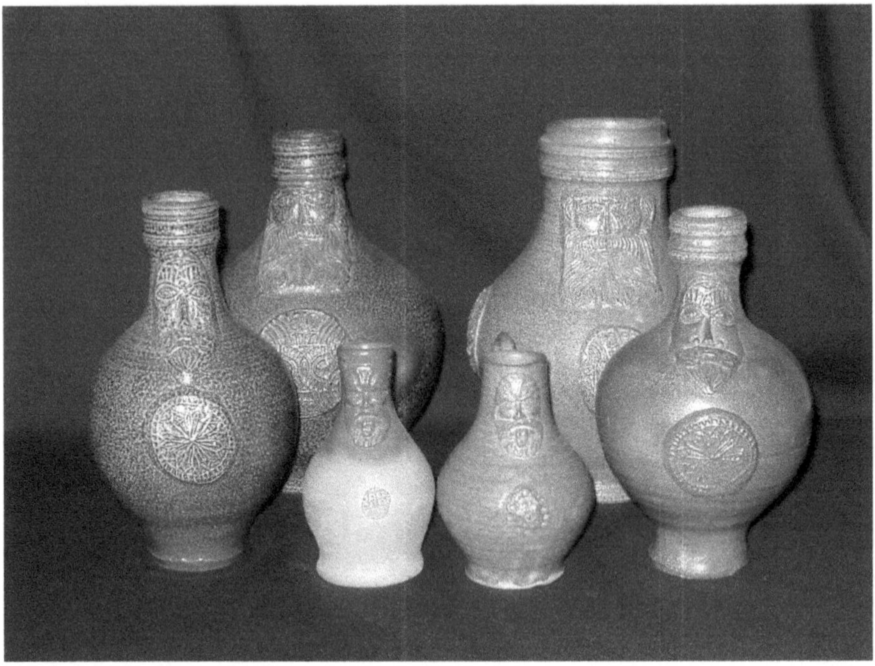

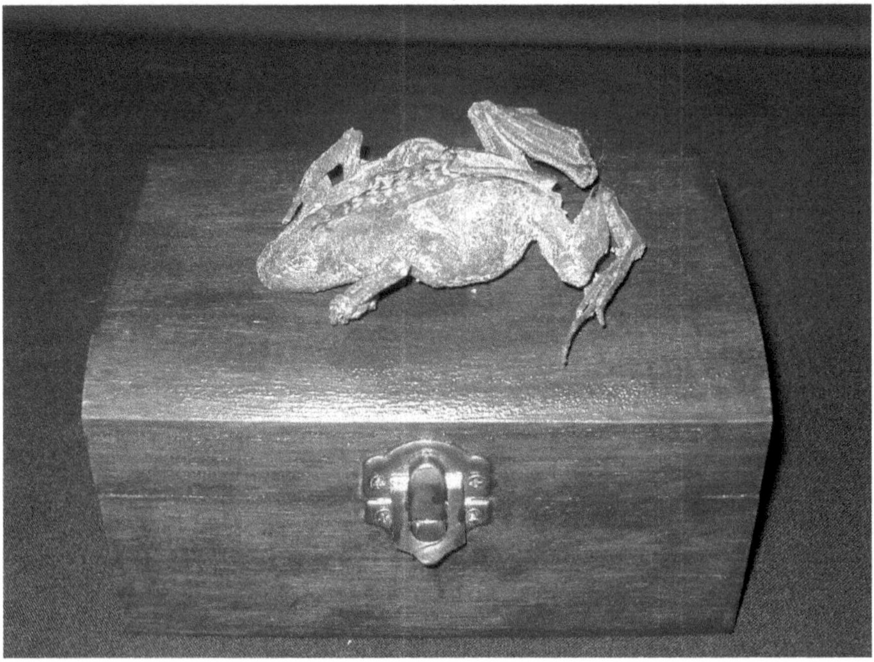

Facing above: Some witch bottles from the author's collection. Used as protective and curse-breaking devices, they are generally incorporated into the fabric of the home.

Facing Below: A mummified toad and the casket in which it is generally housed. A magical device for casting spells and acquiring magical benefits.

Above: A selection of working tools on a typical East Anglian Witch's altar.

Above: The Three Crowns of East Anglia, carved into the font of the parish Church of Saxmundham, Suffolk.

Facing: St. Botolph's Church, situated on an ancient promontory of the river Alde, at Iken, Suffolk, and (below) a 'Frairy Ring', outside the main door of the Church; an indication of earlier inhabitants in the area?

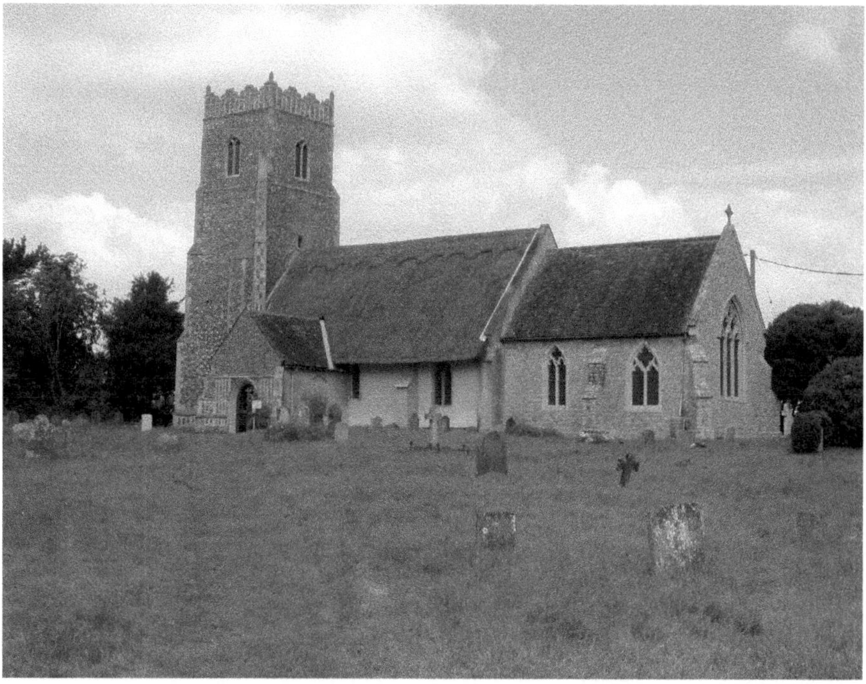

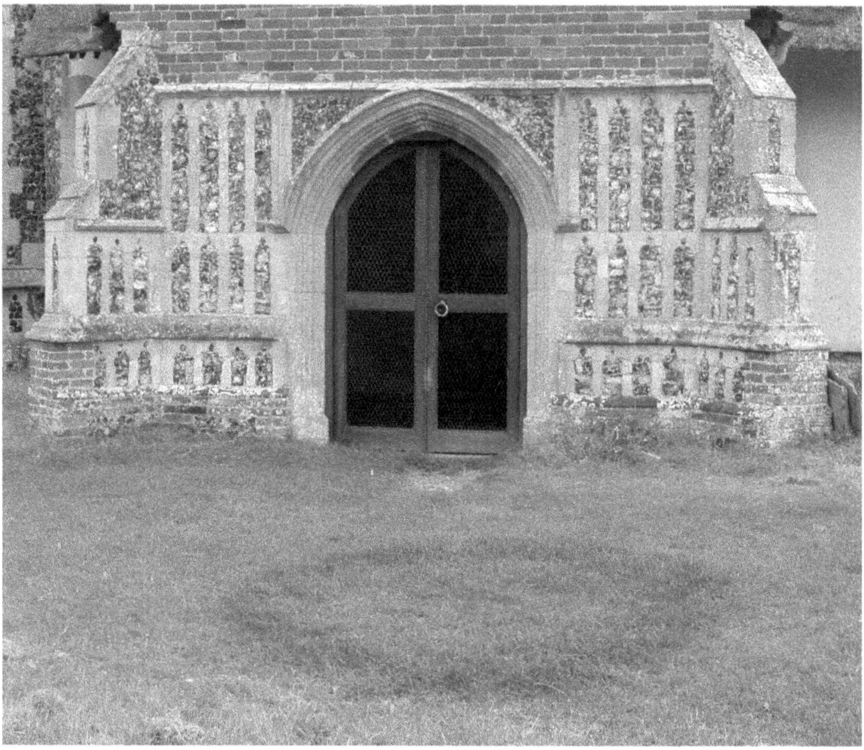

Above: The 1 ½ m. tall limestone cross shaft, discovered during excavations at St. Botolph's Church. Probably the base of the commemorative cross, erected in the 9th or 10th century and decorated with Anglo-Saxon curvilinear work.

Left: St. Withburga. Painted panel, St. Nicholas' Church, East Dereham, Norfolk. Image source: Wikipedia.

Facing: Carving of the martyr King, Edmund, above the entrance of St. Edmunds Church, Southwold, Suffolk.

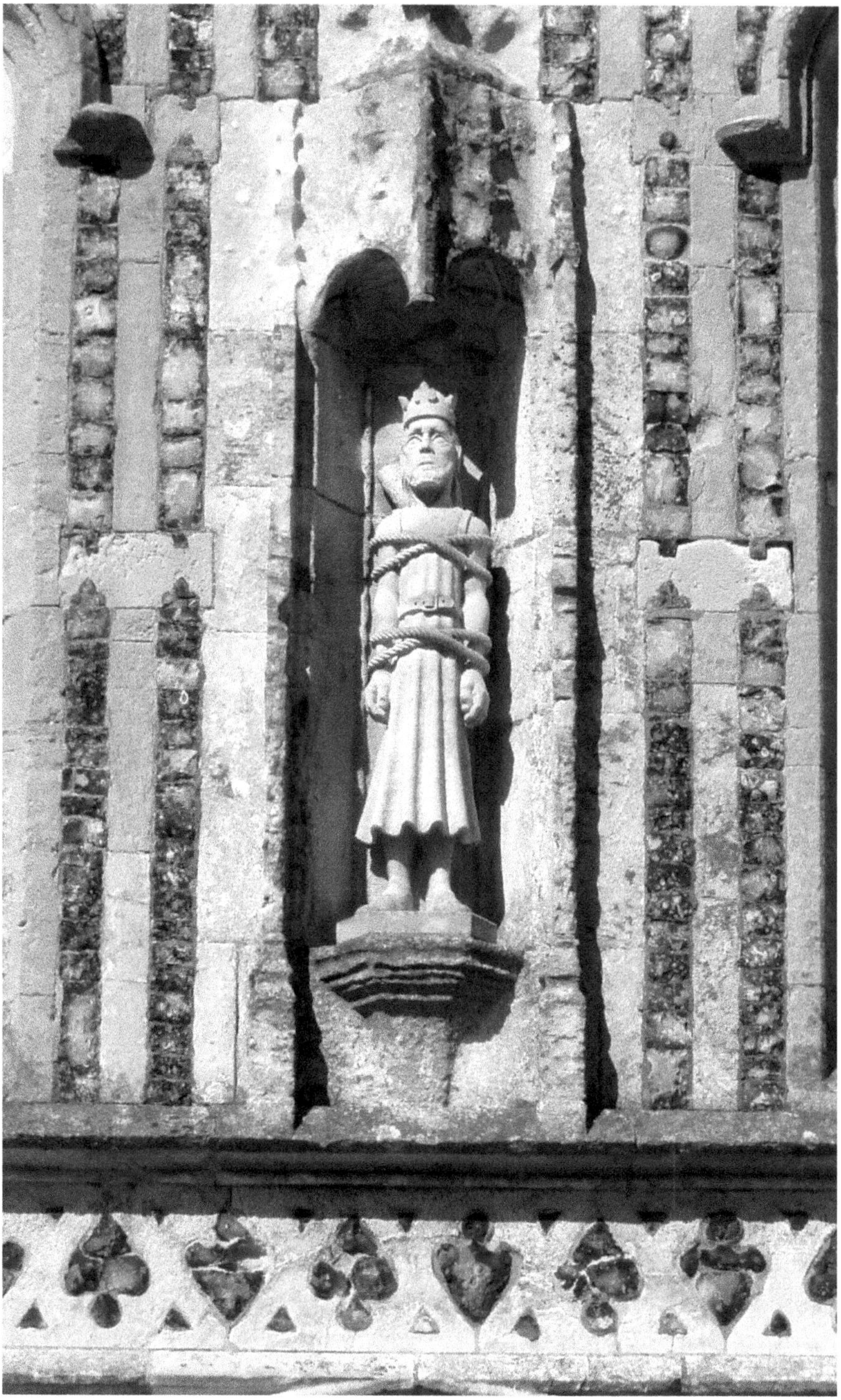

Above: A portrayal of the Wuffingas royal Wolf, in pargetting, from Suffolk.

Facing, above: A magical charm carved into the stonework of Orford Castle, Suffolk. Believed to be to obtain the release of the prisoner.

Facing, below: Mask used by modern East Anglian witches in their rites to honour and impersonate the Devil.

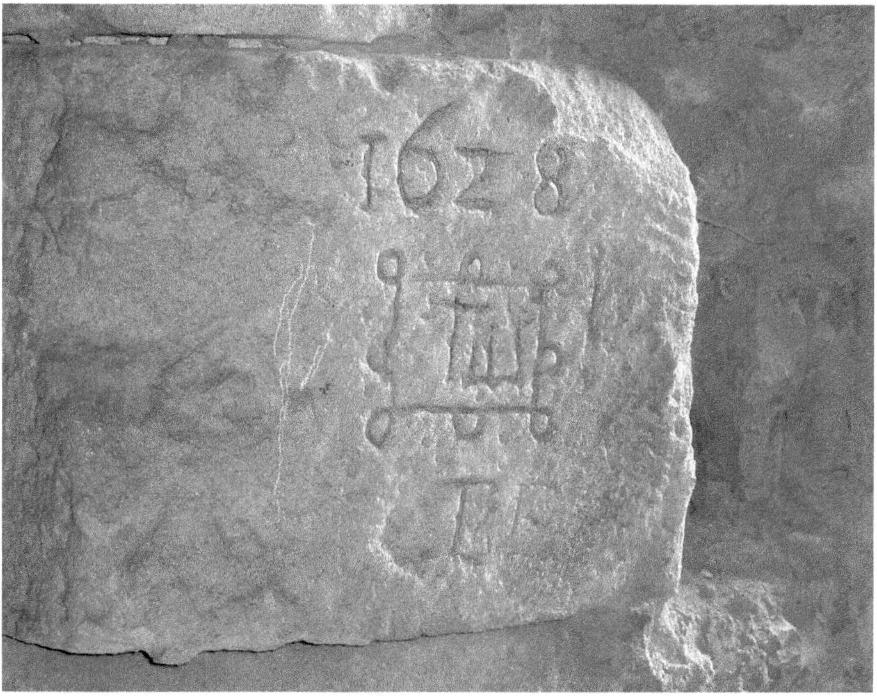
1628

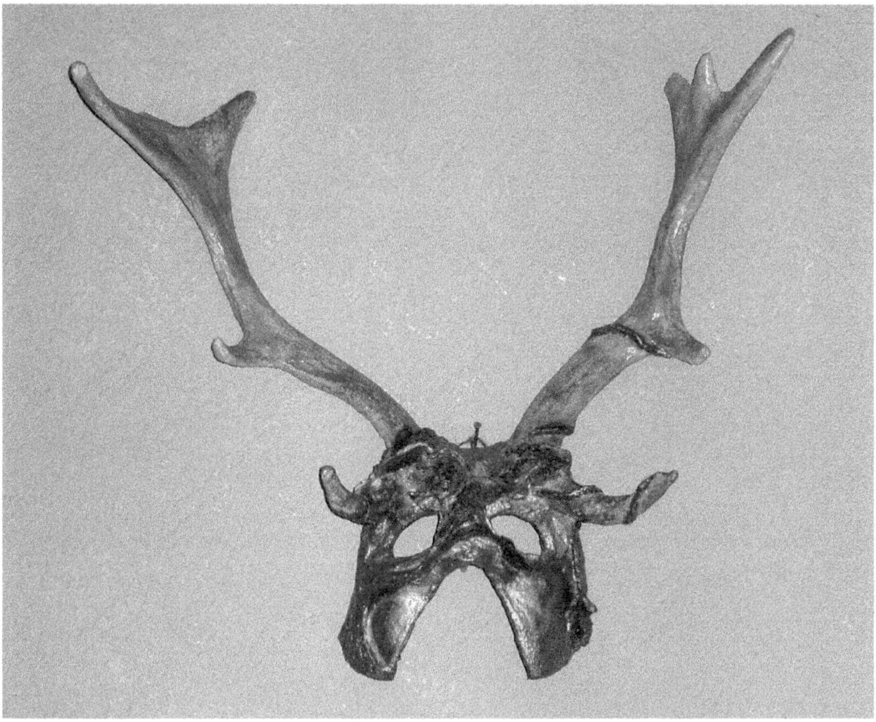

A 'Ferisher Tree'; a tree with three separate openings at its base, said to be the entrance either to the home of the Ferishers, or one of the openings into the 'Green Country'.

Witch Ways

Fetch, to journey out in incorporeal form themselves. All of this work involved creating an extremely close bond between witch and imp, to the extent of sleeping together and feeding the imp on small amounts of the witches' own blood. This is the origin of the stories of witches 'suckling' their familiars, by which means they were able to establish and maintain a psychic bond between them. The imps were also fed on the witches' own food, milk and, occasionally, when it could be obtained, the consecrated host from the Mass or Communion service. The idea of this, although seemingly blasphemous to outsiders, was simple and magically very valid; through the 'magical ceremony' of the Mass/Communion, the wafer had been transformed into a thing of strength and power and also of a supernatural nature, ideally suited to feed and empower a magical servitor.

According to Catherine Parsons in *'Notes on Cambridgeshire Witchcraft'*, 1915, the successor to Daddy Witch in Horseheath, Old Mother Redcap, received her imps from her sister, who lived in a neighbouring village and had recently died. The description is interesting and illustrates many of the points just mentioned, so I shall reproduce it here at length;

> *'It is said that our imps were brought to Horseheath in a box, upon which their owner sat during the journey. Although the box was securely corded no one was allowed to touch it, not even in assisting to lift the box in or out of the cart, for imps are curious creatures, and no cords or even iron bars can keep them in bounds unless they are solely under the control of their owner.*
>
> *We think the names of the Horseheath imps, five in number, are interesting: Bonnie, Blue Cap, Red Cap, Jupiter and Venus. As to their appearance opinions differ, but they are generally said to be something like white mice. Mrs B. has described one sitting on the top of a salt box in old Mrs C.'s chimney corner, as being something like a mouse, with very large eyes, which kept getting large, then small, though she had but a poor view of the creature owing to the curtain which hung across the chimney shelf. In fact she scarcely had time to realize what it was, before the imp turned*

quickly round and scuttled up the chimney calling out "Wee, wee, wee." But, as it turned she did notice that "it had a little mite of a tail about two inches long." It was believed that this particular imp had been sent down the chimney to see what was going on in the cottage, in order to report any item of interest to the witch, for it is useless trying to conceal anything from a witch. What one does not choose to tell, can always be discovered by the parish witch or wizard with the aid of an imp.

We have heard how Mr. E., the late rag and bone man of Horseheath, was asked one day by the witch where he was going, and how he told the old lady to mind her own business. Before this man got half a mile from his house, he heard something coming along in the hedge behind him, and on looking to see what it was, he discovered an imp had been sent by the witch to watch his movements. Mr. E. chased the imp back and tried to catch it, but the faster he ran the faster the imp ran, till at last it reached its owner, who, standing in the doorway of her cottage, quickly caught the creature up and put it in her bosom. Here, or in the armpit, witches are said to carry their imps in safety. We are told, that it is in this way that their owners take them to church to attend the Communion Service, the witch keeping the bread in her mouth to give the imp when the service is over.'

Norfolk witches were known to have 'a way' with snakes, which they had trained as imps. Here is a description of one method of 'charming' a grass snake, but, if you wish to try the technique, it is not advised that you try this on a poisonous variety! The witch would previously have obtained the snake and become quite familiar with it – and vice versa – before using this method;

'Hold the snake lightly head downwards, letting it slip quietly from hand to hand as if you were going to let it slide to the ground, but as it slips through the hand, put the back hand rapidly to the front, so that it is continuously slipping head downwards, through one's half-closed palms. The snake will gradually grow less and less lively, and when it is quiet, coil it in

the palm of one hand with the head resting up the arm towards the crook of the elbow. Breathe on it several times and cover it lightly with your other hand cupped for a moment or two. When you remove your hand the snake will remain perfectly motionless until purposely disturbed.'

It is in such manner that witches gained the confidence, trust and familiarity with their imps, which allowed the deeper, psychic bond to emerge and grow strong. However, Fenland witches from Cambridgeshire were a bit harsher in the usage of their snakes. They were reputed to be able to tame Vipers (Adders), and to extract their fangs by some means known only to themselves. The fangs were then preserved in home-made wine, doses of which were sold to unmarried pregnant girls. So powerful was the concoction claimed to be that it was said only a few drops of it were needed to procure an abortion. The witches' Vipers were fed all during the summer on milk so that by autumn they had a good layer of fat on them. It was said that the witches could slit open the belly, remove the accumulated fat, repair the opening with horsehair and then put the reptiles in a dark cupboard from which they emerged, apparently no worse for the operation, in the following spring. The Viper fat was melted down to make an ointment for the cure of ulcers and running sores.

There was said to be one problem with owning imps and that was they had to be passed on before the witch could die peaceably. A witch might go to great lengths to pass them on, even trying to pass them off as simply domestic pets. If, finally, they were unclaimed upon the death of the witch, the imps were reputed to visit the home of the next blood kin to their former owner and so on, down the line, until they had found a new home. If even this failed, they were reputed to nest in hedgerows, waiting until they could attract the attention of a passing witch, or some other suitable person, and convince them to take them on. This may all sound

The Devil's Plantation

like a load of rubbish, but like a lot of lore, holds the seeds of practical, magical reality. The bond that a witch develops with their imps is a deep and strong one, and the imps rely on this for their direction and purpose in life. Remember, they are magically inspired beings and not just any old stray pet. Once the directing mind of the witch has gone, the imps have no control over them and no outlet for their energies and abilities; this can lead to serious trouble and the witch knows this. An undirected imp can cause magical havoc without control or command, hence the witches desire to pass them on to someone who can control them before they die. As a final resort, some witches were even prepared to destroy their imps, rather than let them remain undirected. At the beginning of the last century, the witch of West Wickham in Cambridgeshire put hers into a hot oven, but they screamed so hideously that she had to take them out. They were found to be unharmed, but the witches' body was covered with burns, which shows the strength of the bond between them. They were eventually buried with her in the churchyard, presumably having expired themselves somehow. On another occasion, some imps were burned in a brick oven where no more bread was to be baked, and when they were in the oven it was as much as two strong men with great pitchforks could do, to keep the imps from bursting the oven door open, and the men were terrified by the strength of the imps, who screamed and cried like a lot of little children.

The imps of Susan Cooper who died at Whittlesford, aged 83, on 25th April 1878, were also thought to have been buried with her; the children from the local school were cruelly encouraged by their elders on the day of her funeral to trample down the soil on her fresh grave 'so the imps wouldn't get out.' There was also some problem in getting rid of the imps of Jacob Few (see chapter 3), when he died; his nephew had to stand over running water with them and let them go, whereupon they scuttled off and disappeared, never to be seen again. This shows a canny piece of work on the part of Jacob's nephew, who presumably possessed some magical knowledge but didn't want to take on his uncle's imps; by releasing them over running water, their magical energy would be dispersed or dissipated and they would no longer be a risk to anyone.

Finally, a graphic description on this subject was published by John Glyde in the *'Norfolk Garland'*, in 1872;

> *'Mr. Henderson in his "Folk Lore of the Northern Counties" says that at Hurstpierpoint there is a cottage in which lived a witch of whom it was said she could not die until she had sold her secret. Her end was dreadful. She was dying for weeks. At last an old man from Cuckfield Workhouse paid a halfpenny for the secret, and she died with the money in her hand. A blue flame appeared on the roof as she breathed her last. I have not heard of anything so marvellous as this, but that a similar belief prevails in the Eastern Counties is proved by information given to a clergyman in this district. The rev. gentleman says: "The ability to practise witchcraft is believed to be handed on from one to another, usually by the witch on her death-bed communicating the important secret to her chosen successor. A parishioner of mine said that she knew of an instance in which a box containing little imps was given by an old witch to a young woman whom she wished to succeed her in the art. The young woman, however, did not at all value the gift, but not knowing how to dispose of the disagreeable legacy, she called in the advice of a neighbour. The latter suggested that all the windows of the house should be closed, the shutters put up, and the doors locked and barred. This was only preliminary to what was to follow. After the windows were closed and the doors barred, a fire was lighted and the oven heated, and then the box which contained the imps was placed in the oven and the door tightly fastened. The yells which soon proceeded from the oven were said to have been frightful, for the imps proved to be no salamanders. At length all was silent, the two women cautiously re-opened*

the oven, and nothing was discovered to be left either of the box or the imps who had just before been so uproarious but a little dust.'

❦ Prevention, Healing & Cure of all Ills ❦

A large part of the work of a witch is in the areas of healing the ills of the mind and body and the curing of other, less specific problems; this was particularly true in the days of poor medical care and provision in a rural society and still continues to be true today. Many of the simpler remedies employed by the village witch have permeated out into the wider world of folk magic and were available to the general populace themselves, but I would like now to look at a few of the more unusual remedies that have been recorded, that would not normally have been employed by the 'uninitiated'.

Keeping in mind the old adage that 'an ounce of prevention is better than a pound of cure', this charm was used in the Norfolk Fens in the last century and probably still is. It was customary for a young couple, just before their wedding day, to present the local witch with a chicken, which she would prepare carefully in a certain manner, cook and then eat. Having saved all the bones, she then returned the wishbone, suitably charmed, a length of red wool wound tightly round it as though to bring the two curved arms of it together, to the bride. She would then sleep with it under her pillow on her wedding night. Eventually the red wool would be transferred to the ankle of each of her newly born children, to ensure that their limbs would never become deformed.

The cures for 'the ague' (malaria and similar), were many and various, as this was a serious complaint in the marshy, boggy areas of East Anglia, before much of the Fenlands was drained for agriculture. A simple charm was to instruct the sufferer to go to a stile – one of those that are placed across footpaths – and to drive a nail into that part over which foot passengers travel in their journeys; the complaint would then be transferred to the next person to use the stile. A more developed form of the charm goes thus;

> *'Go to the four cross ways at night, all alone, and just as the clock strikes twelve, turn yourself about three times and drive a tenpenny nail into the ground up to the head, and walk away from the place backwards before the clock is done striking, and you'll miss the ague; but the next person who passes over the nail will take it in your stead.'*

An alternative to passing the complaint on to someone else is as follows;

> *'Purchase a new, red earthenware pan and in it place finger and toenail clippings, along with a lock of your hair. With these, place a small piece of raw beef, which, to render the charm effective, you must steal and not buy. You must then tie a piece of black silk over the pan and bury it in the centre of a wood, in ground that has never been broken. As the meat decays, the fever of the ague will be broken and finally disappear.'*

A verse from the Gospel of St. John, whispered over a child with the ague, was also believed to be effective, but the verse could never be discovered.

Concerning this secrecy, two preliminaries are given as necessary to be strictly observed in order to achieve the perfect cure. First, that the sufferer should come to the witch with a full and earnest belief that a cure will be effected; and secondly, that the words 'please' and 'thank-you', do not occur during the transaction. The established procedure consists of the witch making a cross over the affected part of the body and whispering over it certain charms. There is a very strongly held belief that if once disclosed, these mysterious words immediately lose their virtue. In consequence of the secrecy, it has always been

The Devil's Plantation

difficult to discover what the actual words employed are, the witch generally being proof against persuasion or bribery.

This brings up an important point here. The witch, generally, does not make a trade of their abilities in East Anglia; on the contrary, it is believed that any offer of financial reward would at once break the spell and render the charm useless and of no avail. This is in marked contrast to magic workers in other regions, where the roles of witch and cunning man tend to overlap and combine. In East Anglia, these two roles tend to be sharply demarcated, and I will look at some of the counter charms and measures employed by the cunning folk – or 'white witches' – in a subsequent chapter.

Some actual witch-charms however, are occasionally recorded and here follows a selection of these. Just over the Norfolk border into the Fenlands of Lincolnshire comes this charm, again for the effects of the ague;

> *'It was communicated to me by that "wise woman" Mary Atkin. In the autumn of 1858 or 1859, I forget which, the ague was particularly prevalent in the Marshes and my Mother's stock of quinine, a thing really wise Marshfolk were never without in those days, was heavily drawn upon by the cottagers. But on taking a second bottle to Mary's grandson, the old maid scornfully refused it, saying she "knawed on a soight better cure then yon mucky bitter stuff". And with that she took me into his room and to the foot of the old four poster bed on which he lay. There, in the centre of the footboard, were nailed three horseshoes, points upwards, with a hammer fixed cross-wise upon them. "Thear lad," she said, "when the Old 'Un comes to shake 'im yon ull fix 'im as fast as t' chu'ch steeaple, he weant niver pars yon." And when I showed signs of incredulity, she added, "Nay, but it's a chawm. Oi teks the mell i' my left hand, and Oi taps they shoes an' Oi says,*

Witch Ways

Feyther, Son and Holy Ghoast,
Naale the divil to this poast.
Throice I smoites with Holy Crok,
With this mell Oi throice dew knock,
One for God
An' one for Wod,
An' one for Lok."

[Mary Atkin took a hammer in her left hand and tapped the shoe's nails, saying the charm. There has been much speculation about "one for Wod and one for Lok", Wod being interpreted as Woden and the other Loki, though "one for luck", although perhaps a relic of not forgetting to invoke Loki, also just means to ensure luck in the action. This spell is to bind "The Old 'Un", who is deemed responsible for giving the ague sufferer the shakes].'

The above is quoted from *'In Field and Fen'*, by Nigel Pennick, who in turn is quoting from *'Examples of Printed Folk-Lore Concerning Lincolnshire'*, by Mrs Gutch and Mabel Peacock, 1908.

In addition to this, rumours still circulate today of old, Traditional coven/s practicing in the Norfolk area who still worship Woden and, possibly Loki, so this charm is not without substance.

And now on to other charms, known to have been used by the wise folk in the region.

To Prevent Swelling from a Thorn

'Christ was of a Virgin born,
And crowned was with a crown of thorns;
He did neither swell nor rebel,
And I hope this never will.'

At the same time, let the middle finger of the right hand keep in motion round the thorn, and at the end of the words, three times repeated, touch it every time with the tip of the finger, and with God's blessing you will find no further trouble.

To Extract a Thorn from the Flesh

'Jesus of a maid was born,
He was pricked with nails and thorn;
Neither blains nor boils did fetch at the bone,
No more shall this, by Christ our Lord. Amen.
Lord bless what I have said. Amen.
So be it unto thee as I have said.'

To Stop Bleeding from Wounds & Arteries Cut or Bruised

'Stand fast; lie as Christ did
When he was crucified upon the cross;
Blood, remain up in the veins,
As Christ's did in all his pains!'

The words are to be repeated three times, all the while desiring the blessing of God.

From the *'Suffolk Garland'* – 'The Rev. Hugh Pigot, late of Hadleigh, says;
 "There was one old woman, of very witch-like appearance, who was supposed to have great skill in curing burns. She prepared a kind of ointment, and when a patient applied to her she placed some of it on the part affected, then made the sign of the cross over it, and muttered certain mysterious words, which she would not disclose to anyone."
 After many inquiries with the view of ascertaining what were the words employed on these occasions, the reverend gentleman heard from a man the following curious formula, the words of which must be repeated three times;

Witch Ways

There were two angels came from the north,
One brought fire, the other brought frost;
Come out fire, go in frost,
Father, Son and Holy Ghost.

There are many variations of this charm, but in substance the above is correct.'

One of these variations goes as follows;

'An Angel came from the north,
And he brought cold and frost;
An angel came from the south,
And he brought heat and fire;
The angel came from the north
And put out the fire.
In the name of the Father, Son and Holy Ghost.'

We see here a remarkable continuation of, essentially, the same charm as was practised by Mother Didge, using her rosary beads in 1562, as described in chapter 3. This gives great credence and value to the idea of a continued line of orally transmitted magical tradition in this area.

To Cure a Cold

Add to wine or liquor the dried and powdered lungs and liver from three frogs. Recite the following three times after taking the potion:

Frogs in my belly
Devour what is bad!
Frogs in my belly
Show the evil the way out!

The Devil's Plantation

To end this section, here are two spells for protection, quoted in the East Anglian Handbook for 1885. It was, and still is, part of the work of the witch to protect people from harm, just as important as the ability to curse and cure.

A Spell Aainst Thieves

To be said three times while walking round the premises;

> *In the name of the Father, Son and Holy Ghost,*
> *This house I bequeath round about,*
> *And all my goods within and without,*
> *In this yard or enclosed piece of land,*
> *Unto Jesus Christ that died on a tree,*
> *The Father, Son, and Holy Ghost, all Three,*
> *Thieves! Thieves! Thieves!*
> *By virtue of the Blessed Trinity.*
> *That you stir not one foot from this place until the rising of the sun next morning with beams full clear. And this I charge you in the name of the Trinity; Jesus save me and mine from them and fetching. Amen.'*

A Spell as a Protection Against Assault

> *'Whoever thou art that meanest me ill,*
> *Stand thou still!*
> *As the river Jordan did*
> *When our Lord and Saviour, Jesus,*
> *Was baptised therein.*
> *In the name of Father, Son, and Holy Ghost.*
> *Amen.'*

The Craft of Contact

The human body is both frail and vulnerable; it has a need for personal contact and reassurance; it is receptive to touch and feel; this trait can be used by those who know how and are willing and capable of exploiting it, for various effects. The witchcraft of East Anglia is well developed in the area of contact magic and there were those that made this art something of a specialty.

A witch could distill an essence of mandrake root mixed into a salve using nine drops of sweet oil and, after anointing each palm sparingly, touch the shoulders or forehead of a woman, and whilst concentrating on the name and image of a particular man, at the same time making gentle, circular strokes, transmit this projection into the mind of the woman. In this manner through personal contact, the witch cast a strong spell designed to make the woman receptive to the projected image of a particular man. The uses of this technique are obviously much wider and were used as such. The witch could inscribe the symbols most likely to affect, for 'good' or 'ill', the fortunes of someone upon their palm, customarily in an appropriate colour, and simply by shaking hands, or by otherwise physically contacting the person, cast their spell. But this type of craft required more than simple contact; there had to be a mental projection of the spell cast, at the same time as passing on the energy by the physical contact.

A system which found favour during the times of greatest persecution, and after, or was employed when the casting of spells was otherwise hazardous or was intended to be secret, involved the use of invisible substances. For a malefice, lemon juice was used; for a benefice, consecrated oil (chrism), was used, with which the appropriate symbols, letters, curses or invocations were inscribed upon the hand, usually a separate number or letter for each fingertip , or an entire diagram upon the palm; the left hand for a curse, the right hand for a blessing.

In East Anglian craft, the chrism was concocted without recourse to prayer, at least in its accepted religious sense.

The Devil's Plantation

The witch commonly employed equal parts of sweet oil (olive oil), extract of lavendar, and no more than four drops of blood from the person casting the spell. Whilst blending this chrism, the witch repeated aloud the name of the person to be touched and defined the purpose of the spell, for good or ill. The chrism was then rubbed into the witches' hand, which was then not allowed to touch anything else, until he person to be contacted appeared and could be touched. This chrism could also be used to inscribe numbers, symbols, letters or diagrams on other items as well, that the witch wished to be charmed. Its invisibility not only did not detract from the power of the cast spell, because it removed any anxiety over discovery, but made total concentration, total projection of force possible.

Contact craft was highly successful, but its greatest successes had to do with human emotions, rather than physical healing or change; emotions such as love, hate, sexuality, aggressiveness, passivity; the directionless instincts inherent in all people. Its power lay in an ability to coalesce these forces, to detect their existence and channel them towards specific ends. Hatred, for example, could be induced by taking sprigs from a live hemlock plant, one for each letter in the person's name to be charmed, or made to hate someone else, by rubbing each sprig very lightly with aconite, then, taking the anointed sprigs two at a time, one for each letter in each name, breaking them violently with one strong blow, until every sprig was shattered. Whilst doing this, the witch chanted a charm that ordered the bewitched person to despise the other person. Finally, rubbing the juice from the sprigs upon the left hand, and being mindful that this hand touched nothing else thereafter, the witch went to the person who was to hate, and stroked his or her head where the hair was thinnest four times, whilst mentioning the name of the person to be hated four times.

A spell to arouse sexuality, which also employed physical contact and a substance to be passed on, was accomplished in the following manner. Using crushed 'gander-goose' root (which was yellow) and six drops of belladonna in equal parts made into an oil by an equal addition of the extract from a living house-leek plant, a syrupy substance was produced. This was then thoroughly rubbed into the palm and fingertips of either the right or left hand and the anointed hand was then placed on the stomach of the person to be aroused – preferably the bare stomach, but not necessarily so – whilst the name of the person towards whom the aroused sexuality was to be directed was mentioned twice in the course of a normal conversation (or as normal a conversation as could be had under the circumstances!)

Contact craft depended less upon incantation than did other forms of witchcraft. Headaches were often exorcised without any audible charm at all, even though some witches preferred to speak aloud, usually using some form of personal spell. Other witches chose to make a silent incantation, but in either case, contact was made with both fingertips and palms to the temples of the sufferer, the base of the head at the back, as well as to the area of both eyes at the front. Commonly the motion was upwards and not circular, beginning at a low point and working upward to the top of the head; beginning again at the base and working gently upwards again, repeating this until the headache departed.

Affliction was caused by touching the part of the charmed person's body where the pain or disease was to take hold, whilst at the same time making the malignant charm in silent concentration.

❦ Seeking the Hidden ❦

A major area of a witches' work consists of divination, i.e. uncovering that which is hidden. In East Anglia, many methods were used, depending on what needed to be found out. There are various recorded folk methods for attempting to find out the faith – or otherwise – of a lover, but here is a technique that was used by a Norfolk wise woman that is a bit different from the rest. It is recorded in *'I Walked by Night'*, mentioned previously, and was used by the author's Grandmother;

> 'There was one charm that old Granny used to try and tell me about – the way to find out if a lover cared anything about you. You must take the door key and put it between the leaves of the Book of Ruth in the Bible, two people balancen the key by the bow on the middle finger of there hands. The one that wished to know if the lover was true holden the key on the finger of there right hand ... Then these words must be repeated; "Many Waters cannot quence true love, neither can the floods drown it. Love is as strong as Death, but Jelousy is as cruele as the Grave, and burneth with a most vehiment flame. If a man should give all the substance of his house for love, it would be utterly consumed." If the book turn to the left the lover will be false and ficcle, but if to the right, the lover will be true. The old Lady could nether read nor rite but had a wonderful memery for that sort of thing.'

Uncovering the whereabouts of lost property was also a valuable ability for a witch, but more valuable was determining the identity of the actual thief. In Suffolk, witches were able to line up the suspects before a pail of water and have them walk past; the witch would see the identity of the thief in the pail as the thief walked by. A more complicated technique goes as follows;

> 'To discover who they are that have stolen from you and make them confess; take quicksilver and the white of an egg. Mingle them together and make an eye on the wall with it. Then gather together all whom you suspect, and tell them to gaze upon the eye. His or her eye that stole from you will water.'

Witch Ways

Having applied to a witch for information on lost goods and receiving a satisfactory answer, it is then as well not to cross them. Here is a cautionary tale from Norfolk where, unusually, payment (perhaps in kind?) was asked and refused. It is recorded in *'The Norfolk Garland'*, by John Glyde in 1872;

> *'Sometimes the revenge of witches was exercised rather in a sportive than a malignant spirit, and of this an instance was told and religiously believed in Norfolk towards the end of the last century. A farmer's wife having lost some feathers, consulted the celebrated "Nan Barrett" on the surest mode of recovering them. The Sybil assured her that they should be brought back, but the niggardly housewife having obtained this assurance, refused to pay the old woman her customary fee. Provoked, as well she might be, at being thus baulked, the prophetess repeated the assurance that the feathers should come back, but added "that the owner should not be the better for them." The enquirer, however, fully satisfied that she should recover her goods, laughed at the threat, and returned in high glee, congratulating herself on having outwitted the witch and obtained the information so cheaply. As soon as she got home, she called her maids to go to milking, and when they had about half done, hearing a slight noise, she raised her head, and saw her feathers come flying into the milking-yard like a swarm of bees; and to her great annoyance beheld them direct their flight towards the cows, and settle themselves snuggly in the half-filled milk pails, thus spoiling at once both milk and feathers. It will readily be imagined that after this catastrophe no one ever ventured to defraud Mrs Barrett of her dues."*

However, if you wished to hide something that could not be found, not even by the divinations of the local witch, then this is the formula;

> *To Keep Things Hid. If any one shall hide gold or silver, or any other precious thing, the Moon being in conjunction with the Sun, and shall fume the hiding place with coriander, saffron,*

The Devil's Plantation

henbane, smallage and the black poppy, of each a like quantity bruised together and tempered with the juice of hemlock, that which is so hid shall never be found out or taken away.'

East Anglian witches made use of many everyday objects to make divinations and not just for lost or stolen goods, but perhaps the most locally relevant were horse brasses. This is a technique relatively unknown these days and mostly fallen into disuse. As a rural area, East Anglia had a large number of working horses (now, sadly, almost vanished), the most famous of breeds being the Suffolk Punch. Horses brought by the Normans may have been the ancestors of this breed, but the first mention of it dates from the 16th century and they were specifically bred to work on the heavy, clay uplands of East Anglian agricultural land.

The brasses used to decorate the horse trappings originate thousands of years ago in amulets designed to ward off evil influences and protect the bearer from all forms of negativity. Designs such as the Sun, Moon, Stars, Equal-armed Cross and Circle have been found on amulets dating from the Iron Age period in Britain and still appear on brasses today. Other designs have been added over the centuries, such as sheaves of wheat, animals, bells, geometric designs, hearts, heraldic crests, farming implements, acorns and, of course, the horse and horse shoe designs. All of these have a meaning and are useful in divination, but the witch would not stick slavishly to one set, definition only; like all good diviners, the witch would have their own meaning attached to the individual brasses and this would be tempered and the meaning vary, depending on subtle factors felt during the casting. The technique was (and is), simple, but can be as deep in meaning as the caster is able to go. Firstly, a light trance state is entered into, whilst the subject of the divination is held in the mind. The brasses are then cast onto a specially prepared cloth on the ground and the divination is made. Factors affecting the result would be; the noise the brasses made whilst falling onto the cloth, what that makes the caster think of, whether it is a positive or a negative sound. Next, the positioning of the brasses would be examined; what was lying where, what was next to what, what was covering, or being covered by, what. Depending on the foregoing, some of the standard meanings of the actual brasses might be altered slightly or greatly, depending on how the witch felt. Light falling onto the brasses and making one shine whilst another was in shadow could affect the meaning, as well as where they had actually fallen on the cloth. Were they all bunched together, or were some off apart from the rest? Maybe there was a pattern of small groups? All these factors and others unmentioned can affect the eventual outcome of the cast. The witch will make their decision and pronouncement based on feelings and intuitions developed over long periods of study of the brasses and of their own internal guidance.

Another variety of divination that was very popular with witches was called 'Cascinomancy'. This employed the use of a key, a ring, or most popular of all, a transparent orb about the size of a small walnut, suspended from a light, metal chain, or similar; these days we would probably call this pendulum dowsing. This implement was used to obtain the correct answers to questions by swinging from left to right (or sometimes right to left), to indicate 'yes', and by swinging forth and back to indicate 'no'.

With the instrument held away from the body a foot or so, in a freely suspended position, the uppermost end of the chain held between the first and second fingers (of either hand), the ball hanging motionless, the witch then formed the question in their mind and concentrated upon it. For example; 'is this a good time to initiate a spell towards John Smith?' Or; 'Can Mary Jones be cured of her ailment with such-and-such a treatment?' The instrument began to move, quite slowly at first, then more noticeably, from side

The Devil's Plantation

to side for an affirmative answer, or from forward to back for a negative one (witches being cantankerous beings, this may be reversed in any individual case).

A number of variations were employed. For example, although the transparent orb was very popular, some witches used a brass or silver key, some used worn wedding rings of gold, others used very elegant little carved ivory or bone balls, suspended from golden chains. The purpose for using a hollow orb was in order that the witch could fold up a drawing of a proposed client, or insert a small scrap of paper with a question written upon it, inside the orb. Some witches believed that to ask the question aloud destroyed or weakened the ritual (stressing one of the key components of East Anglian magic, that of ritual silence), but whether the questions were voiced or projected silently, concentration and focus was most important. When a key (a symbol of secret knowledge) was used, the operation was known as 'Cleidomancy'. Occasionally the key, or orb, was suspended from a silken thread. Silver chains were sometimes used, as was rawhide, yarn, wool and cotton cord, but the most popular was a plain, light steel chain.

A number of witches held the implement out from the body whilst either standing or sitting, while others created a more elaborate ritual; they used an embroidered, square cloth with two bisecting lines sewn, drawn or painted on it. The pendulum was held directly above the spot where the lines crossed as the question was projected. It worked as well if a simple piece of paper with a cross drawn on it was used. The pendulum swung from side to side or back and forth. The only thing which had a direct effect on the tool, was the length of chain or cord. A short cord restricted movement, while a cord or chain of eighteen inches allowed a more sweeping movement to be had, it was generally agreed. In this manner, all sorts of questions could be asked and all manner of hidden secrets revealed.

The Arte of Ligature

A method of spell casting that has many variations in places all over the country, is the use of cords and the tying of knots. However, the practice of ligature, as it is properly known, seems to be very popular in East Anglia and, although applicable to spell casting of all kinds, seems to have been used mostly for purposes of causing sterility or impotence, in both man and animals. As can be imagined, in a rural and agricultural area like East Anglia, this practice was much feared. The workings of ligature have a long history, far pre-dating Chrisitan times and continuing right up to the present, and I include the following, somewhat gruesome, descriptions for the sake of interest and for a more complete record of the types of workings used by East Anglian witches.

In its variations, ligature can be used to cause sterility, a complete inability to perform the physical sexual act and can also impair urination, the purpose of the spell and the manner in which it is cast defining the difference; it is said that amongst East Anglian witches, more than fifty ways of tying ligature knots were known. The basic procedure was to obtain a strip of leather, or a thong of cord or plaited sheep's wool, and tie knots at specific intervals along it. These knots caused corresponding blockages in the afflicted person's genital tract. How the knots were tied determined whether urination, copulation or sterility were affected. Tying a knot in a leather thong whilst the material was wet (preferably rawhide or green, untanned leather), then placing the thong where sunlight would dry it to an unbending stiffness, thus making it impossible to untie the knots, caused sterility and, depending upon the circumstances, impotency. If the thong could be found and the knots worked loose, the curse was broken. For these reasons it was customary to hide the thong well, and to tie the knots in such an intricate manner that, once hardened or dried, they could not be undone.

There were also forms of ligature based on herbs and potions and there were varieties of herbicidal ligature that, when administered, caused temporary retraction of the male's sexual organ, making intercourse impossible for him; other potions caused frigidity and physical contraction in women, preventing them also from the sexual act. A common potion prevented women from conceiving. Another prevented semen from leaving the male. Still another made lovers or married couples detest the very thought of lying with one another.

The proper method to cause impairment in men so that they will not be able to participate in the sex act is to; first, acquire a strip of untanned, opaque, hairless beef hide. This must be no less than 12 inches long. Next, tie double knots together, looping from left to right (to cause sterility, the looping must be from right to left; to impede urination the knots must be tied singly, left to right, and pulled so tightly that beads of moisture appear on the rawhide). The knots should only be tied after the thong has been left overnight under a half, waning moon, upon a barren plot of land where dew will lie heavily. During the procedure of knot-tying, the witch must incant exactly what is the purpose of the working (impotency, sterility, inability to urinate), and at the close of each sentence, pronounce the name of the person to be affected.

The knotted thong must next be put in a secret place where no one else will see it or touch it, but where the hot sunlight can dry it out. It must be left there one day for every knot tied into it. Finally, when it has thoroughly dried out, the witch must take it to the home of the charmed person and hide it where they will come within twenty feet of it every day for each knot tied; the extent of the ligature must be pronounced, along with the full name of the affected person – one week, one month, one year – for each knot. As long as the thong is not found and the knots remain in place, the spell will remain in force.

Witch Ways

To cause a woman to fear or dislike intercourse, or to be unable to complete the act, or to be frigid and incapable of conception, the knots must be tied the same as for the man, but always double. In addition an ennead (a block of nine knots), must be made using shoemaker's wax. The number nine in this instance is considered to have an 'evil' association, as it is formed of an inverted hexad, or 6, which is a sacred number. Into the wax ennead, four black, iron nails must be embedded. When the knotted thong and the ennead are made, the witch must pronounce her spell, stating which specific malefice is to befall the person, stating also the length of time (for each knot). The thong must then be hidden where the bewitched woman will pass it daily from a distance of no more than twenty feet, and the ennead must be hidden inside the mattress of the woman's bed.

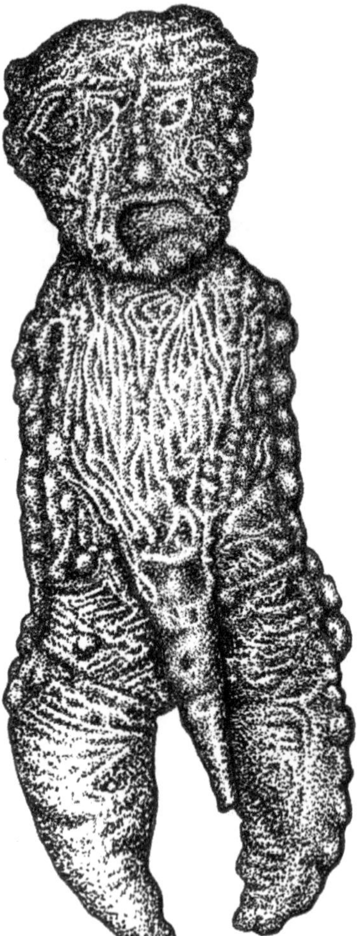

Green Ways

In a predominantly rural society, a knowledge of basic plant lore was common to most people. However, there are always those who specialise and have a deeper knowledge of the plants that grow around them, and East Anglia is no different. The wise folk, the charmers and curers would of course have an intimate knowledge of how to use the green material of their area, for both medicinal and magical effects, and they would also know where and how to find the plants that they needed. I will look at some of the lore pertaining to both of the foresaid categories in due course, but first I would like to make mention of a special class of people, who would seek out and harvest plants and plant material, for those that could not find it for themselves. These were a dedicated category of people, known as the Wild Herb Men.

Specialist Collectors & Gatherers

During the reign of Queen Elizabeth I, it appears that the common right to gather herbs and roots was threatened. To preserve this right, an act was passed, known as 'The Wild Herb Act'. This engendered the guild of medicinal root diggers, known as the Wild Herb Men, who were

The Devil's Plantation

originally active throughout the whole country, but by their latter years, were only working in East Anglia. The season started in November of each year and went on until April of the year following. Groups of men would go out into the lanes and hedgerows of East Anglia, the footpaths and greenways, along cliff tops and the edges of fruit orchards, collecting medicinal herbs and roots. These would be taken back to a central point, sorted and bagged and sent on to the men in the larger towns and cities, who dried, chopped and powdered them, for use in medicines. Reputed to be able to identify each other by a magical password – 'The Herbsman's Word' – they were skilled and knowledgeable plantsmen, who could not only recognise and identify the plants they were after, but also knew where the various types grew best and were to be found.

The roots that were gathered were mainly Dandelion (*Taraxacum officionalis*), Docks (Burdock – *Arctium lappa*, Yellow Dock – *Rumex crispus*), Comfrey (*Symphytum officinale*), Mandrake (*Mandragora officionalis*) and Horseradish (*Cochlearia armoracia*). For a short period of the year, in early spring, the diggers also gathered the tops of the Stinging Nettle (*Urtica dioica*); these were boiled in water and the extract used for the cure of coughs and bronchial troubles. Dock roots were dried and ground into cures for blood disorders. Comfrey roots were made into ointment for the treatment of sprained joints, broken bones and open wounds. Dandelion was used for purification of the blood and to restore the loss of appetite. Mandrake was not used for human cures, but was sold to farmers and veterinarians for the treatment of sick farm stock. Horseradish was the main standby crop because it could be gathered at all times of the year. The roots were made into Horseradish cream to add flavour to cold meat dishes. For a short period of time, when paper was in short supply, the roots of Couch-grass were dug to provide material for paper manufacture.

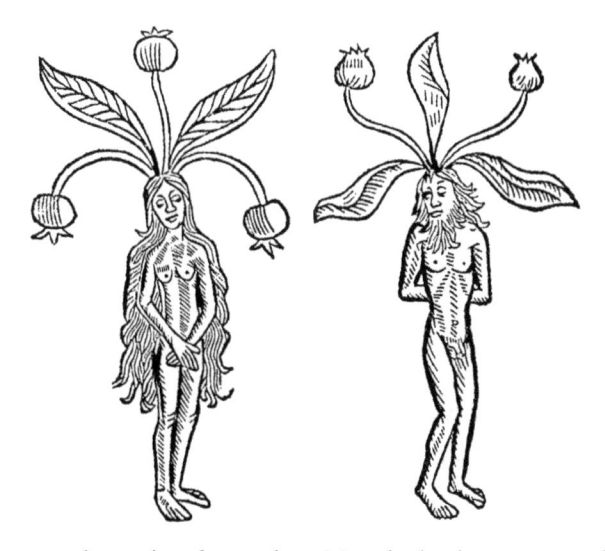

It is worth noting here that Mandrake is not a native of these shores and does not grow well in our climate, although it can be cultivated with great care. The plant referred to is probably White Briony (*Bryonia dioica*), known as English Mandrake, or simply Mandrake in Norfolk. Both plants are toxic in anything over small quantities, but look almost identical and are used for almost the same purposes, both magically and medicinally. Toxic plants were not generally in the remit of the Herb Men, but as there was a demand for this type of plant from some midwives, root doctors, some horsemen and quack doctors, it is likely that some of the younger members of the guild dealt in these too, on the side, so to speak.

In the latter half of the 20th. Century new, chemical methods for manufacturing medicines were developed by the large pharmaceutical companies, and the demand for the root diggers' skills declined rapidly, despite the fact that most modern medicines are based on herbal extracts. Eventually, in 1962, the men who dried and ground the roots for natural medicines finally went out of business. The demand for the Wild Herb Men was no longer there and a whole class and tradition of men became extinct.

The Devil's Plantation

❦ *The Dark Orders* ❦

I would now like to take a look at some of the herbs and plants that were and are used by witches and folk magicians in their work, primarily for magical purposes, but all plants have more than one use. However, before I do, I would like to include a warning here. Many of the plants described in this section and hereafter are highly toxic and can be lethal if taken in anything other than a very small amount. The information I give here is for the sake of interest only and no one should experiment with any of the plants mentioned here without a thorough and deep knowledge of their properties. Witches and herbalists study for many years before they have a competent, working knowledge of plant lore, so take my advice and if you are not qualified to use them, leave them alone.

Before it became illegal to use it (as with many other plants), Opium, derived from either the Blue or White Poppy (*Papaver somniferum*), was used widely as a cure or to relieve the symptoms of malaria and similar disorders (the Ague), particularly in the Fenlands and other marshy areas of East Anglia. Hemp, also known as 'Neckweed' (*Cannabis sativa*), which was grown for making ropes, was also smoked for the same reasons. The problem with both of these plants was that they tended to put you in a stupor most of the time, which was not good for making magic or using the higher faculties of the mind, so they tended not to be used by witches and folk magicians. However, there were other plants that could be used to enter altered states of perception, if you knew what you were doing, and these were frequently employed by magic workers. Known as the 'Weird Plants' (almost certainly deriving from the Anglo-Saxon *'Wyrd'*, meaning Fate or Destiny), they were used by highly skilled practitioners who constituted what some called the 'Dark Orders' within witchcraft. These plants were associated in the popular mind with those that walk on the 'darker' side of life and their lore and use recalls an older kind of wisdom and understanding. The list includes such plants as Foxglove (*Digitalis purpurea*), Monkshood or Wolfsbane (*Aconitum napellus*), Deadly Nightshade/Belladonna (*Atropa belladonna*), Enchanters Nightshade (*Circaea lutetiana*) and Henbane (*Hyoscyamus niger*). All of these plants are highly toxic but, used in minute amounts, can be used to contact the Otherworlds, to heal and to reverse serious disorders. For example, small amounts of Belladonna can be used to reverse the poisonous effects of ingesting Fly Agaric mushrooms (*Amanita muscaria*) and also to prevent miscarriage (but at great risk to the health of both mother and baby). Henbane leaves were burnt on fires, or used in incense during rites to invoke the spirits and as an aid to clairvoyance. Both Belladonna and Monkshood are among the ingredients used in some recipes for the infamous 'Flying Ointment', a trance-inducing salve used by some practitioners when they wished to enter other realms for purposes of searching out hidden knowledge, or to find the answers to some occult problem. While both these plants are deadly poisonous on their own, the fact is that each one is actually the antidote to the other – thus making it possible to use them in conjunction with other ingredients. To create a salve containing these herbs that is effective yet safe would require the knowledge of a highly skilled person, so both are left well alone by the 'uninitiated' (interestingly, the juice from the Belladonna plant, mixed with lard, is also used as a treatment for chilblains). Foxglove also can be used in trance-inducing salves, but as a cardiac depressant can lead to coma and eventual death. It is the origin of the modern, synthetic, drug Digitalin, much used in modern cardiac treatments, and was reputedly 'discovered' by the medical profession by examining the recipe of an infusion given to a rural doctor by a local wisewoman. Another poisonous recipe, used as a cure for sore eyes, consisted of the leaves of true Hemlock (*Conium maculatum*), chopped finely and mixed

The Devil's Plantation

with white of egg, bay salt and red ochre; the magic in this case was that the salve was applied to the sound eye and not to the affected one.

Most of the time however, much more innocuous plants were used, as they would achieve similar results without the accompanying risks. Instead of burning Henbane leaves to enter a trance state, witches could burn Mugwort (*Artemisia vulgaris*), Wormwood (*Artemisia absinthium*), and/or Bay Laurel (*Laurus nobilis*) and inhale the smoke to much the same end. An infusion (tea), could also be made from Mugwort and/or Wormwood and drunk for the same purpose. Both of these latter are also excellent for magically cleansing a site, house, person or thing by making an incense and 'smoking' the particular object with it. On a more mundane level, both were strewn on the ground in the home to discourage the unwelcome presence of fleas, lice and other biting and disease-spreading insects. Trance could also be attained by making infusions from Rosemary (*Rosmarinus officionalis*), Wild Thyme (*Thymus serpyllum*), Rowan Berries (*Sorbus aucuparia*) and/or Yarrow (*Achillea millefolium*). Yarrow tea was used specifically for clairvoyance or sharpening perceptions during divinations. The herb, strewn across the entrance to the home, prevents the entrance of malefic or unwanted magic and using a cushion stuffed with Yarrow negates the powers and abilities of a guest in the home with less than beneficial intentions. Yarrow was sometimes used in conjunction with Rue (*Ruta graveolens*), as in the old charm 'Yarrow and Rue and my Red Cap too!' apparently as a 'flying' tea. Rue was known as 'Witch Broth' in the Fenlands, due to its frequent use for various 'ailments'. It was used as an eyewash for strained and tired eyes, as a cleansing agent and as an ingredient in exorcism incenses to get rid of unwanted spirit visitors. On that note, combined with Pennyroyal (*Mentha pulegium*) and Fennel (*Foeniculum vulgaris*), it was used to procure abortions by country midwives and wisewomen, when extra mouths were impossible to feed.

Green Ways

Returning to Yarrow, on a lighter note, this herb was also used in love charms. To be effective, it must be gathered on July 15th (St. Swithun's Day), stuffed into a pillow and laid beneath the heads of the lovers when they sleep; the relationship will then lead to great happiness. Other herbs used in love potions, charms or pillows are Basil (*Ocimum basilicum*), Rose (*Rosa spp.*), Vervain (*Verbena officionalis*), and Meadowsweet herb (*Filipendula ulmaria*); all of which village girls could procure from the local witch to improve their looks and attract young men. One ingredient that was especially favoured in love magic was Dragon's Blood (*Calamus draco*). This is a bright red powder (sometimes also in granular form), being the resin obtained from the trunk of the plant. Also sometimes used in minute quantities as a purgative, a pinch of it, taken in milk or tea, was used to make even the plainest girl attractive and desirable to the opposite sex.

East Anglian witches used various herbs and plants for cleansing and purifying a place, thing or person. As well as Mugwort and Wormwood mentioned above, Scots Pine (*Pinus sylvestris*), is especially prized, as are Hyssop (*Hyssopus officionalis*), Cedar (*Cedrus spp.*) and Lavendar (*Lavandula angustifolia*). Sage (*Salvia officionalis*) has recently become popular as a cleanser and 'smudge', due to the influence of Native American lore permeating into modern magic, but was never used as such in East Anglia. American Sage (*Artemisia tridentata*), is a different plant entirely to European Sage, and more akin to Mugwort and Wormwood. The cleansing plants would be burnt as incense and the smoke wafted around to cleanse and purify. Another traditional herb used for getting rid of bad 'airs' and spirits is the Groundsel plant, known as Simpson (*Senecio vulgaris*). Once worn as the badge of a witch, it should be burnt on the 6th Full Moon of the year in the home, to cleanse it both spiritually and physically. For spiritual and psychic protection, generally and during magical workings, the traditional Garlic plant (*Allium sativum*), was grown and used widely, and also highly favoured was the Cypress tree (*Cupressus spp.*); the resinous leaves and twigs make an excellent smoke for clearing unwanted energies.

❧ Plant Lore ❧

As well as the witches and folk magicians, the common folk of East Anglia also had knowledge of and worked with plant lore, for various purposes. I would now like to look at a selection of the more interesting and unusual plants featured in the region, the uses to which they were put and the lore surrounding them.

Wild Arum Lily (*Arum maculatum*)
Also known as Cuckoo Pint and Lords and Ladies. This plant is the only native member of the Arum family in East Anglia and has many uses. Most of the plant is highly acrid and poisonous if taken internally, and will bring a burning sensation to the hands if the juice makes contact with the skin, but the tuber roots once baked are edible, high in starch and very nutritious. The starch in the roots was used to stiffen Elizabethan ruffs and collars, but was very hard on the hands. The starch from the powdered root was popular as a cosmetic for the skin and was known as 'Cyprus Powder'; it was also used to remove freckles from the hands and face. In the days of harvesting the corn with a sickle, after sharpening the blade on a grindstone it was often rubbed over with an Arum flower. This was thought to make sure that the cutting edge would remain sharp and keen throughout the harvest. It was believed in eastern Cambridgeshire that Cuckoo Pints, if brought into the house, gave tuberculosis to anyone who went near one. The roots of this plant were named 'heal all' and it was thought that merely by carrying a piece of the root in the pocket that it ensured protection against all human ills.

Green Ways

There is a lovely story concerning the origin of this plant in East Anglia, which I will here relate. It is the traditional belief that when the nuns came over from Normandy to build a convent at Thetford in Norfolk, they brought with them the Wild Arum. When the monks of Ely later stole the body of St. Withburga from East Dereham and paused on their return to rest at Brandon (see chapter 8), the nuns of Thetford came down to the riverside and covered the saint's body with the flowers. During the subsequent journey of the barge down the Little Ouse, bearing the body of St. Withburga, some of the flowers fell off the body into the river, where they threw out roots. Within an hour, they had covered all the banks of the river as far as Ely with a blanket of blooms and, more remarkable still, the flowers gave out a radiant light at night. Much later, during his sermon at the consecration of the newly formed parish of Little Ouse in the 19th. Century, the Bishop of Ely warned the congregation against all Popish superstitions and practices, and stressed that there was no factual foundation to the story of St. Withburga and the lilies. However, whatever the truth of the story, the pollen of the flowers does, in fact, throw off a faint light at dusk. When the Irish labourers came in great numbers to find work in the Fenlands during the famines in their own country, they named the lilies Fairy Lamps; the Fen bargemen had for long referred to them as Shiners.

Blackberry/Bramble (*Rubus fruticosus*)
Although surprisingly possessing a rather sinister reputation, due to its association with witchcraft and its vicious thorns, the Blackberry is one of the most useful edible and medicinal plants found growing wild. Often planted on graves to keep the dead from walking, it is useful as a powerful astringent; it is used to stop diahorrhea, dysentery and bleeding from the bowels. The leaves either chewed or used as a gargle, stop gums bleeding, soothe sore throats and are said to fasten loose teeth. The leaves

boiled with honey, water, allum and white wine are also used as a teeth and mouth cleanser. All parts of the plants can be used as a poultice for cancerous tumours and, added to their feed, the fruit and leaves are used to treat Thrush in horses. The 'Blackberry Cure' was used to heal most minor ailments, boils, hernias, blackheads, jaundice and whooping cough and was achieved as follows; the sufferer had to find an archway formed by a natural growth of Blackberry shoot, rooted on both sides, and crawl under it three times in the same direction, on three consecutive mornings at sunrise.

Borage (*Borago officionalis*) 🌿
Known in the Fens as Virgin's Robe, Borage is recommended by East Anglian herbalists as a remedy for kidney problems; it was often eaten as a midday meal, the chopped leaves sandwiched with bread and butter. The plant was reputed to give courage to those who ate the leaves and was sometimes called the Warriors' Plant. Nonconformist preachers of the 19th. Century used to insist that Borage was one of the plants held up on the point of the spear to the dying Christ on the cross, and another tradition states that Cromwell's men were able to fight day and night without rest, as long as they had Borage leaves to chew.

Bulrushes/ Cat's Tails (*Scirpus lacustris*) 🌿
Another plant that is high in starch, which can also be found in the roots, as with the Wild Arum; roasted in the embers of a fire they make excellent eating. Traditionally considered unlucky to bring into the house, this belief goes back to the days before much of the Fens were drained. Beds of Bulrushes were laid down in boggy trackways – appearing to be solid ground – to ambush unwary travellers daring to penetrate the secret areas of the marshlands. This method was said to have been used by Hereward the Wake in his defiant stand against the Norman invaders in

the 11th century. When the Normans tried to use a local witch, Julia of Brandon, placed at the top of a tower along a causeway, to curse Hereward and his band of resistance fighters, the defenders used the secret pathways through the Fens to attack and set fire to the tower. It fell and the witch with it, bringing an end to that particular magical attack. To be fair, those that claim descent from the Witch of Brandon, say that she was hired by Hereward to curse the Normans and that it was they that set fire to the tower. No one now knows. In drier areas the belief that Bulrushes are unlucky does not persist.

Groundsel (*Senecio vulgaris*)
Mentioned previously and also known as Simpson, this plant has a close association with witches for the common folk. A small patch of the flowers growing beside an ancient trackway traditionally indicated that a witch had stopped there to urinate; large patches of the plant showed that witches had gathered in numbers to revel and plot their deeds. The plant grows freely in many places, sometimes appearing in the thatch of a cottage; this was taken as a sign that a witch had landed and taken off from the roof on one of her nocturnal visits. It was further believed that witches could not die in winter, but only when the Groundsel was in flower, so that they could take a posy of the flowers with them by which the Devil would recognise them as one of His devotees. As stated previously, the smoke of burning Groundsel was used to clear out bad airs and negativity. It was used for getting rid of evil spirits and also for ridding clothes and bedding of vermin and insects. Inhaling the smoke was also believed to be good for the stomach. It could be made into a poultice for boils, a hot poultice was used for Quinsy in horses and softened in milk, it relieved teething pains in babies.

Hemp (*Cannabis sativa*)
Used mostly for making rope and similar products, this

crop was grown from very early times on the Fens in Cambridgeshire and on the isolated island sites where now stand the towns of March, Ely and Chatteris. After the Fens were drained, it became one of the chief crops, although it was a hazardous one for those that grew and harvested it. By ancient tradition, women were not allowed to work in the fields. It was believed that just by touching the plant, a young woman could be made barren while older ones would be affected by a severe rash on the arms; this could only be relieved by the application of caustic soda. Hemp was considered to be the Devil's flower; certainly the harvesting of the crop gave the workers severe headaches. Smoking the dried leaf was an alternative to drinking poppy tea, as a relief from the symptoms of the Ague; both had a similar, stupefying effect.

To show a Fenman how unpopular he was, after having broken the Fenland code of never betraying or letting down his fellows, the following sign was drawn on his door:

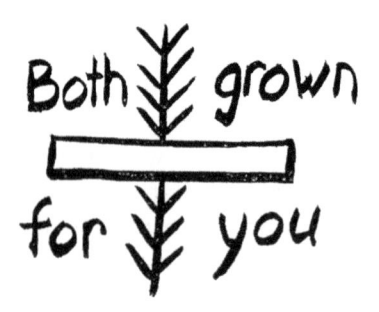

Both ψ grown
for ψ you

This was meant to represent a stem of Hemp and a Willow stake – a reminder of the days when, if a man hanged himself, as a suicide he was buried at the crossroads with a stake through his body, so that his spirit might not wander and affect the living. Hemp was used for making string, cord and rope, so the drawing was a not so subtle hint that the man should go and hang himself.

Honeysuckle *(Lonicera periclymenum)*
Despite its beautiful scent, this flower was traditionally never brought into a house where there were young women, as it was supposed to inspire erotic dreams. If, by chance or accident some was brought in, then it was a sure sign that there would shortly be a wedding.

Horseradish *(Cochlearia armoracia)*
In addition to the uses of Horseradish described above, the plant was of use to many housewives, when their husbands came home from too long a session at the local hostelry. The roots, shredded and infused in hot water, provided a powerful emetic to sober up a man the worse for drink.

House Leek/Sengren *(Sempervivum tectorum)*
Traditionally held to be sacred to the Norse god of thunder and lightning, Thor, the House Leek was frequently planted on or found on East Anglian roofs. Likewise dedicated to the Greek Jupiter, this plant was said to ward off and protect the home from the dreaded lightning flash. It is a small, circular plant often seen growing on house tiles, and held in great esteem in folk-medicine. It is a plant that has a long history in this part of the country and appears under the name of Singrenan in the old English herbal known as the *'Lacnunga'*, where it is recommended as an ingredient in cough-medicine. In East Anglia, it is a sovereign remedy for skin complaints, burns and scalds. The juice is used for insect bites and stings and as a poultice for sore breasts. It is used in an infusion for croup, asthma, shingles and eczema and in an ointment for sores. Mixed with comfrey and marshmallow, it is good to treat inflammations of all kinds.

Ivy *(Hedera helix)*
This was considered to be one of the unluckiest plants to bring into a home. It has a habit of climbing over and

covering derelict buildings and these, in the popular mind, are associated with stories of murder, suicide and witchcraft. Even a small piece of Ivy still adhering to a log brought inside for the fire could cause serious worry. It was often just the variegated variety of Ivy that was considered to be of such ill omen, some people not minding the normal variety at all. Medicinally, the leaves were used, bruised in vinegar for bunions and with oil and vinegar it was used on burns and scalds. In a poultice it can be used on ulcers and sore feet and it was also fed to cows, goats and horses, both for loss of appetite and to expel the afterbirth.

Maidenhair Grass/Quaking Grass (*Briza media*)
Growing freely in damp, marshy conditions, it was an old belief that this Grass grew only in places where a young woman had drowned herself – usually as a result of an unhappy love affair – and so it was another plant that it was considered unlucky to bring into the house. The old people used to declare that they noticed that Maidenhair Grass flourished particularly well wherever a corpse had been dragged from the river and laid on the bank. Cows were supposed to avoid it, and never to eat or trample on it.

White Bryony/'Mandrake' (Brionia dioica)
The name 'Mandrake' is still attached in many parts of East Anglia – in particular Norfolk and Cambridge – to the White Bryony, which is credited with all the powers of the true Mandrake. An old gardener once asked to dig up a clump of Bryony roots refused, saying; *'That's Mandrake, that is; my old dad would never touch it; said it might scream horribly if you did.'*

Up to the end of the 19th. Century, chemists would pay well for 'mandrake roots', which they made into a potion which they guaranteed would make old men strong and put new life into weary women. Men and women working in the harvest fields would wear garlands of Bryony stems to keep off the flies, as the unpleasant smell of the crushed stalks was thought to repel the insects. Leaves of the plant were also placed in the outside toilets as a deodorant in the hot, summer months. Those farmers whose barns and outhouses were overrun by rats would get their men to dig up 'Mandrake' roots, which were then crushed and put into the holes, the scent intended to drive the vermin away. The seeds of the plant were used as a cure for sleeplessness and to relieve pain, while, until 1907, Mandrake pessaries were used to cure constipation in both children and adults.

A Bryony root often resembles the middle and lower portions of the human body, as does a true Mandrake, for which it was useful in making magical servitors known as Alrauns. The dried and charmed root was used by witches to house a spirit that would do their bidding and aid them in their divinations. However, in the areas in which it was found, Bryony root had another function for the common folk. They were dug up, selecting the most human in shape, washed well and marked with the owners sign. On their visits to the local pub, the men would take their roots with them to join with others arranged on the taproom shelf, ready to be judged in a competition, for which a small fee was charged. On the Saturday night, the landlord's wife would be called upon to judge the entries, a prize being awarded for the root which most resembled the female form. These 'Venus Nights' were very popular with both the landlord and his customers, because the entrance fees and prize money were both spent on beer and tobacco. After the prize had been awarded, the winning root stayed on the shelf until ousted by a better example. Even then, the first root was not discarded, as it was then suspended by a string above a sow's sty, which was a sure charm for the beast to produce many fine piglets. When the root was dry and shrivelled, it should be placed among the savings kept in an old sock under the mattress, as it would surely guarantee that the hoard would increase.

Parsley (*Petroselinum crispum*)

It is a widely held belief in East Anglia that Parsley should be sown at the time of the new moon to ensure quicker growth of this notoriously slow to germinate plant. It is also believed that the plant grows and flourishes best when sown by the Housewife, or in households where she is the 'Master'; indeed it is taken as a sign of this if there is a good growth of the herb in anyone's garden. In East Anglia, it is thought that Parsley should be sown in drills running due north to south, the direction being assured by night-sowing, with the guidance of the Pole Star and the constellation of the Plough. It is also believed that chopped Parsley, eaten with boiled pig's brains, gives the consumer the gift of better absorbing knowledge. Made into an ointment, Parsley makes a good eye-salve and was said to be the secret of the exceptionally good eyesight of the Gypsy travellers. It is used as a poultice for boils and the infusion can be taken internally for a weak bladder and to relieve arthritis; externally it is good for swabbing on bruises.

Greater & Lesser Periwinkle/Sorcerer's Violet/Parwynke (*Vinca Major* & *Minor*)

As the name implies, both of these plants were used for magical purposes, but it is the Greater variety that is mainly employed. It is one of the plants that are used for cleansing and warding off serious afflictions and, like many other plants used in magic and healing, it had a prescribed ritual for the taking of it. The collector must be thoroughly cleansed, both inside and out, must pluck it in a pure state of mind when the moon is one, nine, eleven, thirteen or thirty nights old and say the following as they do so;

> '*I pray thee Vinca pervinca, thee that art to be had for many useful qualities, that thou come to me glad blossoming with thy mainfulness, that thou outfit me so that I be shielded and ever prosperous and undamaged by poison and by water.*'

Green Ways

Medically it is an astringent tonic and anti-haemorrhagic, used mainly for excessive menstrual flow, cramps and bed-wetting. The Lesser Periwinkle, although used in a similar fashion to the Greater, had a more popular use in affecting love matches. If a young married couple planted a patch in the first garden of their first home together, then they would be guaranteed a happy life together. However, if the flower were worn as a buttonhole by a young girl of a flirtatious nature or an unchaste wife, then the bloom would quickly fade and die.

Sow-Thistle/Corn (*Sonchus arvensis*)
A little-known and remarked upon plant, but it was believed by common folk that the milky sap of the thistle, when mixed with toad spit, was used by witches for drawing a crooked cross upon their bodies; apparently this would render them invisible and hence safe from harm.

Starwort/Chickweed (*Stellaria media*)
It was believed that if this plant was grown in pots around the house, then it brought good luck to the home. If the plant was gathered when the dew was on it, then crushed and applied to the face, it was thought to turn the plainest woman into a beautiful one. This may not be so strange, as Chickweed is an ancient remedy for skin complaints of all kinds. It relieves the heat of itchy skin, soothes eruptions and abscesses, is good at relieving the symptoms of varicose ulcers and can be made into a poultice or ointment for muscular rheumatism or inflamed, gouty joints.

Stinging Nettles (*Urtica dioica*)
Nettle beer was a well-known remedy for kidney and bladder problems. Many housewives made their own by boiling the leaves, straining the liquor through muslin and fermenting with brewer's yeast. For flavour, honey or sugar (preferably brown), cloves, ginger root and perhaps some lemon peel were added. It is an excellent medicinal plant,

being high in vitamins, minerals and particularly iron. As such it has long been used as a 'spring tonic' and a blood purifier. It is good for arthritis and high blood pressure and the juice from the stalks can be used to treat the sting from the plant itself. A curious use is to beat a mare with the plant after she has been 'served' by the stallion, to ensure a good and safe pregnancy.

Thorn-Apple/Angel's Trumpet/Devil's Apple (*Brugmansia stramonium*) ❦
So-called because of its spiky fruit, this plant is one of the most lethal to grow in East Anglia. Its seeds have the strongest concentration of hallucinogenic substances, which are not destroyed by either drying or boiling and it has been used in minute quantities for obtaining visionary experiences; however, this is a serious risk to health and usually results in the death or serious illness of the person taking it. According to tradition, this plant, which once grew much more profusely in the marshy areas of this region than it does now, was originally brought to East Anglia by the monks of Ely, who bought the original seeds in the market-place in Rome. The seed was reputed to be sacred, having come from the Holy Land, where, especially at Golgotha, the plant was said to reach a height of 10 feet. An alternative legend says that the travelling Romany people brought it with them when they arrived here. This plant was used until about the 1880s as a pain reliever in the Littleport Fens; the top of the fruit in its green stage was cut off, the inside pulped and a teaspoonful of vinegar added. Inhalation of the fumes then brought relief. The scent of the bruised Thorn Apple was so stupefying that it could produce a coma in those who inhaled it; because of this effect, the plant was known formerly as Sopor. The fruit, boiled in pork grease however, was used for inflammations, burns and scald and the leaves were also smoked to relieve the effects of asthma.

Verbena/Shuttleworthia (*Verbena spp*)
It was thought that if Verbena oil was placed in midstream and allowed to float downriver, it would attract large numbers of eels and thus mark the spot where a drowned body lay. Worms used as bait were steeped in Verbena oil and wildfowlers too often baited their snares and traps with crushed verbena leaves. A courting couple used to exchange leaves of this plant and place them carefully in their Bibles. If both leaves remained green, then it was an indication that their love was true; if one or both turned brown, it was a sign that the love of the owner of the discoloured leaf was false. A leaf was often given by a young man to his sweetheart as a token of his love, according to the old rhyme;

> *A Verbena leaf sent to a lover*
> *Carries a message; you need no other.*

An infusion of the leaves was used to treat sunburn.

Arboreal Lore

Trees, as some of the longest living plants, have long been with us and attracted to themselves their own share of lore, magic and healing knowledge. Here are some of the trees that stand out in East Anglian tradition and some of the lore attached to them.

Blackthorn (*Prunus spinosa*)
The wood of the Blackthorn, well known for its viciously sharp and dangerous thorns, has for centuries been used for clubs and stout staves, used both for defence and offence. The tree suckers freely and is used to make impenetrable barriers, both physically and psychically. Its sinister reputation for things dark and dangerous is enhanced by

The Devil's Plantation

the fact that it is traditionally the wood from which comes the renowned 'blasting rod' of malefic witches which is used, when necessary, for cursing or ill-wishing those that have caused their craft harm or who have betrayed their oaths; not in retribution, but purely in self-defence and in protection of their craft ways and practices.

However, the Blackthorn is also the provider of that great fruit, the sloe, which has been used for many years as the basis for sloe gin, a much relished liqueur. It has also been used historically both as a laxative and a digestive (hence drinking a small glass of sloe gin after a large meal) and as a cure for diahorrhea, although it is the leaves in this case that are used. It is a very astringent and sour fruit and is best picked – carefully! – after the first frosts have softened it up a little, making it easier to digest and/or extract the juice from it.

Elder (*Sambucus nigra*)

The Elder tree, or Eldern, was strongly associated with witchcraft and had certain mystical charms. It was considered to be the tree from which the Cross was made and therefore a safe shield and a haven in a thunderstorm, as it would not be struck by lightning. But no labourer would dare to fall asleep under an Elder, as the leaves were thought to give off a toxic scent which, if inhaled for any length of time, sent the sleeper into a coma from which he would never awaken. A cross made of the wood and brought into the house had the same power to protect the home. It was often planted around the house and by old dairy windows, to keep the Devil out of the milk and to prevent him interfering with the butter; it also served as a screen for the retreat in the garden (alias the 'bumby'). It was also planted near sheep pens, the leaves being bruised and rubbed on the sheep by the shepherds, as the smell kept away the flies. Then too, it provided a lotion, made from the flowers and shoots, which was dabbed on the parts of a horse affected by flies. A piece stuck in the gooseberry bushes at the right time prevented the arrival of the magpie moth, and hence the gooseberry caterpillar. In its stages of growth there were three good things to be gained. The green buds could be turned into a tonic, the flowers into an ointment and the fruit into an excellent wine, also often used as a cordial (this applied equally well to the flowers too). The dried blossoms could be brewed into a tea, useful in measles to bring out the spots and in other illnesses to bring on and break the fever with sweats. The flowers, however, were never allowed in the rooms of Fenland houses, because they were supposed to attract snakes and vipers. These reptiles were numerous in the undrained Fens and their habit of coiling up in the roots of the Elder tree made the plant unwelcome with the superstitious. The leaves, mixed with Peppermint, are used in cases of appendicitis and also mixed with suet as a treatment for gout. Then it also grew the 'toothache twigs'; one of the shoots could be held in the mouth of the sufferer and then transferred hurriedly to a hole in a wall, with the exclamation; 'Depart evil spirit!' It was considered most unlucky to cut an Elder and certainly to burn the wood, as bad luck would soon befall the perpetrator; however, some people say that it is common sense not to burn Elder, as it is a wood that spits when placed on the fire and hence dangerous. Elderberries gathered on St. John's Eve (23rd June), were believed to prevent the possessor from suffering from witchcraft; Elderberries and Elder pith were sometimes given in the food of those thought to be bewitched as, like St. John's Wort, they acted as a *fuga daemonum* in putting evil spirits to flight.

Hawthorn/Whitethorn (*Crataegus laevigata/monogyna*)
This much loved tree still has a place in the mythology and lore of the East Anglian countryside, and the taboo on bringing in the May, or Hawthorn blossom, into the house is still well known and regarded, the red and white varieties both being suspect. This may be because the Hawthorn

has always been seen as a tree of the Ferisher folk, and it would not be a good thing to attract their attention by bringing their sacred tree into the house. But in many Suffolk farmhouses there was a custom whereby a servant who first brought a bunch of Hawthorn flowers into the house on the first of May, was rewarded with a dish of cream for breakfast – a great treat in times gone by. The leaves are sometimes used as a quick snack between meals and are known as 'Bread and Cheese' for this reason. In herbal medicine, all parts are used, but it is mostly the berries that are relied on; these can be brewed into a tincture or a tea for cardiac conditions, for raising or lowering blood pressure as the occasion dictates and for easing angina. The peeled, white wood of its branches are used by witches for casting enchantments, and the dried berries have for centuries been used to make rosaries, for both the new religions and the old. Witches were supposed to make their brooms from Hawthorn branches.

Holly (*Ilex aquifolium*)
A Holly tree was considered to be sacred and to have one growing near the house was like having an Elder, a spiritual assurance against evil. Holly was considered very efficacious for the 'touching magic', i.e. touching wood for luck and protection, particularly protection against witchcraft. Pouches were made up for this specific purpose and worn about the body, comprising of Holly, Oak and Ling (a type of Heather) and coachmen did not like to drive at night, unless they had a whip of which the handle was made of Holly wood. To prevent the Ague, fenland people would scratch their legs with Holly, to ward off the shaking and sickness that were symptomatic of the illness; beating chilblains with the leaves until they bled was also popular. The berries, powdered and mixed with lard, were used as an ointment for the same. The beautiful, white wood of a block of Holly, lends itself equally well to carving or whittling and the wood has been used for many

domestic purposes, like bowls, spoons, pegs and platters, as well as door frames and lintels; it ages well like ivory and does not split with age. Like the Elder, it is a protection against being struck by lightning and door handles and sills are made of the wood for this very reason. Holly blossom acts as a magical protection to prevent the entry of harmful people or forces into the house, when fixed to the door lintel and door handles. An East Anglian saying goes;

> *'A bunch of Mistletoe brings all things nice; a sprig of Holly will keep all things nasty away, for if you want to find a witch, look under an Elder tree, never under a Holly hedge.'*

Oak (*Quercus robur*)

Green Oak has been used in construction for centuries, and many is the East Anglian farmhouse and barn that owes its skeleton to this majestic tree. Owing to the shortage of native building stone in this region, the timbered or half-timbered house is historically the typical dwelling in East Anglia and green Oak weathers and ages to an iron-like strength that little can damage. All parts of the construction of the frame of the house can be built from Oak, not even needing nails to keep the beams together, this being done by hammering in pegs made of the same material. Not only the frame of the house, but the floors, staircases, wood panelling and cellars have all been constructed of Oak and show little ageing over the centuries; renovations are still taking place on buildings that have been altered, added to and covered up with plaster and other materials, and the underlying essence is in even better condition than the later alterations. Masons' marks can still be seen carved into lintels, sills and joints, some of which bear striking resemblances to runic signs, designed to protect and defend a building from malignant attacks.

On a more medicinal level, the Oak is a very useful plant and much used in herbal treatments. The bark, when taken young and fresh, can be ground and used in teas, tinctures and even in snuff. It is highly astringent and is particularly useful for ulcers, haemorrhages, haemorrhoids and varicose veins. Acorns, grated into warm milk, can be taken to relieve diarrhoea. The fresh, green leaves make an excellent wine, and no Suffolk cottage would be without a bottle or two in the larder.

Pine (Scots) (*Pinus sylvestris*) ❦
Pine wood is rich in resin and therefore burns hot and long, giving off a sweet scent which imbues the whole house with a fresh and cleansing air. As mentioned previously, Pine is used in witch rites as an incense or smoke to magically cleanse a place or object and has the additional sense of spiritual illumination. As such it is sacred to the Devil in his form of knowledge bringer and opener up of the higher mental faculties of his worshippers. The cones, known as Deal Apples, contain rich, resinous seeds which are highly nutritious, and the cones themselves are used to tip the end of wands used in rites to raise the generative powers, and for blessing the fields. Lone Pines were planted on the tops of burial mounds and hills at the sides of trackways, ancient and modern, to mark the ways for travellers, pilgrims, drovers and merchants, in areas that would otherwise have no significant markings.

Rowan/Mountain Ash (Sorbus aucuparia) ❦
The Rowan was looked upon as one of the most effective defences against witchcraft, just as potent as iron. It is primarily a tree of house protection, being planted by the garden gate or near the door to ward off unwelcome psychic visitations. Rowan twigs removed from the tree without the use of a knife and tied into a cross with red thread, are used to protect stables and byres. In some districts, carters kept a Rowan cross in their pockets or wore a sprig of Rowan in their hats to safeguard their horses, which were supposed to be particularly susceptible to witches. In combination with Birch (*Betula spp.*) and placed over a

doorway on May morning, Rowan gives protection for the whole year, but must be taken down and refreshed with new boughs the next year. Crosses of Rowan are also used to protect freshly planted seed beds, and a necklace of the fresh berries is traditionally considered to be a sure protection against ill health. But in East Anglia, the Rowan was not held to be as effective as the Elder for these protective purposes, the latter being much preferred.

Willow/Sally Tree (*Salix spp.*)
It was an ancient belief that gibbets used to be made by the simple method of planting two young willows a few feet apart in the centre of the crossroads. When the trees were firmly rooted the tops would be bent until they met and then grafted firmly, one to the other, so that there were eventually two trees with only one top, at right-angles to the trunks. From this cross-piece, the bodies of malefactors were hung in iron chains, and a cage riveted around them by the local blacksmith. The creaking of the chains, as the bodies swung in the lightest of breezes, struck terror into many a traveller as he passed by at night, and it may have been this use of the Willow that gave it such a bad reputation in this region. Few people cared to bring Willow wood into the house for burning on the fire or to use the sawn-off limbs of the tree for fencing. When the Willows were felled for cricket-bat wood, it was difficult to get rid of the tops of the trees, even for fire kindling to the poorest of families. Any willow brought into the house had to be adzed, never sawn, adhering to the old belief that to saw the wood was very unlucky. Because of its affinity with water, Willow was considered to be sacred to the Moon and all the powers of the night and hence useful to witches in their craft. In actuality, Willow is a very healing plant, containing high levels of salicylic acid. The green under-bark of the trees was stripped and used as a powerful pain-killing ingredient in teas and tinctures for the sick, and to relieve migraines, fevers and the symptoms

of the Ague. Salicylic acid is the natural compound from which Aspirin was later manufactured.

Yew (*Taxus baccata*)
The Yew is a very long-living tree and is associated with eternal life. Because of this, it was planted in places where the bones or ashes of the dead were buried, like burial mounds and later in churchyards, where many can still be seen today. These were feared in many parts of East Anglia because, in addition to their gloomy, somewhat frightening appearance, especially at night, the trees were thought to afford shelter to witches and to cover up their nocturnal gatherings. The Yew is used in East Anglian witchcraft, both for its association with the dead, as we have seen earlier in this book, and for the qualities of its scent. Although the Yew is a very poisonous tree, all parts being highly toxic, in warm weather (and burnt over charcoal), the tree gives out a resinous vapour that, inhaled in very small amounts can be used to gain visions. It is particularly useful in necromantic rites and in works to gain contact with the ancestors.

Healing Lore

To end this chapter, I would here like to give some more general plant lore, as it is known in East Anglia, and a few original recipes from an old herbal, dating from around the middle of the 18th. Century, purely for interest's sake.

Simples (single herb medicines), were administered in the forms of teas and ointments, draughts and poultices, but if mixed with one other or more herbs and boiled for some time, they were known as decoctions. Chamomile flowers (*Anthemis nobilis*), tinctured with gin, could be made into a poultice helpful in cases of tonsillitis and diphtheria; and the leaves of the plant, mixed with those of Yarrow and Agrimony (*Agrimonia eupatoria*), would make a good herb tea. Coltsfoot (*Tussilago farfara*), alias Foalsfoot, was good for bronchitis and asthma, but the former could also be counteracted by wearing a string of blue beads around the neck, and they were sold for this purpose in shops in Norwich. The leaves and flowers of Marshmallow (*Althaea officinalis*), were made into an ointment to be rubbed on boils, and a decoction of the leaves was good for a strain. A poultice was made from stewed Groundsel and one for sore legs from Chickweed. On the other hand, the roots of Teasel (*Dipsacus spp.*) would cure abscesses. Dock (various), leaves were good for galled feet, green Broom (*Cytisus scoparius*), for the kidneys, Dandelion (*Taraxacum officinalis*), root for the liver, Mistletoe (*Viscum album*), for epilepsy, Daylillies (*Hyperion spp.*), for heart trouble, Parsley and Breakstone (*Spurge spp.*), for the gravel, Pennyroyal (*Mentha pulegium*), for women's complaints, Rue pills for a tonic; and Borage relieved depression. Then again, people were counselled to 'take enough of powdered Horse Beans' for heartburn, and similarly of powdered Acorns for diahorrhea. Cottage homes usually kept a supply of these dried for this purpose. Worms could be treated with chopped leaves of garden Box (*Buxus sempervirens*), or by wearing a raw Carrot (*Daucus carota*), next to the heart, or taken internally first thing in the morning. Snails were a safeguard against consumption! To bring a good night's sleep, stuff a pillow with Hops (*Humulus lupulus*), or Lady's Bedstraw (*Galium verum*), and lay your head upon it. Sage (*Salvia officinalis*), is greatly reputed to be a health-bringer and a promoter of longevity, especially when taken in the month of May. For general healing purposes, Rosemary (*Rosmarinus officinalis*), Thyme (*Thymus vulgaris*), and Peppermint (*Mentha piperita*), were usually recommended and Comfrey (*Symphytum officinale*), is a sovereign remedy for broken bones. Make a poultice of the leaves and bind around the broken limb; it is also excellent for cuts and grazes, healing the flesh rapidly. Arthritis responds well to eating Celery (Apium graveolens), and Primrose (Primula vulgaris), leaves in salads and sandwiches. Headaches can be healed using Valerian (Valeriana officinalis), Ground Ivy (Glechoma hederacea) and Chamomile, but nervous headaches, hysteria, spasms and cramps are better served by Lady's Slipper (Cypripedium calceolus), or Skullcap (Scutellaria lateriflora).

🌿 Some Old Recipes 🌿

For the Siatica
Ragwort boyled in hogs grease till the juce be consumed straine it then put in a little Mastick and olibanum and so make a plaster of it.

For the Dropsey or Green Sickness
Munks Ruborb halfe a pound,
Red mater [Madder] roots halfe a pound,
Seena [Senna] foure ounces,
Anyseeds and Liquorish of each two ounces,
Scabias [Scabious] and Egrimony [Agrimony] of each two good handfull bruise them or steep them in ale or beere three dayes and drink it three weeks together in the morning fasting & at four of the clock in the afternoon.

For the stinging of an Adder
Take garlick and fry it in oyle or may butter and any other butter that hath no salt in it but may butter is the best lay it to the place stinged.

A very good water against any paine in the side the Loynes the brest and heart and it avoideth all distempers
Take a good handfull of Senteway [Centaury], bruised and put into six pennyworth of Ale then distill it then put to it three ounces of Ginger sliced. of Annyseeds & parsley seeds of each three ounces bruised and let them steep in the water twenty foure hours and then distill again.

Green Ways

For a sore mouth in old or young
Take the powder of Sage the powder of allum [Alum] *and temper it with good live honey drop it into your mouth and it will cure you.*

And finally, I leave you with the following, traditional rhyme on the healing artes as considered by the common folk in East Anglia;

Make a black cat spit on mutton fat
Then rub it inside a horse's hat.
Scrape it off within a week
Then go outside a toad to seek
And make it sweat into a pot.
With wooden spoon mix the lot,
And you will have a healing balm
To keep the body free from harm.

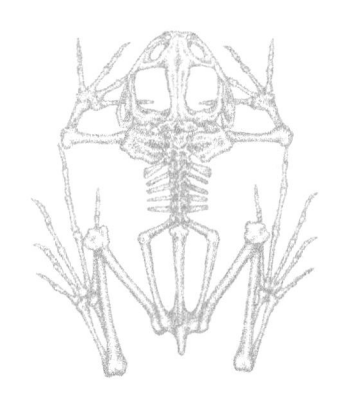

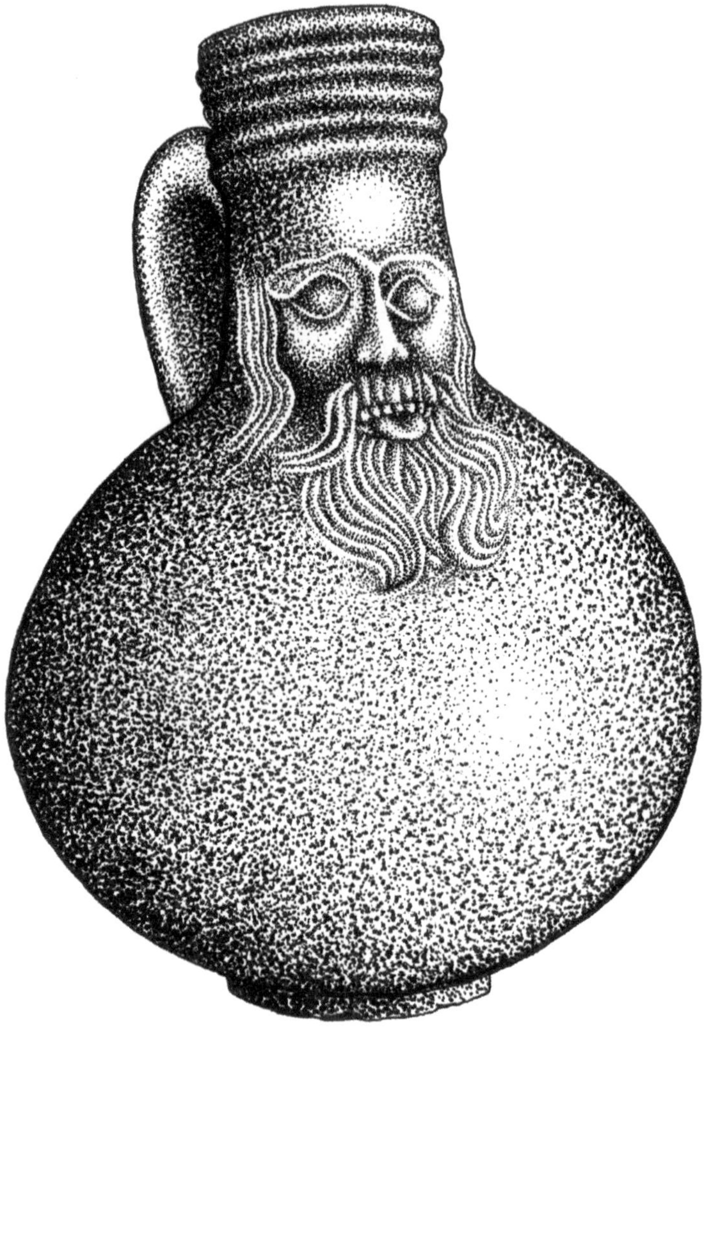

Folk Ways

It is difficult to know where witchcraft ends and folk magic takes over; indeed the methods used by one may very well be used by the other, and the Cunning Folk, or "White Witches", stand squarely in the middle, using every technique in the book. As pointed out previously, in East Anglia, there tended to be a general difference between witches and cunning folk, in that the former tended not to charge for their services, whereas the latter did. There is also the added difference, in that witches tended to look to an alternative authority and Power for the source of their own powers for magic, namely the Being known to us as the Devil; whereas Cunning and common folk would generally look to the Christian God and His Saints for their impetus and inspiration. Of course, all rules are there to be broken, but one of the main features of folk magic in this region was to combat the perceived menace and malignity of the witches, whether they were at fault or not. To this end, various techniques were used and I would here like to look at some of these in some detail.

The Devil's Plantation

❦ *Defense by Boiling & Bottle* ❦

Most counter magics or charms, were based on the premise that there existed a link between the witch and the victim that enabled the sending of the spell, and this link could therefore be used to reverse or send it back. Recorded in the archives of the Eastern Counties Folklore Society from 1936, is the following advice, given by a man who had been bewitched by a woman known as Old Mrs Reeve, of Lake's End, near Wisbech;

> *'Take a stone bottle, make water in it, fill it with your own toe nails and finger nails, iron nails, or anything that belongs to you. Hang the bottle over the fire and keep stirring it. You mustn't speak or make a noise. The old witch'll come to your door and make a lot of noise and beg you to open the door and let her in. If you don't take no notice but keep quiet, the old witch'll burst, but if you speak to her, she'll be free.'*

The same man also related how he had been told of a woman in the village who had been bewitched with lice and how she had succeeded in getting rid of the vermin;

> *'She put one of those bottles over the fire and the old witch come and begged to be let in, and she kept on asking and asking. At last the woman's husband, who was upstairs in bed, shouted down to her "Let the old devil go." That broke the spell. Next morning they see the yard was full of water where that old witch had been walking up and down.'*

A variation on this method is recorded in the Norfolk Garland of 1872;

> *'If in the near neighbourhood, or anywhere indeed within the malignant influence of a known witch ... the most effectual remedy or mode of exorcism is to take a quantity of the patient's urine, and boil with it nine nails from as many old horse shoes. The process is to begin exactly at midnight. The conductress of*

it is to have an assistant to obey orders, but is to touch nothing herself. The orders must be conveyed by signs, for a single word mars the whole charm. At a certain critical point in the process, when three, five or seven of the nails have been put in motion at once by the force of the boiling fluid (for some cases are more difficult than others), the spirit is cast out, at which happy moment the child "squalls", the cow "blores", or the calf "blares", and convalescence immediately commences. The good woman from whom the rev. gentleman obtained this valuable information (not immediately indeed, nor without some little breach of confidence), confirmed it by recounting a failure that once befell herself. She had prevailed on a boy to sit up with her. All was going on most prosperously. The hobnails were in merry motion. The child in the cradle squalled. The boy, in a cold sweat, ventured to look behind him, and he was so overpowered with terror that he forgot all the cautions he had received, and called to his mistress to look at the little black thing that was endeavouring to escape through the keyhole. This was no doubt the evil spirit, which, thus recalled, must have entered the poor child again, for it certainly never recovered.'

Sometimes the counter charm tended to be a bit more dramatic, or even explosive. The use of 'Witch Bottles' is a strong tradition in East Anglia and many have been found and uncovered in old houses. A witch bottle is usually a ceramic bottle of the 'Bellarmine' variety, known locally as 'Greybeards'; these are bulbous, salt-glazed jugs with a squat, round neck, usually of a brown or grey colour and having a crest and bearded face moulded onto the outside. They were imported in large quantities from the Rhinelands in the mediaeval period, containing wine, brandy and other spirits and were subsequently re-used for apotropaic purposes. Various items are placed inside the jar/jug and it is then walled up in the house, placed up the chimney, buried under the hearth or otherwise incorporated into the fabric of the house, for general protection. Alternatively, if there are grounds for thinking that a specific curse has been place on a person, or the house, then a different method needs to be used. Here is an account given in Joseph Glanvil's *'Sadducismus Triumphans'*, or *'A Full and Plain Evidence Concerning Witches and Apparitions'*, published in London in 1689. It is a fairly long account, but worth reproducing for the wealth of detail that it contains;

> *'... which puts me in mind of a very remarkable story of this kind, told by Mr. Brearly, once Fellow of Christ's College in Cambridge, who boarded in a house in Suffolk where his landlady had been ill-handled by witchcraft.*
>
> *For an Old Man that travelled up and down the County and had some acquaintance at that house, calling in and asking the Man of the house how he did and his Wife; he told him that he himself was well, but his Wife had been a long time in a languishing condition, and that she was haunted by a thing in the Shape of a bird that would flurr near her face, and that she could not enjoy her natural rest. The Old Man bid him and his Wife be of good courage. It was but a dead Spright, he said, and he would put him in a course to rid his Wife of this languishment and trouble. He therefore advised him to take a Bottle, and put his Wife's urine into it, together with Pins and Needles and Nails and Cork them up, and set the Bottle to the Fire well cork'd, which when it had felt a little while the heat of the Fire, began to move and joggle a little, but he for sureness took the Fire Shovel and held it hard upon the Cork. And as he thought, he felt something one while on this side, another while on that, shove the Fire Shovel off, which he still quickly put on again; but at last at one shoving the Cork bounced out, and the Urine, Pins, Nails and Needles all flew up, and gave a report like a Pistol, and his Wife continued in the same trouble and languishment still.*
>
> *Not long after that, the Old Man came to the house again and enquired of the Man of the house how his Wife did. Who answered as ill as ever, if not worse. He ask'd him if he had followed his direction. Yes, says he, and told him the event as abovesaid. Ha, quoth he, it seems it was too nimble for you.*

But now I will put you on a way that will make the business sure. Take your Wife's Urine as before, and cork it in a Bottle with Nails, Pins and Needles and bury it in the Earth; and that will do the feat. The Man did accordingly. And his Wife began to mend sensibly and in a competent time was finely well restored. But there came a Woman from a Town some miles off to their house with a lamentable Out-Cry that they had killed her Husband. They ask'd what she meant and thought her distracted, telling her they knew neither her nor her husband. Yes, saith she, you have killed my Husband; he told me so on his Death-Bed. But at last they understood by her that her Husband was a Wizard, and had bewitched this Man's Wife, and that this Counter Practice prescribed by the Old Man which saved the Man's Wife from languishment, was the death of the Wizard that had bewitched her. This story Mr. Brearly heard from the Man and Woman's own Mouth who were concerned, at whose house for a time he Boarded; nor is there any doubt of the truth thereof.'

The 'Old Man' was obviously some form of Cunning man or folk magician and hence recognised both the malady and the cure in this case. Because of the link existing between the Wizard and the woman that he had bewitched, the Old Man was able to advise how to send the curse back and relieve the woman of her problem. The Wizard had presumably acquired something of his prospective victim and by means of this link was able to cast his charm over the woman and the house. However, in so doing, by means of the contagious link, he had himself become indissolubly attached to the object of his curse and therefore the victim also had some form of hold over him in turn. Once the link had been established by the Wizard he was then open to a counter-charm, through the medium of the urine; anything that was done to that would be transmitted back to him and would induce sympathetic pains. The idea was then that the malefactor would be compelled to come to the victim's house, to ask the victim, or helpers, to stop the counter-measures, usually under the promise of the removal of the original curse. That the Wizard died in the process is a sharp warning for all that magic bites both ways and you had better be sure of your powers before you launch into offensive magic.

As most of the East Anglian examples of witch bottles employ the Bellarmine or Greybeard, it is possible that it is meant to be an anthropomorphic representation, a symbol of the figure of the witch. However, it is also possible that the bottle was meant to be a symbol of the witches' bladder. That those bottles that have been discovered buried were invariably placed upside down, with the corked neck bottommost certainly suggests this, as does the finding of pubic hair in the contents of many of the bottles. The heating of the bottle on the fire, making the nails and pins move about in the urine, were meant to transmit intense pain to the witches' bladder. However, some of the contents of the bottles that have been found appear to suggest a sort of 'shot-gun like' blast was intended, to strike the witch however it could. In one bottle that has been discovered, there was a cloth heart with pins stuck into it, amongst the following other contents; sharpened splinters of wood, brass studs, nails, hair, glass chips and a rusted table-fork with no handle. On the occasional jar, there is no face of a Greybeard, but a number of imprinted horse-shoes, or a kind of horse-shoe motif, which obviously had an intended apotropaic significance. Although witch bottles were buried under the threshold and the hearth, they were also buried out of doors, as in the story above. These bottles have been found and dug up in fields and sometimes in hedgerows as well. The purpose of burying them in a field is a final gesture of sympathetic magic; bury the bottle under the ground and the witch will shortly follow it. Also, by doing this, the bottle acts as a protective charm, either against the bewitching of livestock or the blasting of the fertility of the Land itself.

Folk Ways

In 1950, a Soham woman recorded an instance of the bottle ritual being performed, which she witnessed as a child, round about 1900. In this case, the ritual was not performed to break a spell, but to cast one. The woman's mother had recently been widowed and was very put out, because some property and monies from her husband, which she believed should rightly have come to her, had gone instead to her husband's brother. She related this grievance to a gypsy woman who came to the door selling her wares and was advised as follows; she should fill a bottle with her own urine and some nail parings and some snippets of hair. If possible, the hair should come from her brother-in-law, but, failing this, her own would do. She then had to seal the bottle and place it in the middle of a hot fire, at midnight, directing her thoughts towards her brother-in-law as she did so, and wishing him bad luck. If the bottle burst within two minutes, then she would know that her ill-wishing had been successful. The woman did all as she had been advised, even to the extent of making the children stay up with her, telling them to 'think bad thoughts' about their uncle, until the bottle burst. A few days later, the brother-in-law fell from a ladder and broke his leg. This was badly set and failed to mend properly, the man walking with a limp thereafter.

In Cambridgeshire, the most frequent type of bottle employed however, is the glass variety; a long, thin, greenish type of glass bottle, which was usually placed in the wattle and daub of the wall, above the lintel of the door through which the witch was most likely to enter. The purpose of these bottles was the same as the Greybeards, i.e. protective, but the folk-magicians in Cambridgeshire had a different method to draw the power of the witch who had cast her charms on the house or occupants. The glass bottle, after being enchanted of course, was stuffed full of coloured threads, red being the most predominant colour. There are several well-known methods of this apotropaic use of coloured threads; mothers used to tie threads of different colours around the necks of their babies, to stop them being enchanted by the evil eye; and just as horse brasses were first used as amulets and not primarily as decorations, so too the 'hounces' – the coloured, worsted braids worn by farm-horses – originally had the same function. As mentioned already, the witch was thought to be tied indissolubly to her victim by a thin and invisible cord of blood, virtue or life-force; the red thread is an analogue of this cord or filament. What other colour would be more appropriate in this case than red, the colour of blood and hence life? It was also believed in East Anglia that if a witch was suspected of enchanting a person, or was known to have mentioned her intention of doing so, the best preventative was to draw blood from the witch herself; this was best done 'above the breath', i.e. above the nose, or from the forehead. There are many instances of old women, suspected of being witches, being attacked and either scratched to draw blood, or being seriously cut or stabbed, sometimes to the point of death. However, in the case of the Cambridgeshire witch (glass) bottles, the red thread would be a pure instance of sympathetic and defensive magic.

Salt, Shoes & Spheres

Along with witch bottles, there were other methods of protecting the home from malignant magic. Many houses built in the 16th and 17th centuries have been found to contain in their walls small glass phials or bottles; these originally contained salt, and a few, also held iron nails and/or pins. Salt is a well tried and time honoured method of protection from evil and the bottles, full or half-empty, would be considered a very potent safeguard. The addition of the nails or pins shows the great faith being placed in the iron as a safeguard, of which these things were made. Many people considered that if a witch called

Folk Ways

at the house, a pair of scissors, a knife or a key – made of iron – placed under the chair in which she sat would render her powerless. Old horseshoes are of course seen a-plenty hanging on house and stable doors throughout the region, many having been placed there as protective devices many years ago. A somewhat humorous example of the faith placed in horseshoes is given in the *'Cambridge Advertiser'* dating from 1855;

> *'A carpenter residing at Ely, named Bartingale, being lately taken ill, imagined that a woman named Gotobed, whom he had ejected from one of his houses, had bewitched him. Some matrons assembled in the sick man's chamber agreed that the only way to protect him from the sorceries of the witch was to send for the Blacksmith, and have three horseshoes nailed to the door. An operation to this effect was performed, much to the anger of the supposed witch, who at first complained to the Dean [of Ely Cathedral], but was laughed at by his reverence. She then rushed in wrath to the sick man's room and, miraculous to tell, passed the Rubicon despite the horseshoes. But this wonder ceased when it was discovered that, in order to make the most of the job, Vulcan had substituted donkey's shoes ... '* So the moral of the magic is, always make sure of the source of your horseshoes!

Another charm to protect the home was the 'witch ball'. These were balls of coloured glass, usually blue, red, or green, or silvered glass, averaging between six to eight inches in circumference, that were hung in the main window of the home by a metal hook and chain inserted into the top. These balls were originally known as 'watch balls', because they were closely observed, as they hung in the window, by their owners. If the bright surface remained undimmed, then all was well; if it became clouded or tarnished, then sickness, death or some other ill fortune was soon to befall the household. This is a pure case of 'pot calling the kettle black', as the very same charm was used by the witches themselves. In this case, the ball would be enchanted before it was hung in the window, such that any malignity that was cast in their direction would be reflected back upon the sender. It was also used as a scrying device to actually detect who had sent the curse in the first place.

❧ *Blood, Bones, Burning & Baking* ❧

Old houses often have a layer of animal bones placed under the chimney breast or under the floor boards of the main, downstairs room. These were placed there by the builders (often members of the Bonesmen's Guild, another 'secret society' like the Horsemen or Toadmen), as a protection for the occupants; these represent a survival of the old foundation sacrifices, placed to appease the local Land spirits and to invoke their blessing and protection. A Cambridgeshire Fenman recalls that his uncle, a builder, secured the contract in 1897 for building a new Primitive Methodist Chapel. He sent his nephew and his elder brother to the knacker's yard to buy a horse's head. When the two boys brought it back, they watched their uncle and his workmen dig the trench for the foundations and then saw their uncle carefully mark the exact centre of the site, by driving a wooden stake into the ground at the spot. The workmen then gathered around whilst the uncle uncorked a bottle of beer, the horse's head was placed in the trench and the first glass of beer was poured directly over it. The rest of the drink was then shared amongst the men and they afterwards proceeded to cover the head by shovelling bricks and mortar onto it. It was explained to the nephew that this was an old practice to drive off evil and to protect the place from witchcraft. Many of the uncle's fellow builders regularly fetched blood from the butchers and used this to mix the mortar that was used on the brickwork for chimneys and hearths. The blood was

Folk Ways

considered to be a safeguard against witchcraft to those in the know. Salt-glazed bricks were often used, with the same purpose in mind, for building the chimneys.

Other methods of breaking spells were known and were freely put into practice. Catherine Parsons of Horseheath (previously cited), recorded in 1915 the procedure followed by one of the villagers to rid some ducks of vermin, with which so many witches seem to have infested their victims;

> *'Mrs H., formerly of Horseheath, tells how her mother had a beautiful brood of young ducks, and when only a fortnight old, they were bewitched and covered with vermin. These young ducks just turned on their backs, kicked up their little feet, and were dying fast. Fearing she might lose the whole brood, the good woman sent to the shop for an ounce of new pins, and stuck them into one of the dead ducks. Then she made up a good fire, and at twelve o'clock at night, without telling anyone what she was going to do, she put the duck well into the middle of the fire, and before the duck had been burning ten minutes her fears were affirmed. The witch came screaming to the door, making the most agonising noise, for the pain caused by the pins in the burning duck had entered the witch, and we are told the rest of the ducks in the morning were found to be cured of their pest.'*

A similar instance to this was recorded by the Rev. F. Barham Zincke in the *'History of Wherstead'*, published in Ipswich in 1887;

> *Exorcism by Fire*
> *A woman I knew forty-three years ago had been employed by my predecessor to take care of his poultry. At the time I came to make her acquaintance she was a bedridden toothless crone, with chin and nose all but meeting. She did not discourage in her neighbours the idea that she knew more than people ought to know, and had more power than others had. Many years before I knew her it happened one spring that the ducks which were*

a part of her charge, failed to lay eggs ... She at once took it for granted that the ducks had been bewitched. This misbelief involved very shocking consequences, for it necessitated the idea that so diabolical an act could only be combatted by diabolical cruelty. And the most diabolical act of cruelty she could imagine was that of baking alive in a hot oven one of the ducks. And that was what she did. The sequence of thought in her mind was that the spell that had been laid on the ducks was that of preternaturally wicked wilfulness; that this spell could only be broken through intensity of suffering, in this case death by burning; that the intensity of the suffering would break the spell in the one roasted to death; and that the spell broken in one would be altogether broken, that is, in all the ducks .... Shocking, however, as was this method of exorcising the ducks, there was nothing in it original. Just about a hundred years before, everyone in the town and neighbourhood of Ipswich had heard, and many had believed, that a witch had been burnt to death in her own house at Ipswich by the process of burning alive one of the sheep she had bewitched. It was curious, but it was as convincing as curious, that the hands and feet of this witch were the only parts of her that had not been incinerated. This, however, was satisfactorily explained by the fact that the four feet of the sheep, by which it had been suspended over the fire, had not been destroyed in the flames that had consumed its body.

And again in the *'Handbook for Essex, Suffolk, Norfolk and Cambridgeshire'*, by John Murray, 1875;

'1744 – The last of them [the 'Ipswich Witches], *one Grace Pett, laid her hand heavily on a farmer's sheep, who, in order to punish her, fastened one of the sheep in the ground and burnt it, except the feet, which were under the earth. The next morning Grace Pett was found burnt to a cinder, except her feet. Her fate is recorded in the "Philosophical Transactions" as a case of spontaneous combustion.'*

Folk Ways

Not all counter charms were quite so deadly or destructive though. In the book *'A Treatise on Witchcraft'*, by Mr. Roberts, published in London in 1616, there is a section on 'Norfolk Witches', and the method of making a witch cake, according to the prescriptions of a Cunning man in Yarmouth. Here follows the relevant passage;

'It being firmly believed that Elizabeth Hancock, a widow, was bewitched by Maria Smith, her father, Edward Drake, unable to bear any longer the sight of his daughter in pain and torment, determined to go and consult a "cunning man". He told Edward Drake, as soon as he saw him, that he was come to seek help for his daughter, and added that she was so far spent that if he had stayed but one day longer, the woman that had wronged her would have placed her past recovery. He also showed Drake the face of his daughter in a glass, and told him that the witch had accused his daughter of stealing her hen, of which fact Drake was not previously aware. He then gave him the following directions, which, if strictly complied with, would be the means of giving the desired relief to his daughter. "Make a cake with flour from the baker's and mix with the same the patient's urine instead of other liquor, and bake it on the hearth. One half of this cake to be laid on the patient about the region of the heart, and the other half to be applied to the back directly opposite." He also gave a box of ointment, like treacle, which must be spread upon that cake, and a powder to be cast upon the same, and certain words written in a paper to be laid on with the cake. He further told Edward Drake that if his daughter did not exhibit signs of improvement within six hours of the adoption of this remedy, then there was no health or recovery to be looked for. He also wished that silence should be kept, as the woman who had done this would know nothing. The widow, it is said, was by this means freed from the languishing torments that she had endured for six weeks.'

We now have no means of knowing what was in the ointment or the powder, but the written charm may have been something similar to this traditional charm amulet; it was written on parchment and placed under the left breast of a woman, to protect her from all diseases.

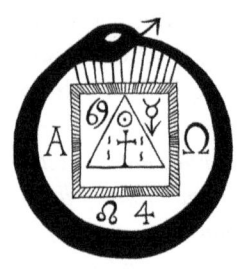

It seems to be similar to many of those given in the mediaeval, and later, grimoires, so was perhaps taken from one of them by a literate and learned Cunning man or woman.

Special Stones

Various other natural charms and measures were used in Folk magic to protect both the home and the individual and one of the most popular, and readily available, of these was different types of stones. We have already seen in a previous chapter how the Hagstone was used to ward off malignant influences from livestock and horses, but it was, and still is, used for personal and domestic protection. The naturally holed stone must be found by the individual, never bought, gifted or swapped for something else, to be truly effective. Giving away a Hagstone gives the luck and protection away as well. Some folk say that the stone is effective all on its own, placed on the hearth or on a windowsill, others maintain that to be fully 'activated', it must be strung on a red thread, cord or string, echoing the threads in the witch bottles above. It must then be hung in a prominent place in the home, or carried about the person if it is for individual protection. It is still possible to see strings of these stones, collected over long periods of time, hung outside along by or under windows, on cottages by the coast, being a protection for fishermen and sailors when they are at sea. Many old houses can still be seen with a Hagstone, threaded onto a red cord, also containing one or more old, iron keys, hanging up at the back door. This is combining the protective powers of iron with the Hagstone for extra effect.

Another popular charm is the 'Fairy' or 'Frairy' loaf. This is a naturally fossilized sea urchin, much resembling the old loaves that would be baked in a country cottage. They were considered to be loaves baked by the Faerie folk and lost, containing all the luck of the small people in them. They were greatly sought after for their protective properties, polished to a high sheen and placed on the mantelshelf over the hearth, or on the outside windowsill. They insured the house protection against witchcraft, poverty, want and storms. Frairy loaves, however, could bring luck to anyone who found one and kept it. A lady walking in 1881 near Hepworth in Suffolk with an old lady of Market Weston, was suddenly told to *'Pick up that thar stone, it's a frairy loaf.'* The woman did as she was bid, the older woman inspected the stone and declared;

> *'That's a stornary lucky one. That's got tew crosses on't, and so that'll preserve yew from the evil doin' of the tempest, and if so be it's a man that finds it he can ax for a hape o' gowd, an' if so be it's a woman she can ax for a good husband so she'll never have to work till her life's end, for sure as I know my name, so sure will that same little Pharisee what lost that loaf come for it, and then you'll see what you'll see. But don't go for to part with it athout his promise, and mind you don't keep it arter he ha' promised, for dew you do that yer luck'll goo, and you'll be as misfortunate as ever you were lucky.'*

It was the stone's resemblance to a loaf, also, that caused the fossil to be used as a charm placed alongside the old brick oven when the weekly batch of bread was baked, especially in north-east Suffolk where it was often picked

The Devil's Plantation

up in the sandy heathlands (known today as The Sandlings and a nationally protected area). Its magic was believed to be an inducement to the bread to rise and imitate the fossil's beautifully domed shape. The weekly bake was critical to the old economic situation of most people; if, after every precaution the bread went 'dumpy', as sometimes happened, the failure was often put down to witchcraft.

Here is a tale from a west Suffolk village, that illustrates this very point, in a time when, if the bread failed, one could not just go to the local shops and buy some more. The cook in the Big House suddenly began to have difficulty with his bread baking. After a succession of failures he roundly ascribed his poor bread to a village woman who was employed part-time at the house. She was a witch, and it was she who was causing the trouble. It was therefore arranged for the local priest to exorcise the oven and take off the malignant spell, with all the members of the household staff standing by. He had not gone far into the ritual, when the apron of the suspected woman caught fire, thus proving her guilt and removing the curse.

Another type of fossil is often found on the sandy heathlands of Suffolk, and this is the Belemnite, otherwise known as the Devil's Finger. Belemnites are pointed, flint cylinders, varying from two to five or six inches in length; they are the fossilized guard of an extinct type of cuttlefish and are frequently found in the soils of East Anglia, where they are also known as Thunderbolts or Thunderpipes. The main beliefs linked with Belemnites are still held by people and this is the origin story of this particular fossil, as given by an older horseman;

> 'As the sun draws up water so the clouds draw up substance from the earth – sulphur and so on. When there's a clap o' thunder, down all this comes as thunderbolts.'

Another farm worker recalls how he was working, when there was a sudden thunderstorm. The lightning struck the ground not far from where he was hoeing in the fields and on examining the spot later, he discovered a little hole. His comment was; *'If I'd ha' dug down that hole, I'd ha' found a thunderbolt, you ma' depend.'* Another farm-worker reported; *'I picked up one of these thunderbolts after a tempest, and it were right warm.'*

The shape of the fossil, like the name, Belemnite, suggests a dart, and in one Suffolk village it is known as a prehistoric arrow. Like the true, Neolithic flint arrow heads, it is sometimes identified with the elf-shot or fairy-darts which were once thought to be the causes of disease in men and cattle. However, a much wider ranging tradition allocates them to the Norse thunder God Thor or his Anglo-Saxon counterpart Thunor. When found, they are eagerly collected and carried in the pocket, or on a string around the neck as an apotropaic charm against all ill, particularly witchcraft, placing the bearer under the Thunderer's protection.

A 'stone' that was used by both witches and folk-magicians alike was Amber. Technically not a stone at all, but the fossilized resin from coniferous plants millions of years old, it was highly prized as a working aid in practical magic and for personal decoration. East Anglia has a very long coastline and, at one time, Amber washed down from the Baltic region was easily picked up on most of the beaches here, in sizes ranging from as small as a little fingernail, to lumps the size of half a brick. Alas, the supply has now mostly dried up and it is a lucky find these days. Because Amber had once been 'alive' and many pieces contained the preserved specimens of the whole or parts of insects, leaves or plants, it was considered to be a potent source of energy or 'virtue'. It was used to enhance and magnify the power of spells and charms in various ways. It could be included, powdered or broken into small pieces, in physical charms; it could be burnt as incense and its sharp, piney smell added to the power of the occasion; an especially large piece could be placed on an altar or work table whilst making magic, to add its energy to the work; and it could be engraved with symbols, charmed and worn as an amulet or talisman. Many magical practitioners also wore it as jewellery to enhance their own powers, or used polished spheres to skry with, considering that its enhanced energy would aid their practice and vision. Nowadays, old pieces of Amber are much sought after but, alas, they are very rare and costly indeed.

The Wake of Freya

East Anglians, in general, are a superstitious folk and many traditions exist for divinations of all sorts, in an attempt to ensure their future good fortune, either in life, health, love or luck.

There was a strange rite surviving in East Anglia, known as the 'Wake of Freya'. It is recorded by the famous author, polyglot and Romany-friend, George Borrow in his book *'Lavengro'*, as being performed by his mother and aunt, on the night of the 5th December, 1783, at Dumpling Green, near East Dereham in Norfolk; the two young ladies were then twelve and seventeen years old respectively. Freya and Frigga were originally two separate Norse goddesses, but in the minds of the people of East Anglia, they seem to have been conflated over a long period of time, as their individual characteristics have become meshed into one. The Freya of the title of this rite is said to have given her name to Friday and be portrayed as veiled and with a spinning wheel, with the power to bestow wedded happiness and bearing the keys to the home; she was also depicted as wearing a costly necklace and a feathered cloak. However, all apart from the last two of these are attributes of Frigga, not Freya, so it would seem that the two goddesses have been remembered as one. The goddess is also depicted as being comely and neat, with a propensity for wearing a snow-white linen dress and it is around this latter that the rite is formed. The power of this pagan goddess was so great that right down to the latter end of the 18th Century and well beyond, the love-

Folk Ways

sick, or just merely curious, young ladies of East Anglia invoked Her name by taking part in the ceremony which was meant to show them their future lovers and husbands.

The rules which had to be observed were these. First, the girl in question had to select a white linen garment from her wardrobe and wash it in pure, running water, such as a local stream or brook. After that, she must hang it up before the fire and watch it drying, between the hours of 11:00pm and the stroke of midnight. Care must be taken to ensure that the outer door is unbolted and left slightly ajar. Never for a minute should the girl take her eyes from off the drying garment, as it was not known exactly when the face of her loved one might appear. All the time she was watching, she must supplicate the name of Freya to show to her her intended.

As recorded in Lavengro, the result of the Wake was as follows; as the clock struck twelve, an outer gate swung to with a resounding crash. One of the girls by the fire leapt instantly to her feet and, flinging herself against the door, locked and bolted it. The next moment she was lying in convulsions on the floor. As the other bent anxiously over her sister, she thought she heard someone press upon the bolted door, and a faint sound of moaning seemed to swell through the cracks in the room.

And what happened eventually to the elder sister? She was ill for many weeks after the Wake, and later on chose for her husband a very unsuitable man. Her whole life was dogged by misfortune, so that she may be said to have been a very good example of what comes of not performing an ancient and time-honoured rite correctly. However, it is in a double sense that the memory of the Wake of Freya has been kept alive in the minds of Norfolk folk, for in addition to the word 'watch', with which the goddess Freya's name is associated, the word 'Wake' also means a 'fayre'. For many years the town of East Dereham in Norfolk held its market or fayre on a Friday, with the result that it, too, became known as the 'Wake of Freya', or Friday's Market.

The Devil's Plantation

A general, East Anglian tradition was observed on Christmas Eve, along similar lines to the above. A maiden wishing for a sight of her future husband must wash out her chemise and hang it before the fire to dry. She must wait in solemn silence until midnight, when he will come in and turn the linen over. This ceremony was also observed on New Year's Eve, another liminal time of all possibility. Sometimes on New Year's Eve also, four girls would prepare a supper for five people; each would then sit in a corner of the room until midnight, when the shade of the future spouse of one of them would come in and join them for supper.

Another similar tradition, albeit not named, seems to have been preserved in Suffolk until fairly recently. An unnamed correspondent to the *Ipswich Journal* in 1887, under the heading of *'Suffolk Notes and Queries'*, gives the following information. Some sixty years previously, he had been told of a ceremony by a person who had been present and the writer also knew some of the other participants himself as well. A group of young ladies had gathered, probably on All Hallow's Eve, to discover who the lover or husband of one of the group would be. They had washed a linen smock and hung it up on the back of a chair to dry. At the stroke of midnight, the shade of the future lover was supposed to appear to turn the smock, but unfortunately, no result of the operation was recorded. The similarity between this and the previous operations is, however, notable. The same correspondent also records another divination to be performed, this time by a lone female, on the Eve of St. Thomas's Day (December 20th). He was present when a young lady, the daughter of a respectable tradesman, came to an old woman of his acquaintance, to enquire about the invocation to be said on St. Thomas's Eve. The writer was very young at the time, and it was thought that he would not take any notice of the matter, so full details were given in front of him, of a rite that seems to have been very clandestine at the time. The lady was to get into bed backwards, repeating the following words as she did so;

Good St. Thomas, use me right,
Bring to me my love this night,
In his apparel, his array,
The clothes he walks in every day.

After getting into bed and speaking the invocation. On no account was she to speak to anyone else until the following day. By following these instructions, she could expect to dream of, and see in her dream, the person who would one day be her husband. The writer records that he saw the young lady the following evening and asked after her results; she said she could remember no more than that she had dreamed of someone who wore trowsers – breeches then being in fashion – so presumed that she had seen a young man who was well known to be her 'walking companion' already.

Charms of Love

To find out whether her pretended lover actually loves her or not, a girl should take an apple-pip and name it for him, then put the pip in the fire. If it makes a noise in bursting from the heat, then it is a proof of love; but if it is all burnt up without a crack, then there is obviously no real regard towards her from the person named.

To bring the sulkiest or most wayward of lovers back, a knife should be thrust violently into the post at the foot of the bed, whilst reciting the following charm;

It's not this post alone I stick,
But (lover's name) heart I wish to prick;
Whether he be asleep or awake,
I'd have him back to me and speak.

The Devil's Plantation

Another formula to gain information about your future husband goes as follows. On three consecutive Friday nights you must say the following charm before going to bed;

To-night, to-night is Friday night,
Lay me down in dirty white,
Dream who my husband is to be,
Lay my children by my side
If I am to live to be his bride.

A somewhat strange verse, but it is sure to bring dreams of the future spouse on the third night of the operation. Again, the expectant young maid writes several male, Christian names, and also her own, on slips of paper, rolls each one up separately in a little ball of clay, and then places them all in a pail of water. As the clay dissolves the slips of paper are liberated and the first that reaches the top is the future spouse. However, should her own name be the first to rise to the surface, then she is sure to remain on the shelf forever!

A spell used in Norfolk goes thus;

A clover, a clover of two, put it in your right shoe,
The first young man you meet in field, street, or lane,
You'll have him or one of his name.

The 'clover of two', means a piece of clover with only two leaves on it, almost as rare as a four-leaved one.

It is considered that if a young woman fills an egg with salt and eats it before going to bed, then her future husband will bring her a drink of water during the night, whilst it is considered that the lover or future husband will be dreamt of, if wedding cake drawn through a ring is placed under the pillow and slept upon.

The first egg laid by a pullet is sought for by young men, who present it to their sweethearts with the idea that it is the luckiest gift that can be bestowed – the girls, however, use the eggs for more mystical purposes. The first egg which a

Folk Ways

hen has laid is made use of by some curious girls to gain a knowledge of the occupation of their future husbands. The egg (it must be a maiden one), is broken into a tumbler of water about noon, when the sun is out, on Midsummer's Day (June 24th). It is allowed to stand for some time in the sun, and the shape which the white assumes denotes the trade of the future husband. For example, if the white looks like a ship, then the girl will marry a sailor; if it looks like a pair of scissors, she will marry a tailor; if a loaf of bread, a grocer; if a shoe, a cobbler, etc. Sometimes the women break the egg when they go to bed, and examine the glass in the morning when they awake.

Another way of finding out the trade of a future spouse is to make a hole in the ground, at a four cross ways, and apply the ear to the hole; and you will hear what you will hear. But in travelling along the road, to see three crows not flying but sitting in the road, surely denotes a coming wedding.

Sometimes a young woman would know perfectly well whom it was that she wished to marry, but was not always successful in getting the attention of the young man of her desires. To encourage him to do so, a girl from the Cambridgeshire/Norfolk fen region would go out at midnight when the moon was full and walk barefooted in a patch of Yarrow. Then, with eyes closed, she would pick a bunch of flowers and, on returning to her home, put them securely away in a drawer or under her bed. If on rising at dawn the next morning, she found that the flowers were still wet with dew, she could be sure that the young man would soon begin to notice her. If, however, the flowers were dry, she would either have to repeat the ritual at the next full moon, or transfer her affections elsewhere.

St. Mark's Eve

Certain rites, having no connection with the commemoration of any Christian martyr, but having co-opted his memory,

The Devil's Plantation

were performed on St. Mark's Eve (April 24th), which is sometimes seen as a peculiarly East Anglian 'All Hallows Eve'. It was important that they were performed on this day and no other, otherwise the rite would not work. These rites were said to reveal certain, sure knowledge sought by the performer, from love divinations and husband seeking, to forecasting deaths and severe illness.

One particular vigil, kept by young women, was for the purpose of divining their future husband. Precisely at midnight on St. Mark's Eve, the girl must go alone into the garden or an empty field, taking with her a quantity of hemp seed. This she is to sow, whilst reciting the following lines;

Hemp seed I sow,
Hemp seed grow;
He that is my true love
Come after me and mow.

Performed with all sincerity and full faith in the efficacy of the charm, the image of her future husband will appear behind the girl as she walks, with a scythe in hand, in the act of mowing down the hemp.

Another rite of divination concerned Dumb Cake, so called because of the rigid silence that must attend its manufacture. This is a species of dreaming bread that is prepared by single girls in the hope of seeing their future husbands, if they followed the directions exactly. These directions – the surviving remnants of some greater witch lore – are given as follows;

An eggshell full of salt,
An eggshell full of wheatmeal,
An eggshell full of barleymeal.

The cake must be baked before a fire, a little before midnight on St. Mark's Eve. The maker must be quite alone, must be fasting and not a word must be spoken. Some girls

Folk Ways

believed that, precisely at midnight, the husband-to-be would come and turn the cake before the fire, but generally the rite followed a more settled pattern. This consisted of cutting the baked cake into three pieces, a part of each to be eaten, the rest to be placed under a pillow. Upon the stroke of midnight the girl would go upstairs backwards, jump into bed and keep a profound silence whatever might happen. Those girls who were to be married would see (or dream of) their future husbands, and those who were to remain single would see nothing at all.

Discovering the trade of future husbands was serious business and the formula consisted of using two pewter pots. Two maidens would scrub the hearthstone absolutely clean before retiring to bed for the night. They would then take two pewter pots, placing one on either side of the hearth stone, upside down, then walk backwards from the room and upstairs. Without a word being spoken they would then undress with their backs to the bed, so as not to break the spell, then climb into it backwards. The next morning, as soon as it was light, they would go downstairs to view the results of their rite. Turning the pewter pots over, they would expect to see the symbols of their future husbands' trade, such as a sprinkling of earth, suggesting that he would be a labourer. If a piece of wood shaving were found, then he would be a carpenter; if metal were found, he would be a blacksmith, stone for a mason, rope for a sailor and so on through all the possible trades a man could follow. Disappointment at finding nothing under the pots did not deter the maidens from trying it out until they were eventually married though!

Regarding portents and signs of death or illness, there was a very strong tradition of 'Watching' on St. Mark's Eve. The belief on this subject is that the shades of those who will die, or be subject to severe illness in the course of the following year, will walk into their parish church on the eve of St. Mark's. Infants and young children not yet able to walk are said to roll in on the pavement. Those who are to die remain in the church and do not re-emerge; those who are to recover return, after a longer or shorter period, in proportion to the length of their future sickness. The shades of those entering singly and remaining denoted death, but those of couples entering together and returning was sure sign of marriage. In some areas though, a slightly different belief was held; in those places it was thought that the forms of those who were to die came out of the church, walked around the graveyard and, having found the site of their future graves, lay down and vanished underground.

And likewise, those who will be wed,
In ghostly pairs emerge; and so
Such as dare watch the door 'tis said,
Their neighbours' destiny may know.

Those who wished to witness these portents and apparitions are to conceal themselves in the church porch and keep watch throughout the night. However, if the watcher fell asleep, then he or she would die during the following year, and many is the tale of a person watching, who has seen their own form pass into the church, not to re-emerge later. The portent has always proven true, as the person observing this unfortunate sign has always died within the year; beware of what you seek to know, as you might just find out!

Finally in this section on divinations, something that does actually have to do with the Christian faith – divination by bible and key. When any property has been stolen and a strong suspicion attaches to a particular person, against whom no strong evidence can be found, this form of divination is sometimes resorted to, which can be performed in two different ways. In both of them, the key to the parish church door and the church bible are the instruments used. In one way of performing the ceremony, the person suspected of the theft and the owner of the stolen goods are the only people to perform the divination. The key is inserted between the leaves of the bible, with the bow and part of the stalk protruding at one end. The book is then tied together very tightly, so that its weight may be supported by the key. The bible is then set on the other end, and is raised from the ground by the supposed thief and the person robbed, each supporting the weight by one or two fingers placed under the bow of the key, opposite to each other. Whilst the bible is thus suspended between them, a form of adjuration is pronounced with all due solemnity. It is believed that if the suspected person be guilty, the bible will, of its own accord, turn towards him, and as it were point out the culprit.

The second method of divination is used when there are more than one, or several suspects. The persons suspected are arranged around a table, on which is laid the bible with the key placed on it. The owner of the stolen goods then takes the key by the middle, and gives it a strong twirl, so that it turns around several times. The person, opposite to whom it stops, i.e. points at, is the thief.

Curious Cures

We have already seen the uses to which some plants are put in East Anglia, both for healing and other purposes, but the folk of this region have many other ways of curing life's ills as well. All manner of animate and inanimate objects are used in the search for a cure, as can be seen from the following examples.

Whooping cough, that old scourge of infancy, had a wide range of folk remedies applied to it. One very common cure was to drink the remains of a saucer of milk, of which the family ferrets had drunk the other part. Norfolk children suffering from this condition were sent to meet the incoming tide, and as it ebbed, so the cough would go with it. Also, if you lived on the coast, you had to get a live flat fish – a 'little dab' would do – and place it alive on the sufferer's bare chest, keeping it there until it died; this was a sure remedy. Then there is the spider remedy. The mother of the child must find a dark spider in her own house and hold it over the head of the child, repeating three times;

Spider as you waste away
Whooping cough no longer stay.

The spider must then be hung up in a bag over the mantelpiece, and when the spider has dried up the cough will be gone.

On the border ground between Suffolk and Norfolk, the following charm has been popular. A hole was dug in a meadow and into this the child was placed in a bent position, head downwards. The flag cut in making the hole was then placed over him, and the child remained in the hole until he coughed. It was thought that if this charm was performed in the evening, with only the father or the mother to witness it, the child would soon recover. In another parish, a variation of the charm was used. The child was laid face downwards on the turf of the meadow; the turf was then cut round the child in the shape of a coffin. The child was taken up and the flag turned roots upwards, and as the grass withered it was believed that the cough wasted. This charm also must be done secretly or it would fail. To eat a roasted mouse was thought to be a certain cure for this cough, as was passing a number of live snails through the hands of the invalid; they were then suspended in the chimney on a string in order that as they died, the ailment would leave the child. A less cruel method was to take some hairs from the cross on the back of a donkey, and having placed them in a bag, hang them around the neck of the patient. If this is done secretly, a speedy cure will result.

Warts, or 'writs' as they are sometimes known, are a perennial problem and one that has spawned numerous cures. The patient needs to steal a piece of beef (it must be stolen or the charm will have no effect), rub it on the warts and then bury it in the ground; as the beef decays the warts will vanish. Make the sign of the cross on each wart with a pin or pebble stone, then throw the pin or pebble away. Or go to an ash tree that has its 'keys' on it and cut the initial letter of both your first and surnames onto the bark. You must then count the exact number of warts and in addition to the letters, cut a notch for each. As the bark grows up to cover the notches, the warts will go away. Or take the froth of new beer and apply it on three consecutive mornings to the warts, when no one can see you. The froth must not be wiped away, but allowed to work off by itself, and then the warts will disappear. Another cruel one this; get as many snails (or dodmen/hodmidods in East Anglia) as you have warts and stick each one on a Blackthorn spike, having first touched the wart with each one. As the snails die and decay the warts will be taken from you.

Cramp could be cured by wearing finger rings made from the handles of coffins. Alternatively, keep in your pocket the knee bone or patella of a sheep or a lamb. The right foot of a female hare is also considered useful for cramp, as it is for rheumatism. On this point there is a wonderful tale told concerning a one-time Bishop of Norwich at one of his Confirmation sessions. Many East Anglians believe that a child never thrives until it is properly named; and this is one cause of the earnest desire to have their children duly baptised. If the child is sick, it is even supposed to speed the cure; and this virtue is also believed to be equally inherent in the rite of Confirmation. At one such rite being performed by the Bishop, an old woman was seen eagerly pressing forwards into the church. A standerby, struck by the contrast in age between the woman and the other youthful candidates for the rite, asked her if she was going to be confirmed. When the old woman replied that she was, the enquirer expressed his surprise that she should have left it so late to take the confirmation. The old woman replied with some degree of asperity, 'that it was not so; that she had been bishopped seven times already and had every intention of doing so again; because, you see, it was so good for her rheumatism.'

Alternatively, the first new potato, the size of a small egg, should be carried in a pocket, or else a piece of sulphur. A particularly favourite remedy was a piece of brass, a piece of zinc and a piece of copper, placed in a flannel bag next to the skin. Wear this until the flannel wore away and you would surely be cured of your ailment. Eelskin garters were worn by both men and women to ward off rheumatism and eelskin belts, especially by fishermen, to ward off lumbago. Norfolk folk swore by a necklace of Horse Chestnuts, but they must be gathered by children who had never suffered from the malady. A snake's 'avel' (skin), was worn inside of the hat band to cure headaches; you had to keep it there until it was worn to a powder and the headaches would never return.

For typhus fever, a dangerous disease for country folk as well as town-dwellers, the milt or spleen of a cow, or the skirt of a sheep, applied to the feet, is supposed to 'draw' the fever from the head and thus bring about a speedy cure. Some article of church plate, placed upon the patient's stomach is also deemed of great value in this and other similar diseases.

It used to be a tradition in Suffolk that if a young woman suffered from fits of epilepsy or hysteria, she applied to ten or a dozen unmarried men (if the sufferer was a man he applied to as many unmarried women), to obtain from each of them a small piece of silver of some kind; this could be a piece of broken spoon, or ring, or brooch or buckle, or even sometimes small coin, and a penny (without telling the purpose for which the pieces are wanted). The twelve pieces of silver were taken to a silversmith or other worker in metal, who formed them into a ring, which was worn by the sufferer on the fourth finger of the left hand. If any of the silver remained after the ring was made, the workman had it as a bonus, and the twelve pennies collected from each person were intended as the wages for doing the work, and he must charge no more.

Ringworm, on the other hand, could be cured by the sweat of an axe. For this it was necessary to make a bonfire and put green stuff on it to make smoke rather than flame. The axe was held in the smoke and then applied to the affected part of the body, drawing it along to leave the sweat behind. For shingles, you went to the blacksmith's forge and put a handful of wheat into his iron ladle, holding it over the fire of the forge, until the oil melted out of the grains. This was then applied to the body.

The Tides of Life

Acknowledging the cycles of life has always been very important to East Anglian folk and there are various traditions concerning how they are marked. The most

The Devil's Plantation

attention was paid either at the beginning or ending of time on this earth, these being the two most liminal points in a person's life. East Anglian mothers, for example, consider that a child born with its head covered by the membrane commonly called a 'Caul', are extra lucky and will never die by drowning. After the birth, the caul must be kept, lest the luck and the immunity of the person born in it disappears; a Cambridgeshire woman in 1910, was known to have blamed the midwife for the ill health and early death (at age 20), of her son, as the poor woman had carelessly burned the caul in which he was born. If a caul is sold then its power is transferred to the new owner; there are still sailors to be found on the East Anglian coast who are willing to purchase, for a price, an intact caul, which will not only keep them from drowning, but will also prevent any ship that it is aboard from sinking. A caul can also be lent, however, the borrower then coming under its protection for however long it is in their possession. The caul, in which a Norfolk child was born in 1891, was borrowed by relatives and friends of the family when they were travelling by sea, and by soldiers going to South Africa to fight in the Boer War. In the First World War it was again borrowed on several occasions, by soldiers returning home on leave. They never asked to take it to France, however, presumably thinking that a possible death by drowning en route would be better than enduring the horrors and the afflictions of the trenches if they arrived there unscathed. It was a common belief in East Anglia, until the last decades of the 19th century, that a caul could, in addition to its other benefits, endow its possessor with the gift of reasoned, well-delivered argument. Lawyers, therefore, were very anxious to obtain one, either by loan or purchase.

In Cambridgeshire the placenta, or after-birth, was often burned by the midwife in the hearth of the new child's home (when home births were more the norm); she then reported to the mother how many times it had crackled in the fire, this number indicating how many more children she was to have under that roof.

In Suffolk, it was considered unlucky to weigh a new baby right away, for this meant that they would probably die young and certainly would not thrive. To ensure a successful life, a baby born at home used to be carried upstairs when it left its mother for the first time. This made certain that it would 'rise in life'. If the mother's room were at the top of the house, the midwife would carefully climb on a chair and raise the baby up in her arms. On the Norfolk and Suffolk coasts, the belief is still strong that the tides influence both birth and death. Births are most common when the tide is coming in, whilst a child born at ebb tide is thought to suffer adversity and ill luck throughout its whole life. For some strange, unknown reason, brown-eyed children have always been desired by East Anglian parents. To ensure that the, usually, blue eyes of their newly-born babies would eventually turn brown, the parents would bind a small hazel twig to the baby's back, or hang bunches of the twigs in the room in which it was born.

However, sometimes the thought of another baby, of whatever sex, arriving in a family where there were already too many mouths to feed was something that the parents could not bear to think about. In such cases, a Norfolk fenwoman would take any opportunity that arose to hold a dead man's hand for two minutes, considering that this would prevent her having another child for at least two years. Alternatively, she could try to obtain a piece of Corpse Money. This was the florin piece that, until the middle of the 19th century, was placed by the village wise woman on the forehead of a corpse immediately after death, in order that it would pay for the sins of the deceased. 'Wise woman' in this case was another name for the village nurse and/or midwife, who was also referred to as the handy-woman. She was usually credited with also being the local witch, who was known to be of a definite 'grey' persuasion,

The Devil's Plantation

rather than practising purely black or white magic. The florin would remain on the forehead of the deceased until just before the coffin lid was nailed down, when the wise woman would retrieve it; she was then at liberty to sell it, at a profit, to any woman who wished to have no more children, for at least a while. The procedure was to sleep with the coin under the pillow and to keep it there for as long as she wished to remain 'without child'.

In the same region, until roughly the same time as the custom of the placing of the Corpse Money died out, the practice of Sin Eating was still extant in some of the more remote parishes. This involved the consumption by a self-appointed Sin Eater of bread and salt that had been placed on the chest of the corpse, the idea being that they would take upon themselves the sins of the deceased, hence easing their passage to heaven. A schoolmistress who was appointed in 1870 to the new Board School in Little Ouse, gave to the local vicar a notebook containing an account of this practice; she had heard it from an old woman who had not only witnessed it in her youth, but was able to describe how the Sin Eater herself, who was shunned by all her neighbours, had come to undertake her office.

She had, in the beginning, drunk herself stupid with poppy tea until her neighbour, getting anxious, sent for the parson. He, on seeing her, came to the conclusion that she was past all human aid, so he did his duty by reading the church's prayer for the dying and giving her absolution...

Slowly the fumes of the poppy passed off and she sat up, and her neighbour informed her that, so far as the church was concerned, she was dead. All her past sins had been wiped away and so, as she did not exist any longer in the eyes of the church, she could not commit any more. Hereafter she could earn her living as a Sin Eater.

Under the silent gaze of the bereaved family and neighbours, the woman would eat the slice of bread and the little pile of salt placed on the dead person's shroud, and would then be handed, on a shovel, her fee of thirty pennies, which had been dipped in whitewash so that they looked like silver.

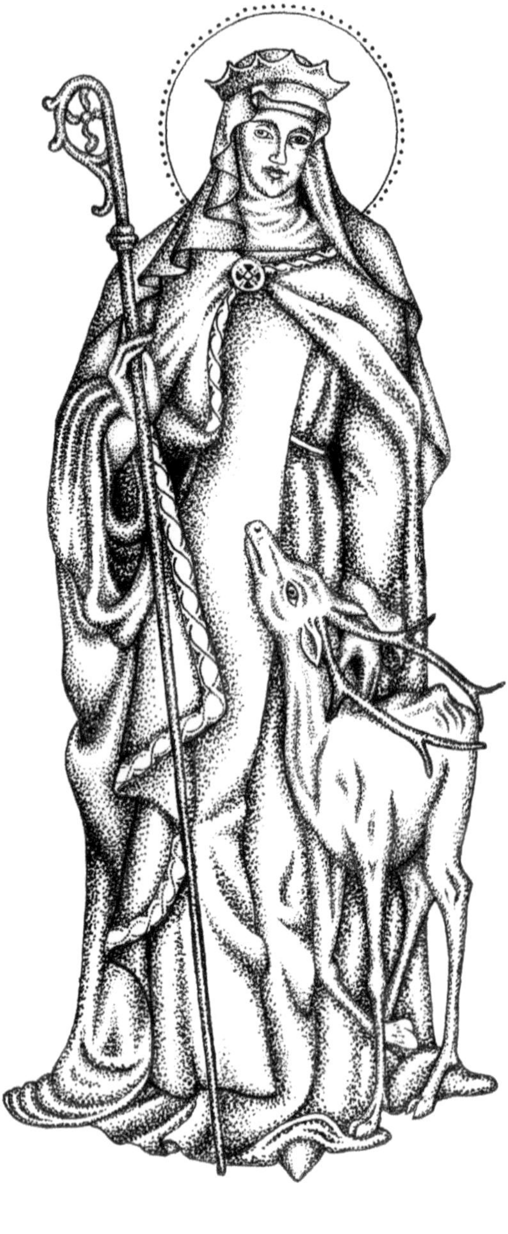

Three Crowns & Several Halos

It may be said that the spirit of a region can be encapsulated and displayed in the signs and insignia by which it chooses to represent itself to the rest of the world. Although East Anglia has no official insignia recognised by the College of Heralds, an East Anglian flag was designed by George Henry Langham at the end of the 19th century and first mentioned in print in 1900. Although not especially well known, even in its 'native' region, the design attempts to capture the spirit, history, mythology and magic of the place it aims to represent. It draws upon the coat of arms of the Wuffingas dynasty (the ancient, Anglo-Saxon royal clan of East Anglia): three crowns in a blue shield, the colour of the Swedish flag, superimposed on a St. George's cross. The technical terminology is; Argent, a cross gules, surmounted by an escutcheon azure charged with three ducal crowns two and one or. The device refers to an old legend of the three crowns of East Anglia, and the blue colour represents the Anglo-Scandinavian heritage of much of East Anglia.

The Devil's Plantation

On the 15th. Century font of the church of St. John the Baptist, in Saxmundham, Suffolk, the shield and three crowns can be seen carved into the stone.

❧ *Legendary Regalia* ❧

Regarding the Three Crowns of the flag, there are various explanations as to just what exactly they refer to or represent. Some say that they refer to the three counties of East Anglia; Suffolk, Norfolk and Cambridgeshire. Some say they refer to the three crowns of the See of Ely, regarded as symbols of the first three Abbesses of the monastery; Etheldreda, Saxburga and Ermenilda. All three were known as Queens in their own right, and the first two were the daughters of Anna, King of East Anglia from 635 to 654, who was slain by King Penda of Mercia. Others say the three crowns refer to the saintly virtues of King Edmund; his chastity, martyrdom and kingship. This, however, is contradicted by the Tudor antiquarian and officer of the College of Arms, John Guillim, who ascribes the shield of King Edmund to an earlier king; he states that it belonged either to the Celtic King Belinus or the god Belenus, as he was mythically crowned in each of three different counties, supposedly circa 401 BCE. Then again there is the theory that the crowns belong to, or represent, the 'three Odins', a trinity named in an ancient Icelandic document and worshipped by the Swedish Kings, who at one time ruled East Anglia. An alternative to this is that the crowns represent the three gods Odin, Thor and Freyr, still thought to be represented by the three crowns on the national flag in Sweden to this day.

However, the best and most popular claim to the Three Crowns of East Anglia is the legend of the buried crowns. According to tradition, three holy crowns were buried along the coast of East Anglia to protect England from foreign invasion, and as long as there is still a single crown hidden, England will remain safe. One of the crowns is believed to have been placed at Dunwich and to have disappeared into the sea, along with most of the rest of that ancient city. It may, perhaps, have been the crown which St. Felix placed on the head of Sigeberht, son of King Raedwald of Rendlesham, who built his own palace at Dunwich ('Dummoc'), in 630 CE (Unfortunately, Sigeberht was also killed by Penda, in 637 CE). In the early 18th century another ancient, silver crown was dug up at Rendlesham; this is believed to be the site of Raedwald's capital and where he was reported as having a temple/church with one altar for the worship of Christ and another, smaller, one for 'sacrifices to devils'. The crown was thought to have belonged to the East Anglian Kings, weighed about 60 ounces and was sold and melted down before its historical value and importance was recognised. The third possible crown is said to have belonged to King Anna, but no one knows its whereabouts now. However, there is still a strong tradition concerning this crown existing in Suffolk, centred around the town of Blythburgh, very near to where King Anna was reputed to have been slain; the tradition states that the third crown is still safely hidden and that it was this crown that prevented the German forces from invading in the Second World War.

Like many founding or foundation myths, the exact reality and history of the three crowns is unlikely ever to be discovered. However, this does not detract from the validity of their use; that they had and still have a living, vibrant and meaningful presence in and for East Anglia is undeniable. Like all symbols they represent that which is desired to be shown and, if only on this level, the Three Crowns embody the very magic and bedrock of East Anglian individuality.

The Devil's Plantation

❦ East Anglian Holy Land ❦

That very magic, as we have seen, derives from various sources, one of which I have yet to look at in any detail. Christianity, although having a dubious date of origin in this region and a varying degree of adherence amongst its residents, has long been incorporated into both the witchcraft and folk-magic of East Anglia. That Christianity arrived here during the Roman occupation is undeniable, but what impact it made on the general populace is very difficult to determine. After the Romans left and the Germanic tribes arrived, the predominant belief systems of the time would have been dictated by the incomers, combined with whatever indigenous Romano-Celtic beliefs were still practised. The old idea that the 'invading' Anglo-Saxons wiped out the local populations and took over wholesale has been discredited for some time now; it is much more likely that they initially arrived in small numbers to raid, eventually settled in larger numbers within the region, mixing with the remains of the Iron Age tribes and Roman veterans, the newcomers' culture and language gradually becoming dominant. That did not mean that they wiped out all trace of the preceding cultures, as we have seen already in the remains of place names, counting words and forms of local devotion. Likewise, with the subsequent re-arrival of any concerted form of Christianity, probably in the 6-7th centuries CE, total and complete conversion was a long time coming, dual faith being the norm for at least several centuries afterwards. This can be amply demonstrated by King Raedwald's two altars, previously referred to; if the King was doing it, how much more so the general populace, not subject to such strong political pressures to convert totally?

However, that Christianity arrived and gradually became absorbed into the general magical and spiritual framework of the region is a fact. East Anglia has a wealth of saints, either native or finding fame in their work here, and I would now like to look at the lives, and myths, of some of the more important early ones. As an example of the impact that these people made on the native culture, we only have to turn to the old nickname for the county of Suffolk, namely 'Silly Suffolk'. This derives from the Old English 'Selig Suffolc', the word 'selig' having the meaning of blessed, fortunate or holy, the whole referring to the number of saints and holy places to be found in the county. Not only that, large parts of East Anglia, rural as it is, still retain a quiet, brooding and especially spiritual and magical atmosphere, contributed to by those long ago holy folk. 'Selig Suffolk' can still be sensed in the allure of its hedgerows, meadows and country lanes; there is an Otherworldly feel to the cornfields, farms, the very land itself, as well as the flint-towered churches and holy wells, a powerful Spirit of Place that intimately joins the present to its especial past. There is a strange and inexplicable quality to the atmosphere, a subtle magic is present in the air occasionally and in certain qualities of light, at different times of day and night and throughout the year, walking along an ancient drover's lane, by a lone tree or a church. This has been created by the combination of all the magical spiritualties that have lived in East Anglia, Christian saints having played no little part in this themselves. That their lives and myths have been mixed with, into and continue the energies of previous deities, spirits and sacred locations, is undeniable; the whole forming a rich and vibrant tapestry which is the magical energy and foundation of the Land of East Anglia.

Saint Felix

The early history of Christianity in East Anglia is rich with the names of many saints, the first of whom was notably St. Felix, Bishop of Dunwich and the first to the East Angles. Felix is mentioned in the Anglo-Saxon Chronicle, a collection of annals that was originally compiled in the late 9th century. The annal for 633 CE states simply that Felix, *'preached the faith of Christ to the East Angles'*. Another version of the Chronicle, written in the eleventh century in both Old English and Latin, elaborates upon the short statement contained in the earlier version: *'Here there came from the region of Burgundy a Bishop who was called Felix, who preached the faith to the people of East Anglia; called here by King Sigeberht; he received a bishopric in Dommoc, in which he remained for seventeen years.'*

The Venerable Bede, of Jarrow Monastery in Northumbria, describes how the exertions of King Sigeberht of East Anglia, *'were nobly promoted by Bishop Felix, who, coming to Honorius, the archbishop, from the parts of Burgundy, where he had been born and, ordained, and having told him what he desired, was sent by him to preach the Word of life to the aforesaid nation of the Angles'*. Bede also praised Felix for delivering, *'all the province of East Anglia from long-standing unrighteousness and unhappiness'*.

Later sources tend to differ from the version of events described by Bede and the Anglo-Saxon Chronicle. The Liber Eliensis, an English chronicle and history written at Ely Abbey in the 12th century, states that Felix came with Sigeberht from Francia and was then made Bishop of East Anglia. According to another version of the story, Felix travelled from Gaul and reached the hamlet of Babingley, via the River Babingley. He then made his way to Canterbury. He was ordained as a Bishop in about 630 or 631 CE by the Archbishop of Canterbury, Honorius. Felix's arrival in East Anglia seems to have coincided with the start of a new period of order established by Sigeberht, which followed the assassination of his predecessor Eorthwald and the three years of apostasy that followed it. Sigeberht had become a devout Christian before returning from exile in Francia to become king and his accession may have been decisive in bringing Felix to East Anglia. Soon after his arrival at Sigeberht's court,

Three Crowns & Several Halos

Felix established a church at Dommoc, his episcopal see, which is widely taken to mean Dunwich, on the Suffolk coast. Dunwich has since been almost totally destroyed by the effects of coastal erosion, but was at one time a major and powerful city, housing many religious orders, their priories, monasteries and chapter houses. Bede related that Felix started a school, 'where boys could be taught letters', to provide Sigeberht with teachers. According to the mediaeval customary of Bury St Edmunds, known as the Liber Albus, Felix is said to have visited Babingley, in the north west of Norfolk, and 'maden ... the halige kirke' – 'built the holy church', which ties in with the earlier description of his arrival. During his years as Bishop, the East Anglian Church was made still stronger when St. Fursey arrived from Ireland and founded a monastery, at Cnobheresburg, probably located at Burgh Castle, in Norfolk.

Felix died in 647 or 648 CE, after he had been Bishop for seventeen years and was buried at Dommoc, but his relics were at a later date removed to Soham, according to the twelfth century English historian William of Malmesbury. His shrine was later desecrated by the Vikings when the church was destroyed. Some time later, 'the body of the saint was looked for and found, and buried at Ramsey Abbey'. Ramsey was noted for its enthusiasm for collecting saints' relics, and in an apparent attempt to out-compete their rivals from the abbey at Ely, the Ramsey monks escaped from Soham by rowing their boats through thick Fenland fog, carrying with them the Bishop's precious remains. His only remaining memorial in Suffolk was the '*Red Book of Eye*', which was his gospel book. It was preserved by the monks of Eye priory and after the Reformation, it fell into the hands of the town corporation, who used it for the swearing of oaths. Unfortunately, in the 18th or early 19th century it disappeared – there is a scandalous story that the owner of Brome Hall caused it to be cut up for game labels!

The memory of St. Felix is enshrined in the words of Chronicler Harding;

And in the yere VI hundred thyrty and two
...by holy doctryne
Of saynt Felix, an holy preyste...
And preaching...
Of Chryste's worde and verteous disciplyn...
At Domok then was Felyx fyrste byshop
Of Estangle and taught the Chrysten faith,
(That is full hye in heaven, I hope).

Felix's feast day is celebrated on March the 8th. There are six churches dedicated to the saint, located both in North Yorkshire and East Anglia; in the East Anglian region alone, he is remembered also in the names of various schools, shrines and also possibly in the seaside town of Felixstowe in Suffolk, which some say bears his name (although this is debated, other origins for the name being possible). To some practitioners of the magical arts in East Anglia, he is remembered for his strength, fortitude and learning and is petitioned for help in these areas. He is depicted as a Bishop, wearing three rings on his right hand.

Saint Fursey

As mentioned briefly above, during the time that St. Felix was Bishop, there arrived from Ireland another future saint, St. Fursey, who also made his mark in East Anglia, in more ways than one. St Fursey (also known as Fursa, Fursy and Forseus), was the first recorded Irish missionary to Anglo-Saxon England; he arrived in East Anglia with his brothers, Foillan and Ultan, during the 630s CE shortly before St. Aidan founded his monastery on Holy Island. This fact alone is interesting, in that it is generally thought that the south and much of the rest of England was re-Christianised purely by priests from Rome. This was as a result of St. Augustine's mission to Kent, having famously been sent there by Pope Gregory the Great, remembering his meeting with the 'Angels' (Angles), in the Forum in Rome. However, certainly – and quite deeply – at least in East Anglia, there was a strong vein of Irish Christianity initially, as St. Fursey was not the only person with Gaelic heritage and training to preach here. St. Felix himself is thought to have been trained in a monastery founded by, or at least based on, the principles of St. Columba of Ireland, whilst in Francia. Further to this, the royal house of East Anglia, the Wuffingas, of whom King Sigeberht was a member, had close ties with Abbess Burgundofara of Faremoutiers Abbey and she had been inspired to found this abbey by the influence and teaching of none other than St. Columba himself. It has even been suggested that a connection between the disciples of Columba and Felix, helps to explain how the Wuffingas dynasty established its links with Faremoutiers in the first place. This Irish connection would certainly have found favour with the culture of the remaining 'Celtic' folk and been readily absorbed into the existing fabric of magical and spiritual life in the region.

St. Fursey is reputed to have been baptised by St. Brendan whilst still in Ireland, and to have gone on to found a monastery of his own in County Galway. He was said to have been something of an ascetic, wearing thin clothing all year round. Aspirants came in numbers to place themselves under his rule, but he wished to secure also some of his relatives for the new monastery. For this purpose he set out with some monks for Munster, but on coming near his father's home he was seized with an apparently mortal illness. He fell into a trance from the ninth hour of the day to cock-crow, and while in this state received the first of the ecstatic visions which have made him famous in medieval literature. An injunction was laid on him by the two angels who appeared to restore him to his body to become a more zealous labourer for the Lord. Three nights later, the ecstasy was renewed. He was taken to the heavens by three angels who contended six times with demons for his soul. Among the spirits of those just made perfect he recognized Saints Meldan and Beoan. They entertained him with much spiritual instruction concerning the duties of ecclesiastics and monks, the dreadful effects of pride and disobedience, and the heinousness of spiritual and internal sins. After this, his brothers Foillan and Ultan then joined his monastic community, but Fursey seems to have renounced the administration of the monastery and to have devoted himself to preaching throughout the land, frequently exorcising evil spirits. Exactly twelve months later he received a third vision. This time, the angel remained with him a whole day, instructed him for his preaching, and prescribed for him twelve years of apostolic labour. This he faithfully fulfilled in Ireland, and then stripping himself of all earthly goods he retired for a time to a small island in the ocean.

As we know, the conversion of East Anglia to Christianity had begun under King Raedwald, but halted with the martyrdom of Raedwald's successor, his son Eorthwald. When Fursey arrived with his brothers, as well as other brethren, bearing the relics of Saints Meldan and Beoan from Ireland, he had been welcomed by the new King Sigeberht, who gave him land to establish an abbey at Cnobheresburg, where there was an abandoned Roman fort, traditionally identified with Burgh Castle in Norfolk; here he laboured for some years in helping to convert the local Angles and Saxons. This is what Bede has to say of Fursey in his *A History of the English Church and People*:

> *'Whilst Sigeberht still governed the kingdom, there came out of Ireland a holy man called Fursey, renowned both for his words and actions, and remarkable for singular virtues, being desirous to live as a stranger and pilgrim for the Lord's sake, wherever*

an opportunity should offer. On coming into the province of the East Angles, he was honourably received by the aforesaid king, and performing his wonted task of preaching the Gospel, by the example of his virtue and the influence of his words, converted many unbelievers to Christ, and confirmed in the faith and love of Christ those that already believed. Here he fell into some infirmity of body, and was thought worthy to see a vision of angels; in which he was admonished diligently to persevere in the ministry of the Word which he had undertaken, and indefatigably to apply himself to his usual watching and prayers; inasmuch as his end was certain, but the hour thereof uncertain, according to the saying of our Lord, "Watch therefore, for ye know neither the day nor the hour." Being confirmed by this vision, he set himself with all speed to build a monastery on the ground which had been given him by King Sigeberht, and to establish a rule of life therein. This monastery was pleasantly situated in the woods, near the sea; it was built within the area of a fort, which in the English language is called Cnobheresburg, that is, Cnobhere's Town; afterwards, Anna, king of that province, and certain of the nobles, embellished it with more stately buildings and with gifts".

During this period, such was the religious and spiritual influence of Fursey on the King, that Sigeberht abdicated his power to his co-ruler, King Ecgric and retired to lead a religious life within a monastery he had built for his own use; this is reputed to be the very one that he gave to St. Fursey at Cnobheresburg. In the year 642 CE, East Anglia was attacked by King Penda and his Mercian army and King Ecgric was obliged to defend it with a much smaller force, though one that was not negligible. The East Angles appealed to Sigeberht to leave his monastery and lead them in battle, hoping that his presence and the memory of his former military exploits would encourage the army and make them less likely to flee. Sigeberht refused, saying that he had renounced his worldly kingdom and now lived only for the heavenly kingdom. However, he was dragged from the monastery to the battlefield where, unwilling to bear arms, he went into battle carrying only a white staff. The Mercians were victorious and Sigeberht, Ecgric and many of the East Angles were slain and their army was routed. In this way Sigeberht became a Christian martyr and saint himself.

After Sigeberht was slain, it is recorded that his successor, , and his nobles further endowed the monastery at Cnobheresburg. Three miracles are recorded of Fursey's life in this monastery, the most notable of which involved relieving a famine which had hit the whole of East Anglia. He then retired for a year to live the life of an anchorite with his brother Ultan. However, as great numbers continued to visit him, and as war threatened in East Anglia, he left Foillan as Abbot and proceeded to Lagny, in France around 644, where he died in the year 650 CE. His feast day is January 16th. Fursey is credited with having established a strong visionary genre in East Anglia and is looked to by some magical practitioners for this ability. He is called upon to give guidance during trance or spirit vision, concerning religious matters or those of a spiritual nature; magical practitioners sometimes help their clients by calling on him for guidance. He is usually depicted with two oxen at his feet; beholding a vision of angels, and/or gazing into the fires of purgatory and hell.

❧ *Saint Botolph* ❧

Just after the events described above, another saint arrived on the local scene. Known variously as Botwulf, Botulph or Botulf, St. Botolph (as he is more usually known), was born of Anglo-Saxon, probably noble, parentage and entered a monastery in England as a youth to begin his spiritual training. As an adolescent or young adult, St Botolph travelled to Francia to complete his monastic training. In the turbulent period of the early 7th century this may have been as much about protection as it was about piety or education. We know that many young members of the Anglo-Saxon nobility – both young men and women – were sent across to monasteries and convents in Francia to escape the dangerous threat of the rampaging Mercians. From the sources it seems that he spent a significant period of time at the abbey of Faremoutiers, an important connection with previous missionaries to East Anglia. Here he met the saintly daughters of King Anna of East Anglia, Saethyrth and Aethelburga, and formed a spiritual friendship with both of them. Jointly they persuaded him to go back to their father's kingdom to establish a monastery and wrote letters of recommendation. It is therefore possible to say that his time at Faremoutiers would have been strongly influenced by the Celtic Rule of the Irish missionary St Columba, which we know was observed there in conjunction with the Rule of St Benedict as well as other Frankish monastic rules of the period. This would have entailed that St Botolph's monastic training was of a highly ascetical character, combining extensive monastic services, together with rigorous emphasis on spiritual discipline and obedience as well as the importance of intellectual study.

In 647 CE Botolph returned to England and travelled to Rendlesham in Suffolk, the ancient capital of the East Anglian Wuffingas Court, taking with him recommendations from Anna's daughters. After some negotiation, King Anna allocated him land at Icanho (Iken), a marshy spur, surrounded on all sides by the branches of the River Alde, which would have made it something of an East Anglian 'Holy Island'. Strategically, the monastery was ideally placed through being close to the royal court in Rendlesham, and just a few miles south of the diocesan see that St Felix had established at Dommoc (Dunwich).

Soon after this the raiding of Penda, King of the Mercians, caused Anna to go into exile as well as leading to the ransack and destruction of many East Anglian monasteries and churches, including St Fursey's monastery at Cnobheresburg. It is likely that St Botolph travelled widely over these years by river and land, preaching the Gospel and establishing churches. The entry from the Anglo-Saxon Chronicle for 654CE states, *'In this year Anna was slain and Botwulf began to timber his minster at Icanho'*.

In 1977, as well as uncovering the 1 ½ meter limestone cross shaft from the base of the tower, excavations on the North wall of the nave of the current St. Botolph's church at Iken, discovered the clay foundations of a wooden building which dates to the Middle Saxon Period; this is in all likelihood the very minster that St Botolph himself constructed and worshipped in. During the ensuing years, St Botolph's monastery became an important monastic and missionary centre, no doubt with a good sized library and scriptorium. Whilst no styluses have been found at Iken to date, important examples have been found at Blythburgh and Brandon, both within the Suffolk area. In this period, St Botolph developed a reputation as a holy elder and in particular as a powerful intercessor and excorcist, conquering the 'demon-filled' marshlands for Christ by the sign of the Cross, as we saw in a previous chapter.

Whilst the later medieval 'Lives' may have employed a certain amount of poetic licence, it is recognised that St Botolph's life would have involved real spiritual struggle, considering the then current political and religious climate, especially given the success of his missionary work throughout East Anglia. This missionary success has been indicated recently through further archaeological excavations in the local vicinity of Iken. There is evidence of another small church directly across the river from the minster at Iken on Barber's Point, as well as a possible church just next to the minster on top of the ancient pagan earthwork at Yarn Hill, in addition to a larger monastic site a few miles South at Burrow Hill in Butley; in Anglo-Saxon times this was an island cut off from the mainland by tidal mudflats crossed by a causeway. In this sense, we are talking more about a monastic archipelago centred around Iken rather than just an isolated monastery, and it is just possible that there were already existing shrines and temples to the preceding deities, onto which the monastic communities were grafted. This would make it a place of especial sanctity and continued magico-spiritual use for many centuries. Unsurprising then, that Botolph would have found the area already inhabited with 'spirits and demons' when he arrived there.

During these years, apparently following a snake bite, no doubt from a distant ancestor of the adders which can still be found in Iken's marshes, St Botolph made a further missionary journey to a place 'remote from the sea, in a vast solitude, with a river flowing through the valley, and accessible through forests or jungle', where he dedicated two churches to St.'s Peter and Paul. In 670 CE, Bede's teacher, Abbot Coelfrith of Jarrow, visited Botolph's monastery in Ikanho following his ordination by Bishop Wilfred. The author of Coelfrith's Life describes St Botolph as *'a man of unparalleled life and learning, and full of the grace of the Holy Spirit'*. It's likely that Bede's silence on Botolph may give further weight to St Botolph's Irish, as opposed to directly Ionian or Roman, influences which were aspects of the story of England's conversion to Christianity outside of the Venerable Bede's Romano-centric narrative.

On June the 17th 680, in the words of his Norman biographer Abbot Folcard, St Botolph reposed, *'in the presence of the brethren, in the monastery which he had built'*. The reference in the later Life to his 'age and infirmities' suggests that he was well over sixty at the time of his death. Sadly, around 870 the same Viking hoard who martyred King Edmund, also raised Iken to the ground, presumably killed its monks and looted the monastery of its sacred possessions, books and relics. The Anglo-Saxon cross that was discovered at the base of the West tower by Dr. Stanley West in 1977 is thought to have been erected in his memory around the 9th to the 10th century. St. Botolph's feast day is June the 17th in England and he is the patron saint of travellers and farming. Strange that such an ascetic and 'bookish' saint should be associated with farming and the Land in general, but he is petitioned with great success by modern folk-magicians in cases pertaining to the fertility of crops and animals within this region.

Saint Etheldreda

King Anna of the East Angles, as well as being a devout man himself, had several daughters who were devoted to the Church, most of whom became saints themselves. Prominent amongst them was St. Etheldreda (also known as Æthelthryth, Ediltrudis and Audrey), who was also a queen in her own right and foundress and Abbess of Ely. She was probably born at Exning, near Newmarket in Suffolk, and at an early age she was married (c.652) to Tondberht, Ealdorman of the South Gyrwas, but because of her deep religious faith, it was agreed that she could remain a virgin. On his death, (c.655) she retired to the Isle of Ely, part of her dowry. In 660, for political reasons, she was married to Ecgfrith, the young king of Northumbria who was then only 15 years old, and several years younger than her. He agreed that she should remain a virgin, as in her previous marriage and, with his consent, she entered the monastery at Coldingham and became a nun, under her aunt Ebbe. Ecgfrith, however, later repented having given her leave to do so and, with a band of followers, journeyed to Coldingham with the intention of taking her back by force. Etheldreda then fled back to Ely with two faithful nuns and managed to evade capture, thanks in part to the miraculous rising of the tide. Another version of the legend related that she halted on the journey at 'Stow' and sheltered under a miraculously growing ash tree which came from her staff planted in the ground. Stow came to be known as 'St Etheldreda's Stow', when a church was built to commemorate this event. According to the Anglo-Saxon Chronicle, Etheldreda founded a double monastery at Ely in 673, which was later destroyed in the Danish invasion of 870, like many others. The double monastery created by Etheldreda came from a restored old church at Ely, reputedly destroyed by Penda, pagan king of the Mercians, and built on the site of what is now Ely Cathedral. After its restoration in 970 by Ethelwold it became the richest abbey in England except for Glastonbury. Etheldreda died c.680 CE from a tumour on the neck, reputedly as a divine punishment for her vanity in wearing necklaces in her younger days; in reality it was the result of the plague which also killed several of her nuns, many of whom were her sisters or nieces. At St Audrey's Fair necklaces of silk and lace were sold, often of very inferior quality, hence the derivation of the word tawdry from St Audrey. It is also said, however, that these laces replaced the miniature iron shackles which the Ely monks had earlier given to pilgrims visiting the saint's shrine, as mementoes of their visit and in commemoration of one of her miracles. This involved St. Audrey appearing after her death to a man in chains in a dungeon in London, falsely accused of illegal moneylending transactions. In this vision she (and St. Benedict), agreed to free the man, if he agreed to become a monk at Ely and serve them, as he had previously vowed to do. He willingly did so, whereupon the chains that bound him broke asunder and fell to the ground, causing such a clatter that the guards outside his cell came in and found him freed. On hearing his story, Queen Matilda sent her chaplain to examine the man and he subsequently declared that a miracle had happened. The man, whose name was Brystan, was sent home to Ely, with the broken shackles, to live out his vow to the Saints as a monk; the iron chains were preserved and hung above the altar in the church at Ely.

The Devil's Plantation

In 695CE, Seaxburh translated the remains of her sister Etheldreda, who had been dead for sixteen years, from a common grave to the new church at Ely. The Liber Eliensis describes these events in detail. When her grave was opened, Etheldreda's body was discovered to be uncorrupted and her coffin and clothes proved to possess miraculous powers. A sarcophagus made of white marble was taken from the Roman ruins at Grantchester, which was found to be the right fit for Etheldreda. Seaxburh supervised the preparation of her sister's body, which was washed and wrapped in new robes before being reburied in the marble sarcophagus. She apparently oversaw the translation of her sister's remains without the supervision of her Bishop, using her knowledge of procedures gained from her family's links with the Faremoutiers Abbey as a basis for the ceremony. This demonstrates another piece of Irish influence, as women were not allowed to act independently of their Bishop in the Roman Church, whereas they had much greater autonomy in the Irish faith. After Seaxburh, Etheldreda's niece and her great-niece, both of whom were royal princesses, succeeded her as Abbess of Ely.

Her Feast Day is June 23rd, and she is the patron of throat complaints. However, according to Bede, due to her great sanctity she was thought to possess the spirit of prophecy, and it is for this ability and her help in matters of divination that she is petitioned by modern magical practitioners. She is usually depicted as an Abbess, holding a model of Ely Cathedral.

Saint Withburga

Tradition describes Withburga as the youngest of the daughters of King Anna. After her father's death, and many years spent devotedly in the amelioration of the ills of the people in the district, Withburga built a convent in

Three Crowns & Several Halos

East Dereham, in Norfolk and herself became its Abbess. A traditional story relates that while she was building the convent she had nothing but dry bread to give to the workmen. She prayed to the Virgin Mary and was told to send her maids to a local well each morning. There they found two wild does which provided milk for the workers. This allowed the workers to be fed. The local overseer did not like Withburga or her miracles and decided to hunt these does down with dogs and prevent them from coming to be milked. He was punished for his cruelty when he was thrown from his horse and broke his neck. This story is commemorated in the large town sign in the centre of East Dereham. St. Withburga eventually died in 743 CE and was buried in the nunnery burial-ground, until a suitable shrine could be constructed.

Some 50 years later it was decided to remove the body into the nunnery church. The grave was opened and, to the amazement of everybody present, just like her sister, her body was found to be miraculously preserved. One story tells of how one of the men reached and touched her cheek with his finger, whereupon the maiden saint blushed at the sacrilege! After removal of her body to the church, many miracles were wrought through it and its fame spread throughout the Land; for generations the relic brought pilgrims to worship at the shrine of St. Withburga. In 870 CE, King Edgar granted Ely, Dereham and all the other monasteries destroyed by the Danes to the Bishop of Winchester. He restored Ely, and at Dereham had a prison and court-house built. During the Danish invasion, the nunnery had been destroyed, but the church and shrine escaped and, when peace returned, became the parish church.

In 974 CE, Ethelwold, Bishop of Winchester, and Brithnoth, Abbot of Ely, wishing to gain possession of St. Withburga's body and remove it to Ely, on account of the revenues gained from pilgrims, gained the King's permission to do so. However, they thought it advisable to proceed with caution, as it was likely that the inhabitants of Dereham would not part very easily, if at all, with so venerable and valuable a treasure without much resistance, if their plan were known. Therefore, they decided to carry out the transfer of the body with as much secrecy as they could muster. On the day decided upon, therefore, the Abbot and some of the most 'suitable' monks set out with some well-armed servants. They were received with honour by the people of Dereham, who thought that they had only come to take legal possession of the town. The Abbot, having held his customary court of justice, invited the people to a sumptuous feast, during which he and the monks went into the church, under the pretext of saying office, to make their preparations. When night fell and the town was quiet – sleeping off the generous Abbot's feast – the monks forced open the saint's tomb to satisfy themselves that the coffin inside it really did contain her body; they then transferred the coffin to a waiting carriage and, with the Abbot's servants guarding it, set off for Brandon, about twenty miles away. Here boats were ready for them and on these they set sail for Ely with their stolen, holy treasure.

Meanwhile the people of Dereham had discovered the theft and had raised the alarm. Arming themselves with whatever weapons they could get hold of, they made straight for Brandon; however, they were too late, as the monks had already embarked and proceeded a considerable way down the river. Dividing themselves into two groups, each taking a different side of the river, the townsfolk marched forward and at length overtook the thieves. But not having boats themselves, the people could not reach the monks in the middle of the river, so that after spending some time in vain threats and dire warnings, they exhausted themselves and were forced to give up the pursuit and return home again; this left the monks free to continue the rest of their journey to Ely without further molestation. They landed safely the same day at a place called Turbotsey, where they were received with great joy and triumph by all sorts of people who had come with the rest of the monks and the clergy to meet them. The body of St. Withburga was transferred with solemn procession and praises being sung to God, to the church at Ely, where it was deposited next to Saints Etheldreda, Sedburga and Ermenilda, her holy sisters, all daughters of King Anna.

When the Dereham men returned home, however, they found that a spring had appeared in Withburga's violated tomb. The water in this spring was considered to be compensation for the loss of their saint, and pilgrims continued to come and drink from the water, miracles of healing still happening there. The spring has never run dry and the water, in Withburga's violated tomb, can be visited to this day in the, now, churchyard of St. Nicholas at East Dereham.

St. Withburga's feast day is celebrated on July the 8th and she is petitioned for her compassion and intercession with other saints as well as for her healing powers. She is sometimes depicted as an Abbess, bearing wild lilies.

Saint Edmund

Eadmund (Edmund), King, Martyr, Saint, Patron of East Anglia and the first and one-time Patron of all England; probably the most important historical character in the history of this region to its people. Considering his importance, almost nothing is factually known of Edmund, although many conflicting versions of his history exist; here are some of the basic facts and I will present the myth anon. He is thought to be of East Anglian origin and was first mentioned in an annal of the *Anglo-Saxon Chronicle*, written some years after his death. Unfortunately for history, the kingdom of East Anglia was devastated by the Vikings, who destroyed any contemporary evidence of his reign, including books or charters referring to Edmund. Later writers produced various accounts of his life, asserting that he was born in 841 CE, the son of Aethelweard, an obscure East Anglian king, whom it was said that Edmund succeeded when he was fourteen (alternatively that he was the youngest son of a Germanic king named 'Alcmund' and was adopted into the royal family of East Anglia). Later versions of Edmund's life relate that he was crowned on 25 December 855 at Burva (probably Bures St. Mary in Suffolk), which at that time functioned as the royal capital, and that he became a model king.

In 869, the 'Great Heathen Army', comprised of many thousands of Danish Vikings, advanced on East Anglia and killed Edmund. He may have been slain by the Danes in battle, but by tradition he met his death at an unidentified place known as Haegelisdun, after he refused the Danes' demand that he renounce Christ: the Danes beat him, shot him with arrows and then beheaded him. A coinage commemorating Edmund was minted from around the time East Anglia was absorbed by the kingdom of Wessex and a popular cult emerged. In about 986, Abbo of Fleury wrote of his life and martyrdom. The saint's remains were temporarily moved from Bury St Edmunds to London for safekeeping in 1010. His shrine at Bury was visited by many kings, including Canute, who was responsible for rebuilding the abbey: the stone church was rebuilt again in 1095. During the Middle Ages, when Edmund was the patron saint of England, Bury and its magnificent abbey grew wealthy, but during the Dissolution of the Monasteries, his shrine was destroyed. The mediaeval manuscripts and other works of art relating to Edmund that have survived include Abbo's *Passio Sancti Eadmundi*, John Lydgate's 14th century *Life*, the Wilton Diptych and a number of church wall paintings.

However, over the centuries, the mythology of Edmund has grown in proportion with his importance and who can say where fact ends and fiction begins; often a story is the best way to preserve and convey truths that would be lost as 'mere facts'. The following is an amalgamation of the major themes in the mythological life of Edmund, which blends many 'truths' together.

In the late 9th century, East Anglia was ruled by a king named Aethelweard. He had but one son, named Edmund, who was a noble, pious and kindly child. Unfortunately, Aethelweard died when Edmund was still only a boy so, when he was just 14 years old, he was crowned by Bishop Humbert on Christmas Day, at a place now called Bures St. Mary in Suffolk; some say he was elected king by consent of the populace, despite his youth, as he was loved so much by the people. For a decade, Edmund grew in virtue and stature among his devoted people, being widely loved for his wisdom, strength and Christian kindliness. Then the heathen and barbaric Danes landed with their armies, first in the north, led by two brothers named Hinvar and Ubba. While Ubba wrought destruction across Northumbria, Hinvar came to East Anglia, secretly entering a city, slaughtering its entire population, and burning it to the ground. Other battles and sieges followed, including one where Edmund escaped his enemies by using a ford known only to him. Finally Ubba came with another army to join his brother Hinvar, and they met the King in battle somewhere near Thetford, the Danes winning the day. Edmund fled 20 miles east to his royal town of 'Haegelisdun', now known as Hoxne in Suffolk, with his foes following.

Some say that Edmund threw down his weapons, vowing to stay true to his people and his faith, and he was seized in his own hall. Many say that he hid beneath a bridge, but was betrayed by a newly-married couple who saw the golden glint of his spurs reflected by moonlight in the water, and gave him up to the Danes. Couples going to get married in Hoxne to this day try to avoid going over the very same bridge, to avert the curse pronounced by the King, indignant at his betrayal, on any couple who afterwards passed over the bridge, either on their way to or from the marriage altar. The Danes called on him to yield up his treasures and his kingdom, to reject Christ, to swear homage to their gods and to bow down before them; Edmund refused to submit, saying that he alone must die for his people and his God. Dragging him out to a field, they beat him and scourged him with whips, then tied him to a tree and fired dozens of arrows into him, ostensibly making him a sacrifice to their own gods and a saviour to his own Land.

Even then the King defied them, calling upon God for help, so they struck off his head and threw it into deep brambles in a nearby wood, leaving his body where it had fallen. After the Danes had departed, Edmund's folk came out of hiding, and found the mutilated corpse of their lord still bound to the tree - but the head was nowhere to be seen. Although they searched by day and night for weeks, nothing could be found until a voice came out of the wood, calling 'here, here, here!' Following the voice, they found that it was coming from the lips of the severed head itself, which was being cradled between the paws of a huge grey wolf, the very symbol and meaning of the Wuffingas, the East Anglian Royal dynasty. The wolf allowed the people to gently retrieve the head and take it back to the town, the wolf walking tamely behind until it was sure that all was safe, then disappearing back into the forest. Behind them, a miraculous fresh-water spring broke through the soil where the head had been discovered. With huge sorrow and reverence the head was placed back upon its shoulders, whereupon the two miraculously became whole again. The body of the king was buried in a grave, and a simple wooden chapel hastily erected over the spot.

Over the years miraculous healings occurred at the little chapel, including a pillar of light emerging from the grave that restored sight to a blind man. As peace returned to the land pilgrims began to make their way there, and Edmund's fame and saintliness spread. In time, the martyred king's body was transferred to a new and grander church built for it some miles away at 'Beodricesworth', or 'Bedericsgueord', the town that would later become Bury St. Edmunds. But when the grave was opened, not only was Edmund's body found to be incorrupt, but all the wounds on his body had healed, and all that was left to show where his head had been severed was a thin red crease on the neck. More miracles followed over the centuries at the new shrine, and as his fame spread, so princes, kings and a host of other pilgrims came to the abbey that was built around him, to give him honour and pray for his blessing. Although his exact place of burial is now unknown, it's said that Edmund's body still lies somewhere under the abbey ruins, even now whole and incorrupt, and a treasure buried with him.

As the patron saint of East Anglia, Edmund is of extreme importance in the spiritual and magical make-up of this region. At the height of his fame and glory, the shrine at Bury St. Edmunds was rivalled as a site of pilgrimage in England only by Glastonbury and vied with Walsingham as the most pre-eminent in East Anglia; it held huge power and riches, both spiritual and temporal. Edmund can be seen as achieving almost god-like status from some perspectives, but certainly at least a 'totemic' value from others, whether from a purely Chrisitan view point, or a folk-magical and metaphysical one. In his myth and person, he exemplifies the image of the Slain King, dying for his Land and People, his blood fertilising and blessing the soil; this is a theme common to both 'Celtic' and Scandinavian religion, remnants of which are the substratum of much of East Anglian magic today. He may also be seen to embody both Christian and pagan imagery in himself, being born of a dynasty, claiming Wodan as an ancestor, being a follower of the Christ, but being martyred bound to a tree and pierced, just like both 'Lords'. He was even venerated by the Danish Vikings of

East Anglia who killed him; they later took up his sacred cult and produced a coinage to commemorate him.

The site of the remains of the Abbey at Bury St. Edmunds are claimed by some people to lie on the proposed St. Michael's Ley Line, which runs from the West of the country in Cornwall, passing through many ancient sites on its way across the country, and exiting our Isles on the East Anglian coast at Hopton. The site of Edmund's shrine is considered to be a major power point along its route. Edmund can be said to embody the essence of 'East Anglian-ness' and is certainly a power house of energy and spirituality to be called upon for those working within the magical framework of this region; this energy has been built up over a period of many centuries, and is still available to be used today.

King/Saint Edmund's feast day is November the 20th, his flag is three golden crowns on a blue shield, and he may be called upon for help in anything pertaining to the matter of East Anglia. He is depicted as being crowned and robed as a king, holding a sceptre, arrow, orb or sword. His 'badge' is a crown containing two crossed arrows.

Saint Walstan

The patron saint of agricultural workers and sick animals, St. Walstan, is said to have been born in the year 965 CE, either in Bawburgh in Norfolk, or Blythburgh in Suffolk. He was the son of Benedict, who was either a minor and obscure East Anglian King, or of a wealthy and noble family. His mother, named Blida or Blitha, was a kinswoman of King Ethelred and his son, Edmund Ironside, and was herself considered a saint. At the age of seven Walstan received instruction from Bishop Theodred of Elmham with the assistance of Father Aelred, the parish priest of Bawburgh. When he was only twelve he left his parents' home and travelled to Taverham in Norfolk where he worked as a farm labourer. Here he became so charitable that he would even give away his own food to the poor; he applied himself to the meanest and most painful labour in a perfect spirit of penance and humility; he fasted much, and spent time in fervent prayer. He made a vow of celibacy, but never embraced a monastic state. On one occasion, he even gave away the very shoes that he was wearing to a woman who had asked him for alms.

His employer's wife, hearing of this, went to remonstrate with him for his foolish generosity, and found him loading a cart with thorns and bushes, barefooted but showing no signs of pain or injury. Overcome by the sight, the woman fell at his feet and begged his forgiveness. Her husband, told of the incident, wanted to make Walstan his heir, but the saint asked for only one thing, the promise of the calf which would be born to a certain cow on the farm. In the event, the cow had two calves, which Walstan tended carefully, as he had been told by an angel that the beasts would, at his death, take him to his place of burial. This prophecy occurred one day when he was working in the fields. He heard the music of an angelic choir and a voice giving him the time of his death. He called his fellow ploughman to come and listen but the man could hear nothing till his foot touched the young man's. Then he heard the chiming of bells and the song of the angels. This touching of the person experiencing the vision and then becoming able to experience it yourself is a marked feature of advanced seership techniques, known to have been practiced within certain Irish and Scottish faerie traditions; the practice continues today.

On the 30th May, 1016, while he was scything a hay crop, the angel again appeared to Walstan to warn him of his approaching end, but he went on with his work, knowing that his death was very near. Finally, he asked his master and his fellow workers to place his body in a cart after he had died, yoke it to the two oxen, and to allow the two animals to go where they would. Walstan died in the fields at the appointed time, praying for the sick and all animals, promising that all who sought cures for their own infirmities and for those of their cattle would find them at his tomb. Walstan breathed his last and, as he did so, a white dove flew from his mouth.

His body was placed on the cart which the pair of oxen, unbidden, began to pull in the direction of Bawburgh. Passing through Costessey Wood, they crossed a pond without sinking into it, on the water of which the animals' hooves and the marks of the cart wheels were imprinted, as though on solid ground; they then mounted a hill from whose summit a spring miraculously issued. Then the oxen continued on to Bawburgh, passing over the Wensum stream, again without sinking into the waters, where they rested a while, another spring issuing from the spot. On the site of their final resting place, a little further on, another spring started to flow and a church came to be built. By popular demand, Walstan was declared a saint and a small chapel was built off the existing church of St Mary, giving it a new dedication of St Mary and St Walstan. Since then St Walstan has been honoured as a special saint of farm workers, farmers and farm animals. Until the time of the Reformation, the shrine of St. Walstan, which once had six chantry priests, was visited by many pilgrims who found at it the cures promised by the saint before he died. The water of the well at Bawburgh (which is still flowing today), much prized as a remedy for sick animals, was at one time sold in the streets of Norwich.

St Walstan is represented in religious art by a crown and sceptre and with a scythe in his hand and cattle near him. Icons dating from before the English Reformation occur mostly in Norfolk and Suffolk, but in modern times his cult has extended much further. St Walstan's Day is celebrated each year in Bawburgh when a special Patronal Service takes place on the nearest Sunday to May the 30th, his feast date.

Three Crowns & Several Halos

❦ Walsingham ❦

As mentioned above, the only real rival to the shrine of St. Edmund at Bury St. Edmunds in Suffolk, up to the Reformation, was the Shrine of Our Lady, at Walsingham in Norfolk. In 1061 the young widow, Richeldis de Favarches, Lady of the Manor of Little Walsingham, prayed that she might undertake some special work in honour of the Virgin Mary. In response to her petition, the Blessed Virgin apparently took her in spirit form, whilst asleep, and showed her a vision of the Holy House in Nazareth, scene of the Annunciation. Bidding her to mark well the measurements of the house, the Virgin commanded Richeldis to build an exact counterpart of it at Walsingham, so that England might have its own Nazareth. When she awoke, craftsmen were at once called in to produce a replica of the Holy House as it had appeared to her in her vision. But when the little wooden building was completed, she was at a loss as to where to have it placed. While she wondered, praying for guidance, a heavy dew fell one night on a nearby meadow, leaving however, two small areas quite dry over two wells. This strange occurrence Richeldis took to be a sign from the Virgin Mary that the replica of the house should be placed on one of them. But naturally she did not know which one. Eventually, when she did reach a decision, it proved to be the wrong one, for although all measurements for the house had been carefully adhered to, the craftsmen were unable to fit it to the foundations prepared for it. They tried in vain for a long while then, wearied by their unsuccessful efforts, they returned home disheartened, intending to tackle the project again after a good night's sleep.

However, further effort was not required of the carpenters. The next morning they discovered that, during the night, the little wooden structure had been moved to the other site, not haphazardly by wind or weather, but presumably by supernatural hands, as it was firmly fixed, each part of the building joined together better than they themselves could have done it. There was in fact nothing more for them to do and this, then Richeldis decided, was the chosen site. She had the little house enclosed in a stone chapel, while in later years, her son Geoffrey endowed it with money and lands and a priory was founded there.

In this way the Holy House of Walsingham came into being, not on the site of the modern Anglican replica of it, now enclosed in a large church, but as the legend stated and excavations in 1961 proved, to the west of the wells, the chapel which was later built over it leading from the north of the church of the Augustinian Priory founded in 1155. A well, discovered in 1931 during the building of the Anglican shrine, water from which is now bottled and eagerly collected by pilgrims, was known to local people previously as a secular well.

From the foundation of the priory until, in 1538, the famous statue of Our Lady of Walsingham was taken to London to be burned at Smithfield, the little Holy House was torn down and the Priory buildings were robbed and ruined, Walsingham steadily increased in fame. Kings, Princes and commoners all found their way there, both from England and abroad, until the road to the Holy House became one of the main highways in the country; the cluster of stars called the Milky Way was renamed the Walsingham Way, because it was said to point to England's Nazareth and miracles of all kinds were wrought there. Unfortunately, no image of the statue of Our Lady now remains and no description of it has ever been found, but it was supposed that the figure on the seal of Walsingham Priory would naturally bear a close resemblance to it. On that seal, the Virgin, crowned, is shown seated upon a throne, supporting the Christ Child with one arm as he sits on her knee and holding in the other a Lily sceptre; most modern representations of Our Lady of Walsingham take this form.

Three Crowns & Several Halos

Apart from such notables as Henry III, Edwards I and II, the young Henry VIII, Catherine of Aragon and Anne Boleyn (herself of Norfolk stock), the learned scholar Erasmus visited the shrine in the year 1511. Thirteen years later he wrote his famous Colloquy, *'A Pilgrimage for Religion's Sake'*, in which he satirised mediaeval pilgrimages in general and the members of the Augustinian Order to which he had once belonged, and which he had left without permission, in particular. Nowhere in his work did he mention Walsingham by name, but made his fictional pilgrim describe his visit to 'the famous Virgin-by-Sea… by the North-West coast of England only thirteen miles from the sea'. Erasmus declared that the water of the twin wells came from a stream of water which issued from the ground at the command of the Blessed Virgin (a story of his own invention, for the water table in the area is such that any deep hole immediately fills with water). The stream, he said, was *'wonderfully cold fluid, good for headache and stomach trouble.'* Over the wells was a shed which, he was told, had been brought suddenly, from far away, one winter when everything was covered with snow. When he pointed out that the shed had been repaired so often that little of the original structure remained, his attention was drawn to an old bearskin hanging on the rafters, as proof of the building's antiquity.

Several centuries later, the Rev. Robert Forby, writing in *'The Vocabulary of East Anglia'* (pub. 1830), had this to say concerning the wells at Walsingham;

> *'Amongst the slender remains of this once celebrated seat of superstitious devotion, are two small circular basons of stone, a little to the north-east of the site of the conventual church, (exactly in the place described by Erasmus in his "Peregrinatio religionis ergo"), and connected with the chapel of the Virgin, which was on the north side of the choir. The water of these wells had at that time a miraculous efficacy in curing disorders of the head and stomach, the special gift, no doubt, of the Holy Virgin: who has probably*

since that time resumed it, for the waters have no such quality now. She has substituted, however, another of far more comprehensive virtue. This is nothing less than the power of accomplishing all human wishes, which miraculous property the water is still believed to possess. In order to attain this desirable end, the votary, with a due qualification of faith and pious awe, must apply the right knee, bare, to a stone placed for that purpose between the wells. He must then plunge to the wrist each hand, bare also, into the water of the wells, which are near enough to admit of this immersion. A wish must then be formed, but not uttered with the lips, either at the time or afterwards, even in confidential communication to the dearest friend. The hands are then to be withdrawn, and as much of the water as can be contained in the hollow of each is to be swallowed. Formerly the object of desire was most probably expressed in a prayer to the Virgin. It is now only a silent wish: which will certainly be accomplished within twelvemonths, if the efficacy of the solemn rite be not frustrated by the incredulity or some other fault of the votary.'

The Walsingham excavations of 1961 showed that where Richeldis built her Holy House, an early Anglo-Saxon shrine had once existed, the choice of its site being governed, no doubt, by the presence of the already sacred wells nearby, long before they later received their Christian 'hallowing'. However, it is here that the Virgin Mary chose to make Her presence felt and it is still a sacred, powerful and holy site to many. The waters are still used for many healing rituals and not a few witches and folk-magicians have been known to bow the knee there. It is an excellent and graphic example of the many spiritual and religious levels that go to make up the East Anglian tradition.

Petitioning the Saints

It may well be asked, exactly how does the folk magician, or other magic-maker, work with the saints, or indeed the

Virgin? Every practitioner will have their own particular way of working, but in general, the procedure is very simple and, as ever, relies on the focus and attention of the worker to build up the contact and the energy.

The worker will either have a small statue or picture of the saint that they work with, or be able to build a very clear image of same in their mind. They may wish to collect together some of the items associated with the saint, such as agricultural tools, plants, representations of animals, etc. and have them present also. Initially, one or more candles may be lit before the image and or other items, and a simple prayer will be said, calling on the presence of the saint.

The worker will then take up a set of rosary beads, or similar (as we have seen used in a previous chapter), and will then begin to chant, using the beads to keep track of the repetitions. What is chanted will be appropriate to the saint and the practitioner; some like to chant a part of one of the psalms associated with the saint; some have particular prayers passed to them for use with the different saints; some, again, will have other words that they use. The chanting continues, whilst the worker focuses on the image – mental or actual – of the saint, and until a palpable presence can be felt. At this stage, once a spiritual rapport has been achieved, the practitioner will make their request or petition of the saint and will also most likely make some offering too. This can simply be some flowers, some wine or some food, some incense or perfumed oil, or a promise of a certain act or work in honour of the saint and in payment for the favour requested. Thanks are given in expectation of a favourable outcome and the candles are extinguished. The offerings are left for a period where they are, for the saint to absorb their essence.

It is claimed that great things can be done using this method, but the key – like all forms of magic with another entity – is a good working relationship with the saint that is petitioned and a willingness to stick to what has been promised.

APPENDIX

Removing a Witch's Curse

W.H. Barrett was a Cambridgeshire Fenman and spent most of his adult life collecting the folklore and history of his native region. This has been published in several of his volumes of tales (see Bibliography), but the following story stands out as being of especial interest for this particular book and I would therefore like to reproduce it here in its entirety. It is one of the few eye witness accounts of old-style witchcraft in action, and is remarkable for the wealth of information it contains. Very few accounts have come down to us of the details of witch practices in this area, and this tale is a valuable addition to the stock of knowledge available to us. I have mentioned in previous chapters that Barrett's grandmother had been a great source of information for him in his researches, being a local girl and, shortly before she died in 1904, at the age of 90, she told him the following tale;

> 'When I was a gal witches were very real and everybody believed they had the power to do harm. I myself have never seen a witch flying through the air, but I did once see one being dragged across the river because she had bewitched a farmer's wife. She told her, you see, that all her children would be born with dog's paws instead of hands and this had so upset the woman that

Appendix

she went clean out of her mind. When her husband knew what had made her like this he was furious and one night he made four of his labourers get hold of the witch, strip her to her shift and tie her hands and legs together. Then they threw her into the river and dragged her across with a cart rope until she was three parts drowned, then they hauled her out and laid her on the bank, face downwards, to let the water drain out of her. She recovered after a bit and the men were just getting ready to give her another swim when she started begging and pleading for mercy and promising that she would take the curse off the farmer's wife. So they untied her and let her go after she'd promised to be at the farmer's house the next evening, after dark, when they were all to be there, too, to see her take her curse off.

Next morning the old witch, having her own ways of getting things done, ordered the Littleport blacksmith to make her a Trinity Bottle – that's a three-sided one, not a round one – out of sheet iron and she told him that while he was shaping it he was only to heat the iron three times. She stood over him as he worked and before he put the red-hot iron on the anvil she spat on it three times. The sweat poured off him as he shaped the bottle, for the old woman told him that, from start to finish, the job must not take more than three-quarters of an hour; if it did then he would have a cold hearth and a silent anvil because his strength would leave him and for the rest of his life he would be too weak to lift a hammer.

When the bottle was finished the blacksmith was told to take it along to the nearby inn and have it filled with a quart of ale to see that it did not leak. The test showed that all was well, so then he had to drink the ale, emptying the bottle in three long draughts, no more and no less.

That night the witch went to the farmer's house where she found the four labourers, the farmer and his wife all waiting for her. First of all she ordered one of the men to go outside and bring in a hen from the yard, and she cut its throat so that the blood ran into the Trinity Bottle. Next she cut a lock of hair from the farmer and his wife and took clippings from their toenails; these she sprinkled with salt before putting them into the bottle along with the insides of the hen and three of her tail and wing feathers. After that she rubbed some of the gizzard fat on the wife's forehead and bandaged her eyes then, putting her hand up the chimney, brought down some soot which she sprinkled on both the farmer and his wife who were ordered to go outside and fill the bottle with their urine.

When the couple came back into the room the witch stopped up the bottle with a piece of wet clay and put it in the middle of the fire. The candle was blown out and everyone sat in the dark waiting for the spell to be broken. Suddenly, with a loud bang, the clay cork and most of what was inside the bottle went flying up the chimney and a horrible smell filled the room. The charm worked, though, for when the bandage was taken off the woman's eyes she was as right as rain.

The farmer kicked that old witch out of the house, though, and picking the bottle out of the fire with the tongs hurled it after her. His wife had one child – a girl – and there was nothing wrong with her, but do you know that when her first baby was born, twenty-five years later, it had deformed hands, just like paws.'

We can recognise in this tale several features that are common to other charms, curses and counter measures already encountered in this book. The repeated insistence on the number three; the use of iron and salt; the use of the urine, hair and nail clippings from both the farmer and his wife; certain time constrictions in the making and performing of the ritual; placing the bottle in the fire; and the – presumed – insistence on silence in the dark. There is also the – to us nowadays – seemingly cruel use of the chicken, its blood and entrails. However, this is very much in keeping with other practices that we have already seen and it must be remembered that most people would keep poultry in those days, and that they would kill them themselves to eat and use every part anyway.

Appendix

It remains unknown as to exactly why the farmer's grandchild was born with hands like paws; maybe the witch's curse was not effectively removed, or maybe it was deliberately delayed to save her own skin. However, the essential point here is, I think, that the witch had genuine power and ability and herself chose how, when and in what way to use it.

Select Bibliography & Suggested Reading

A History of the English Church and People. Bede. Penguin Classics, 1978.

An Hour-Glass On The Run. Jobson, Allan. Robert Hale & Co. 1975.

Ask the Fellows who Cut the Hay. Evans, George Ewart. Faber & Faber, 1965.

Cambridgeshire Customs & Folklore. Porter, Edith & Barrett, W.H. Routledge & Kegan Paul, 1969.

Children of Cain: A Study of Modern Traditional Witches. Howard, Michael. Three Hands Press, 2011.

Country Remedies: Traditional East Anglian Plant Remedies in the Twentieth Century. Hatfield, Gabrielle. The Boydell Press, 1994/2002.

East Anglian Folklore and Other Tales. Barrett, W.H. & Garrod, R.P. Routledge & Kegan Paul, 1976.

County Folk-Lore: Suffolk. Gurdon, Lady Eveline Camilla. The Folklore Society, ND.

East Anglian Magazine. Manifold contributors. East Anglian Magazine Ltd. 1948 – 1972.

East Anglian Superstitions. Forby, Robert. Oakmagic Publications, 2005. (First published as part of 'The Vocabulary of East Anglia', by J.B. Nichols & Son, 1830).

Edmund: The Story of the Martyr-King and His Kingdom. Taylor, Mark. Fordaro, 2014.

Folk-Lore of East Anglia and Adjoining Counties. Pennick, Nigel. Spiritual Arts & Crafts Publishing, 2006.

Genuine Witchcraft is Explained. John of Monmouth. Capall Bann, 2012.

Hikey Sprites; The Twilight of a Norfolk Tradition. Loveday, Ray. Published by the author, 2009.

Gogmagog. Lethbridge, T.C. Routledge & Kegan Paul, 1957.

Bibliography

Gypsy Sorcery and Fortune Telling. Leland, Charles Godfrey. Kessinger Publishing, ND.

Horseheath: Some Recollections of a Cambridgeshire Parish. Parsons, Catherine E. 1952. Unpublished manuscript; Cambridgeshire Archives Service.

Horse Power & Magic. Evans, George Ewart. Faber & Faber 1979/Faber Finds 1988.

In Field & Fen. Pennick, Nigel. Lear Books, 2011.

In The Footsteps of Borrow & Fitzgerald. Adams, Morley. Jarrold & Sons, ND.

I Walked by Night. By Himself, Ed. Lilias Rider Haggard. Nicholson & Watson, 1935.

Lavengro: The Scholar, The Gypsy, The Priest. Borrow, George. Oxford University Press, 1982. (Originally published, 1851).

Men of Dunwich. Parker, Rowland. Granada Publishing, 1980.

Norfolk Witches, Superstitions & Legends. Glyde, John. Oakmagic Publications, 2005. (First published by Jarrold & Sons, 1872).

Notes on Cambridgeshire Witchcraft. Parsons, Catherine E. Cambridgeshire Antiquarian Society, 1915.

Old Suffolk Love & Cure Charms (And Other Folklore Relics). Ed. Eveline Camilla Gurdon. Oakmagic Publications, 2005. (First published by Pawsey & Hayes, 1893).

One: The Grimoire of the Golden Toad. Chumbley, Andrew. Xoanon Publishing, 2000.

Operative Witchcraft. Pennick, Nigel. Lear Books, 2011.

Secrets of East Anglian Magic. Pennick, Nigel. Capall Bann, 2004.

Suffolk Miscellany. Jobson, Allan. Robert Hale & Co. 1975.

Tales from the Fens. Barrett, W.H. Routledge & Kegan Paul, ND.

The Folklore & Witchcraft of Suffolk. Glyde, John. Oakmagic Publications, 2005. (First published as part of 'The New Suffolk Garland', Suffolk, 1866).

The Folklore of East Anglia. Porter, Enid. B.T. Batsford Ltd. 1974.

The Leaper Between. Chumbley, Andrew. Three Hands Press, 2013.

The Lore of the Land. Westwood, Jenifer & Simpson, Jacqueline. Penguin Books, 2006.

The New Suffolk Garland. Glyde, John. Forgotten Books, 2012. (Originally published 1865).

The Pattern Under the Plough. Evans, George Ewart. Faber & Faber, 1967.

The Society of the Horseman's Word. Fernee, Ben. The Society of Esoteric Endeavour/Caduceus Books, 2009.

The Suffolk Dialect of the Twentieth Century. Claxton, A.O.D. Boydell Press, 1968.

Under Three Crowns. Forrest, A.J. Norman Adlard & Co. Ltd. 1961.

Online Resources

www.foxearth.org.uk – Website and archives on the lore of the Essex/Suffolk border region.
www.gippeswic.demon.co.uk – Homepage of Pete Jennings online; folklore, paganism & more.
www.hiddenea.com – Landscape Legends of Eastern England; Black Shuck, St. Edmund, etc.
www.museumofwitchcraft.com – The website of the Witchcraft Museum in Boscastle, Cornwall. World's largest collection of witchcraft and related items.
www.secretsuffolk.com – Suffolk and East Anglia's Anglo-Saxon heritage.
www.the-cauldron.co.uk – Witchcraft, folklore and paganism; excellent archive articles.
www.traditionsofsuffolk.com – Oral Traditions, Music & Song, Horsemanship.
www.wuffings.co.uk – Dr. Sam Newton's website on the East Anglian Kingdom of the Wuffings.
All of the above have links to further sites of interest to readers of this book.

Index

Aconite, 150
Adder, 139, 188, 241
Ague, 142-145, 164, 172, 182, 186
All Hallows Eve, 93, 241
Amber, 207-208
Ancestors, 19-22, 132, 154, 186
Anglo-Saxon Chronicle, 231-232, 240, 243, 247

Ballingdon Hill, 36
Bargus, 112
Barrett, W.H., 89, 260, 264-265
Basil, 167
Bawburgh, 252, 254
Bay Laurel, 166
Beccles, 77
Bede, 232-233, 236, 241, 244, 264
Beechamwell, 105
Bel (god), 105
Belemnite, 206-207
Belenos (god), 111
Belladonna, 151, 165
Bellarmine, 193, 196
Beowulf, 40, 59
Bet Cross, 85-86
Bible, The, 152, 179, 216-217
Blackberry, 169-170
Black Book, 11, 64
Black Shuck, 52-53, 55, 57, 60, 266
Blackthorn, 127, 179-180, 219
Blickling Hall, 58
Blythburgh, 55, 57, 229, 240, 252
Bones, 21, 23, 44, 123, 133-134, 142, 146, 156, 162, 186-187, 200, 220
Borage, 170, 187
Brandon, 169, 171, 240, 246
Brandon Creek, 89-90
Brickett Wood, 92, 94
Bull, 23, 65-66
Bulrushes, 170-171
Bungay, 55-57, 102, 104
Bures St. Mary, 35, 248-249
Burial Mound, 101, 132-133, 184, 186
Bury St. Edmunds, 65, 251-252, 255

Calirius (god), 111
Callow Pit, 109
Cambridge, 11-12, 14-16, 20, 23, 26, 41, 59, 69, 83-86, 88, 99-100, 115, 121, 130, 137, 139-140, 168, 172, 174, 194, 197, 200, 202, 213, 222, 228, 260, 264-265
Canute, 248
Cascinomancy, 155
Castle Acre, 96, 121
Castle Hill, 107-108
Castle Rising, 67-68
Catherine Parsons, 84-85, 121, 130, 137, 201
Caul, 222
Cedar, 167
Cemetery, 109, 126
Cernunnos (god), 111
Charms, 66, 71, 74-75, 78-79, 82, 84, 89, 115, 124, 133-136, 138, 142-145, 147, 150-152, 158, 166-167, 175, 180, 192-193, 195-197, 199-200, 203-205, 207-208, 211-212, 214, 218-219, 262, 265
Chrism, 149-150

❖ 267 ❖

Christianity, 13, 64, 112, 230-231, 235-236, 241
Christmas Eve, 210
Circle, 20-21, 90-92, 95-97, 120-122, 132, 134, 154
Claypole, 82
Cleidomancy, 156
Cnobheresburg, 233, 236-238, 240
Comfrey, 162, 173, 187
Communion, 137-138
Corpse Money, 223-224
Cottenham, 101
Cottie Burland, 91, 93
Cramp, 177, 188, 219-220
Crown, 145, 227-229, 252, 254
Cunning Man, 74, 81-83, 144, 195, 203-204
Cypress, 168

Daddy Witch, 11, 83-85, 115, 137
Dandelion, 162, 187
Danish/Dane, 13-14, 44, 64, 95, 87, 107, 243, 245, 248-251
Devil, The, 11-12, 58, 60-61, 67-69, 71-72, 75, 83-84, 89, 99-116, 119-122, 124-127, 129, 136, 171-172, 178, 180, 184, 191, 206, 229
Devil's Dish, 106
Devil's Ditch, 105
Devil's Dyke, 99-100
Devil's Hills, 106
Devil's Hole, 108
Devil's Plantation, 11-12, 64, 82, 84, 104
Devil's Stone, 102-104
Diana (goddess), 105

Divination, 13, 115, 151, 153-155, 166, 175, 208, 210, 214, 216-217, 244
Dock, 162, 187
Downham Market, 45
Dowsing, 155
Dragons, 35-57
Dragon's Blood, 167
Dumb Cake, 214
Dunwich, 21, 229, 231, 233, 239, 265

East Dereham, 82-83, 169, 208-209, 245, 247
East Wreatham, 106
Elder, 180-183, 185
Ely, 86, 89, 169, 172, 178, 199, 228, 232-233, 242-247
Epilepsy, 81, 187, 221
Epona, 93
Erasmus, 257

Fairy/Faerie/Frairy/Ferisher/Feriers/Pharisees, 25, 28-32, 34, 40, 104, 169, 182, 205, 207, 253 Familiars, 69, 75-76, 115, 136-137
Faremoutiers, 235, 239, 244
Fendyke, 109
Fennel, 166
Fetch, 59, 137
Flash Boys (Girls), 112
Flitcham, 87-88
Fly Agaric, 165
Fossditch, 109
Foxglove, 165
Frairy Loaf, 205
Frigga (goddess), 208
Freya/Freyja (goddess), 95, 111, 208, 209
Freyr (god), 228

Index

Garlic, 167, 188
Gayton, 91, 93
Gerald Gardner, 92-93
Gervase of Tilbury, 23
Giants, 20, 23-25, 39, 43-50, 100, 102
Glastonbury, 243, 251
Gogmagog, 23, 43, 51, 264
Going to the River, 123
Graveyard, 21-22, 59-60, 104, 106, 109, 126-127, 132, 216
Great Heathen Army, 13, 248
Green Children, 32-34
Grendel's Dam, 40, 60
Greybeards, 193, 197
Groundsel, 167, 171, 187
Gypsy, 114, 176, 197, 265

Haegelisdun, 248-249
Hagstone, 30, 204-205
Hawthorn, 181-182
Hell Hole, 108
Hemlock, 150, 154
Hemp, 164, 171-172, 214
Henbane, 154, 165-166
Hermits of Mole End, 95
Hikey Sprite, 26, 34, 264
Hinvar, 249
Holly, 182-183
Honeysuckle, 126, 173
Horned God, 83, 93, 97
Horse Brasses, 154, 198
Horseheath, 11, 83-85, 115, 121, 130, 137-138, 201, 265
Horsemen, 78, 114, 123, 163, 200
Horseradish, 162, 173
Horse shoes, 134, 154, 192
Huntingtoft, 77, 125
Hyssop, 167

Iken, 101, 239-241
Imps, 68-70, 72-73, 75-76, 84, 115, 136-142
Induction, 93-94
Initiation, 94, 96, 104, 113, 116, 119-120, 122, 136
Ipswich, 71, 72-75, 133, 201-202, 210
Iron, 30, 35, 104, 107, 137, 159, 178, 183-185, 192, 198-199, 205, 221, 243, 261-262
Ivy, 173-174, 188

Jabez Few, 76
Jack O' Lantern, 27, 104

Kelsale, 66
Key, 152, 155-156, 199, 205, 208, 216-217, 219
Killingdon Hill, 36
King Anna, 229, 238-239, 242, 244, 247
King Penda, 228, 237
King Raedwald, 13, 229-230, 236
King Sigeberht, 232, 236-237
King's Lynn, 33, 45, 47

Langmere, 106
Lavendar, 150, 167
Lavengro, 208-209, 265
Leiston, 57
Lemon juice, 149
Lethbridge, T.C. 24-25, 51, 264
Liber Eliensis, 232, 244
Ligature, 157-158
Littleport, 178, 261
Loddon, 115
Lois Bourne, 92-94

❋ 269 ❋

Loki (god), 95, 111, 145
Ludham, 35-36, 106

Magister, 93, 115
Maidenhair Grass, 147
Malaria, 142, 164
Malekin, 31-32
Mandrake, 88, 149, 162-163, 174-175
Man in Black, 115
March, 100, 172
Mary Atkin, 144-145
Matthew Hopkins, 14, 68
Meadowsweet, 167
Meremaids, 39-40, 42
Middleton, 102
Midsummer's Day, 213
Milky Way, 256
Monica English, 91-94
Monkshood, 165
Mossymere Wood, 105
Mother Didge, 147
Mother Lakeland, 71-72
Mother Staselton, 79
Mr. Rix, 83
Mrs Mullinger, 80
Mugwort, 166-167

Nails, 145-146, 159, 183, 192-196, 198, 262
Nazareth, 255-256
Neckweed, 164
New Year's Eve, 210
Nightshade, 165
Noah's Ark, 54
North Walsham, 81

Oak, 104, 106, 182-183
Odin (god), 59, 228
Old Harry, 112
Old Mother Redcap, 137

Old Mrs Reeve, 192
Old Ragusan, 112
Old Winter, 73-75, 78
Opium, 164
Orford, 42
Osbert FitzHugh, 24
Otherworld, 22, 59-60, 97, 110, 114, 119, 131, 165, 231
Oulton, 104

Parsley, 133, 176, 187, 188
Pendulum, 155-156
Pennyroyal, 166, 187
Peries (Perries, Perry Dancers), 30
Periwinkle, 176-177
Placenta, 222
Pliny the Elder, 123
Poppy, 154, 164, 172, 224
Prickwillow, 89, 91
Prince of Wales, 86-88

Ralph of Coggeshall, 31, 42
Recipes (herbal), 165, 186, 188
Reformation, the, 64, 66, 72, 108, 233, 254-255
Rendlesham, 40, 229, 239
Richeldis de Favarches, 255-256, 258
Ringworm, 221
River Gipping, 40
Romany, 114, 178, 208
Rose, 167
Rosemary, 166, 187
Rowan, 166, 184-185
Rue, 88, 166, 187

Sage, 167, 187, 189
Salt, 131, 137, 166, 188, 193, 198, 201, 212, 214, 224-225, 262

Index

Sandringham, 86
Scissors, 199, 213
Scots Pine, 167, 184
Secret Granary, 64, 82-83
Simples, 186
Simpson, 167, 171
Sin Eating, 224
Snake, 36, 138-139, 181, 220, 241
Sow thistle, 177
Spirament, 19
St. Audrey, 242-243
St. Botolph, 101-102, 238, 240, 242
St. Columba, 235-239
St. Edmund, 65-66, 100, 251-252, 255, 266
St. Etheldreda, 242-244, 247
St. Felix, 229, 231-235, 239
St. Fursey, 233-238, 240
St. John's Eve, 127, 181
St. John's Wort, 181
St. Mark's Eve, 213-215
St. Martins Land, 33
St. Thomas, 210-211
St. Walstan, 252-254
St. Withburga, 169, 244-245, 247
Starwort, 177
Stile, 142-143
Stinging Nettle, 162, 177
Suffolk Punch, 154
Susan Cooper, 140
Sutton Hoo, 13, 20
Syleham, 104

Taranis (god), 111
The Broads, 15, 52
The Confraternity of the Plough, 116
The Deben, 52

The 'Eye', 79-81, 87, 129, 198
The Horseman's Word, 122, 266
The Millers Fraternity, 116
The Smeeth, 45, 47-49
Thetford, 52-53, 96, 107, 109, 169, 249
The Wash, 15-16, 52
Thomas Colson, 133
Thor, 173, 207, 228
Thornapple, 178
Thriplow, 100
Thunderbolt, 206-207
Thunor, 207
Thyme, 166, 187
Tilly Baldrey, 77-79, 125
Toad, 76, 115, 121-125, 127-131, 136, 177, 189
Toad Bone, 77, 122-123, 127-128
Toadsman, 126, 128, 200
Toadswoman, 77, 79
Tom Hickathrift, 45-46, 49-52
Tuddy, 129
Tumour, 130-131, 135, 170, 243
Tunstall, 108
Tydd St. Giles, 101
Typhus, 220

Ubba, 249
Urine, 192, 194-197, 203, 262

Venus (goddess), 105
Verbena, 167, 179
Vervain, 167
Vikings, 13, 59, 233, 241, 247-248, 251
Viper, 90, 139, 181

Virgin Mary, 245, 255, 258
Virtue, 19-21, 34, 143, 148, 198, 207, 220, 228, 237, 249, 258

Wake, 208, 209
Walsingham, 96, 251, 255-258
Wandil, 24-25
Wandlebury, 23-24
Wangford, 104
Ward, The, 34
Warts, 69, 130, 219
Watching, 215-216
Waters of the Moon, 123
Wenhaston, 103
Westleton, 103
White Briony, 163
White Witches, 144, 191
Whooping Cough, 130, 170, 218
Wicca, 92, 119
Wight, 11, 25, 27, 34
Wild Arum Lily, 168
Wild Herb Men, 161, 163
William of Malmesbury, 233
William of Newburgh, 32
Willingham, 76
Will O' the Wisp, 26-27
Willow, 172, 185
Wisbech, 45, 47, 50, 192
Witch Ball, 199
Witch Bottle, 193, 196, 198, 204
Witch's Stone, 103
Wizard, 73-76, 85, 134-135, 138, 195-196
Woden/Wodan, 95, 111, 145, 251
Wodewose, 42
Wolfsbane, 165

Woodbridge, 13, 30
Woolpit, 32-33, 53
Wormwood, 166-167
Wuffings/Wuffingas, 12, 227, 235, 239, 250, 266

Yarrow, 166-167, 186, 213
Yarthkins, 26
Yew, 21, 186